CW01513139

Palgrave Studies in Prisons and Penology

Series Editors
Ben Crewe
Institute of Criminology
University of Cambridge
Cambridge, UK

Yvonne Jewkes
Social & Policy Sciences
University of Bath
Bath, UK

Thomas Ugelvik
Faculty of Law
University of Oslo
Oslo, Norway

This is a unique and innovative series, the first of its kind dedicated entirely to prison scholarship. At a historical point in which the prison population has reached an all-time high, the series seeks to analyse the form, nature and consequences of incarceration and related forms of punishment. Palgrave Studies in Prisons and Penology provides an important forum for burgeoning prison research across the world.

Series Advisory Board
Anna Eriksson (Monash University)
Andrew M. Jefferson (DIGNITY - Danish Institute Against Torture)
Shadd Maruna (Rutgers University)
Jonathon Simon (Berkeley Law, University of California)
Michael Welch (Rutgers University)

More information about this series at
http://www.palgrave.com/gp/series/14596

David Maguire

Male, Failed, Jailed

Masculinities and "Revolving-Door" Imprisonment
in the UK

David Maguire
Institute of Education
University College London
London, UK

Palgrave Studies in Prisons and Penology
ISBN 978-3-030-61058-6   ISBN 978-3-030-61059-3   (eBook)
https://doi.org/10.1007/978-3-030-61059-3

© The Editor(s) (if applicable) and The Author(s), under exclusive license to Springer
Nature Switzerland AG 2021, corrected publication 2021
This work is subject to copyright. All rights are solely and exclusively licensed by the
Publisher, whether the whole or part of the material is concerned, specifically the rights
of translation, reprinting, reuse of illustrations, recitation, broadcasting, reproduction on
microfilms or in any other physical way, and transmission or information storage and
retrieval, electronic adaptation, computer software, or by similar or dissimilar methodology
now known or hereafter developed.
The use of general descriptive names, registered names, trademarks, service marks, etc.
in this publication does not imply, even in the absence of a specific statement, that such
names are exempt from the relevant protective laws and regulations and therefore free for
general use.
The publisher, the authors and the editors are safe to assume that the advice and information in this book are believed to be true and accurate at the date of publication. Neither
the publisher nor the authors or the editors give a warranty, expressed or implied, with
respect to the material contained herein or for any errors or omissions that may have been
made. The publisher remains neutral with regard to jurisdictional claims in published maps
and institutional affiliations.

Cover illustration: Contributor: Lankowsky/Alamy Stock Photo

This Palgrave Macmillan imprint is published by the registered company Springer Nature
Switzerland AG
The registered company address is: Gewerbestrasse 11, 6330 Cham, Switzerland

The original version of this book was revised. Missed corrections have been updated in all the chapters. The corrections to the book can be found at https://doi.org/10.1007/978-3-030-61059-3_10

ACKNOWLEDGMENTS

I am most indebted to the men that gave up their time to take part in this research and shared so openly and courageously their life stories.

I would like to thank Deborah Drake, Rod Earl, Katherine Fender, Jane Hurry, Yvonne Jewkes, Linda McDowell, Peter Ramsay and Anita Wilson all of whom have given this project so much of their time and have been a constant source of encouragement and support.

I am so grateful to Benny and Neil for the time they gave me during my research in Hull, and I would like to extend a special thank you to Norman and Eleanor Griffin for their ongoing support and belief.

I would like to thank Micheal Maguire, whose long and enduring friendship has been integral to this journey.

I would like to acknowledge and thank my son, Dylan Maguire, who through the course of this project has made his own transitions from childhood into an amazing young man.

This book is dedicated to my wife, Natasha Kidd. Thank you, Natasha for taking me to "places that I couldn't have reached without you".

PRAISE FOR MALE, FAILED, JAILED

"Maguire's book is a triumph on so many levels. The culmination of a long personal journey, it offers anyone concerned about prisons, social justice and men's lives a rich and provocative new resource. Academic books are often the result of impressive scholarship and searching intelligence. This is all of that, but I also defy anyone not to be moved by Maguire's account of young men looping in and out of jail. Hurting inside and out, they have rarely been so well drawn or their predicaments so acutely analysed."

—Rod Earle, *Senior Lecturer in Youth Justice, The Open University, UK*

"Complicating new arguments that young men no longer 'learn to labour', but instead 'learn to serve', this book charts the ways that places and spaces come to bear on constructions and performances of masculinity and result in young men 'learning to serve' at her Majesty's pleasure. Sensitive and sophisticated, the sociological insights developed by David Maguire are in keeping with the traditions of the famous Teesside studies, upon which this book excellently builds."

—Steven Roberts, *Associate Professor of Sociology, Monash University, Australia*

CONTENTS

CHAPTER 1

Introduction: Failing Masculinities

Shortly after being released from what would be my last time in prison, I started a journey in higher education that has culminated in the publication of this book. It was the close of the 1990s and the beginning of the millennium: a time when an interest in masculinities and a so-called "crisis in masculinity" had for a number of years been fiercely debated both in the academy and in popular media. The late 1990s marked the height of oversimplified media and political representations of the crisis discourse that positioned boys and men as a homogenous group who were suffering as a result of the success of women/girls in education and the workplace. I spent a large part of this decade in and out of a Manchester prison, encountering time and time again the same types of men. There were no noticeable changes in this population to reflect this crisis among **all** men; we all came from very similar environments.

I was born and raised on a council estate in Greater Manchester. I lived with my mother and stepfather who—after a number of redundancies (before I was old enough to remember them ever being employed)—survived on benefits that were occasionally topped up with "fiddly" cash-in-hand work. After being expelled from school at the age of 15—having become involved in low-level criminality and accumulating several convictions during my childhood and early teens—I sought out legitimate forms of employment once I was old enough to. For a number of years, as a young man without qualifications and with a criminal record, I moved

© The Author(s) 2021
D. Maguire, *Male, Failed, Jailed,*
Palgrave Studies in Prisons and Penology,
https://doi.org/10.1007/978-3-030-61059-3_1

between exploitive—and, in some cases, abusive—employment positions, unemployment and sporadic crime. With growing disillusionment at my prospects of finding legitimate work and falling ever deeper into local drug and criminal cultures, criminality took over as my main activity and source of income. Inevitably, periods of incarceration followed.

In the concluding chapter, I discuss the critical moment that prompted my transition from a prisoner to an academic. The important point to emphasise here—and the reason for this disclosure—is to highlight how central my introduction to feminist-inspired theory and research was in the early stages of my higher education career. As I explain in Chapter 2, this scholarship—largely influenced by the work of Connell (1995, 2000)—challenges the idea of a singular or homogenous masculinity espoused by the proponents of crisis discourses and instead recognises the intersection of class, place and other social categories in creating multiple and hierarchically positioned masculinities. Most importantly, it profoundly captures many of my experiences as a boy and then a young man negotiating the challenges of the streets, education and employment. This personal identification with writing on masculinities is what has both nurtured and sustained my interest. It is what inspired this project and in doing so it has afforded me the necessary capital(s) to be able to contribute to "doing masculinity" differently.

Having been out of prison for almost two decades, my research career has been punctuated by—and enriched by—my experiences of working with excluded boys and men in various contexts: on the streets of impoverished estates, in schools' exclusion centres and in prisons. Unfortunately, in doing this work I have not seen enough research on gender and masculinities that has been conducted outside of the academy in order to inform and improve the lives of the men who it represents.

Over the same period, academic interest in boys, men and masculinities has grown at a remarkable rate and there has been increasing rates of recognition of the cost of constructing masculinities under profound structural disadvantages. With this the UK has witnessed some of the highest rates of academic underachievement among often "bright, working-class boys" (see Allen et al. 2015; House of Commons Educational Committee 2014). During this period, England and Wales have also seen surging incarceration rates, with numbers more than doubling from 41,800 in 1993 to a record 88,179 at the close of 2011 (Sturge 2020). The vast majority of this population—indeed, of all prisoners around the world—are male. Mostly undereducated men were drawn from some of the most impoverished working-class neighbourhoods (Crewe 2009; Jewkes 2002; McAra and McVie 2013; Phillips 2012).

A recent sweep of the longitudinal study, *The Edinburgh Study of Youth Transitions and Crime*, for instance, has found that pupils who have been excluded from school at the age of 12 are four times more likely to end up in prison than other children (McAra and McVie 2013). Kennedy (2013) discovered that 900 of the 942 young male prisoners who were surveyed had, at some point, been excluded from school; more than a third of these individuals were aged just 14 when they last attended school. Sally Coates (2016), in her *Review of Education in Prison*, noted that 42% of individuals across the prison estate report having been excluded from school. In the same review, she points out that more than half of those who enter prison are assessed as having the literacy and numeracy abilities of primary school age children and that 47% of them have no qualifications (ibid.).

Data released from the Ministry of Justice's (MOJ) recent analysis of the *Surveying Prisoner Crime Reduction (SPCR)* longitudinal cohort study found that over two-thirds of newly sentenced prisoners were unemployed four weeks before they had been taken into custody. Those who had worked reported being paid lower wages than the average rate of pay for the working-age population (Brunton-Smith and Hopkins 2013). In their 2018 Employment and Education Strategy, the Ministry of Justice highlight the fact that just 17% of people who leave prison have managed to secure paid, P45 employment a year after their release (MoJ 2018).

There is a body of rich empirical research looking at masculinities of marginalised (young) men in education (Corrigan 1979; Evans 2006; Frosh et al. 2002; Mac an Ghaill 1994; O'Donnell and Sharpe 2000; Willis 1977), on the streets (Anderson 1999; Alexander 2000; Bourgois 2003; Gunter 2010), in employment and in the workplace (McDowell 2003; McDowell et al. 2014; Nayak 2006; Roberts 2018). Largely, this scholarship has explored how the relationship between structural disadvantages and (restricted) agency generates cultures or identities that reproduce and amplify existing forms of marginalisation that for many—as the data above suggest—lead to imprisonment.

Scholarship on schooling in poor neighbourhoods has shown, for instance, how some schools are under-resourced. Consequently, they are failing to equip many of their pupils—particularly boys—with adequate social capital to transcend the barriers of poverty. Instead these schools become key sites in which patterns of exclusion are reproduced (Ball

2003; Reay 2018). Paul Willis's (1977) and Paul Corrigan's (1979) studies in the mid to late 1970s and the surge of interest in masculinities over the last three decades have generated an impressive interdisciplinary scholarship that has shown how schools are crucial sites in the formation and reproduction of versions of working-class masculinities constructed through having a "laff" (Willis 1977) fighting, fucking and football (Mac an Ghaill 1994).

Previously having a "laff" and resisting the formal curriculum were key parts of the working-class cultural processes of learning to labour (Willis 1977). Regardless of their levels of academic attainment, few would have had trouble finding a position on the shop floor. Now though, it is poorly educated boys who are found to be the most adversely affected by—and the most vulnerable to experiencing—unemployment in neoliberal labour markets (McDowell 2014; McDowell and Bonner-Thompson 2020; McDowell et al. 2014).

In this time of economic change, we have seen a shift from "masculine" heavy manual work to a "feminised" service sector that is increasingly dependent on "doing deference" (ibid.); forms of labour are typically part-time, poorly paid and insecure. Many young working-class men—still invested in outdated macho, working class, masculine culture—are struggling to adapt. Consequently, these men are "trapped" in deindustrialised neighbourhoods that offer them a limited range of legitimate routes to attaining respectable adult masculinities (Nayak 2006).

A cluster of longitudinal studies by Teesside University's Youth Research Unit, referred to as the "Teesside School", draws on the concept of (youth) transitions in order to show how young adults—often described as being "hard to reach"—navigate varying youth-to-adult transitions under similar economic conditions in the deindustrialised and disadvantaged neighbourhoods of the Northeast (see Johnston et al. 2000; MacDonald and Marsh 2005; Webster et al. 2004). The economic developments of recent decades have had a significant impact on the post-schooling trajectories of many young people—including those who come from more affluent backgrounds. However, as the Teesside studies show, it is the transitions of young people who are at the higher end of the poverty spectrum that are the most adversely affected.

While the Teesside School and others have provided excellent insights into youth-to-adulthood transitions in places of extreme poverty—and a vast amount of qualitative enquiries have documented the gendered experiences of schooling among working-class boys—there is not the same level of academic focus that explicitly explores the gender and construction of masculinities among criminals and prisoners. Serious crime, as Cockburn and Oakley (2013) have pointed out, is overwhelmingly committed by men. Likewise, DeKeseredy and Schwartz (2005) have suggested that men commit almost 100% of all violent crime. It follows that, in England and Wales, the prison population at any one time during the last century has been over 90% male (Sturge 2020).

Carlsson (2013) notes that, given the sheer extent of the presence of men in official figures on crime and imprisonment, it is "remarkable that so little focus has been directed on gender and masculinities" (2013, p. 662). There are some notable exceptions, though, where scholars have positioned gender and masculinity as being central to their analysis of crime (see Collier 1998; Messerschmidt 1994; Messerschmidt and Tomsen 2018; Winlow 2001, 2004).

Other work has also been undertaken in which researchers have recognised the importance of masculinity in generating street identity or cultures (Barker 2005; Bourgois 2003; Mullins 2006). James Messerschmidt (1997)—a leading scholar in this area and a close collaborator of the major protagonist behind masculinity studies, Connell—argues that gender is situationally constructed. Moreover, he contends that—in the absence of legitimate avenues for constructing masculinities, such as paid work—many (young) men will use whatever resources are available to them, including crime and violence, as a means of "doing masculinity".

As with the relatively low number of qualitative studies that currently exist on crime and masculinities, the dearth of empirical research that explores the gender and masculinities of prisoners is surprising, considering that prisons are among the last official institutions still segregated by gender. This is not to argue that there is a lack of penal research, but rather, that there is a notable lack of focus on the gendered nature of prisoners.

There is a plethora of rich classical sociological studies on prisons. These either centre on debates that claim prison culture and identities are generated as a result of prisoner adaptation to the deprivation of the prison space (Clemmer 1958; Sykes 2007) or, alternatively, focus on importation debates: the notion that criminal hierarchies or street subcultures are directly imported into the prison space (Irwin and Cressey 1962). Although such studies do not explicitly draw upon ideas of gender by way of an analytical framework, the attention that they typically afford to prison subcultures concerns the ways in which these serve to signpost hierarchised masculinities, thereby recognising the role of the prison space in sustaining and reproducing prison/criminal masculinities.

Among more recent penal scholarships, a scattering of studies has appeared with an encouraging growth in contemporary academic interest in the gendered nature of male prisoners. Writing predominantly from an American penal perspective, Sabo et al. (2001) published their edited collection, *Prison Masculinities*, almost two decades ago. In this volume, they highlighted how masculinities in the hyper violent male space of the prison have to be continuously worked—and competed—for, showing that they are organised around the adherence to and policing of a universal prisoner/criminal code.

More recently Maycock's and Hunt's (2018) *New Perspectives on Prison Masculinities* offers 13 chapters that have been primarily written by UK prison scholars. They cover a broad spectrum of topics from the well-observed hypermasculine to the lesser-explored, spiritual prisoner masculinities. Jewkes' (2005) widely cited research shows how proving one's male credentials on the streets—which for many working-class young men, often leads to criminal behaviour and, consequently, incarceration—is itself a prerequisite for successfully adapting to life "inside".

Other research into UK prisons illustrates how prison masculinities prove to be detrimental to the health of men in prison (de Viggiani 2012). Prison masculinities are not so much constructed against the backdrop of prison structures and authority as they were in the context of classical penal scholarship; rather, they are now much more complex and fluid. They are often organised in the prison arena around matters of faith, race and ethnicity (Phillips 2012), the type of offence committed (Evans and Wallace 2008), possessions (clothes), in-cell possessions (electrical), outside (criminal) contacts and a relationship to drugs (Crewe 2009).

Scholarship on prison and criminal masculinities—and transition studies in impoverished neighbourhoods, masculinity and schooling—provides a valuable lens into classed and gendered trajectories over one or two specific sites such as locality and employment or class and schooling, for example. Although most of the existing research speaks closely to my own experiences of these crucial spaces, confirming that my pathway to prison was determined many years before I was handed my first sentence, few qualitative studies explicitly employ a gender analysis in order to explore how these key sites interconnect and serve to construct and maintain marginalised and prison masculinities.

In her paper "Autoethnography and Emotion as Intellectual Resources", Jewkes (2012) has argued that our subjective experiences and life histories impact every aspect of the research process: from how we choose our object of enquiry to how we accumulate and analyse the data, right up to the presentation of our findings. This was certainly the case for me and for this study. Drawing on both my personal experiences and existing literature, my ambition was to use the method of partial observation and life history interviews so as to provide a complete picture of (mainly) adult male prisoners' classed and gendered trajectories across the multiple spaces of neighbourhood, education, employment and incarceration. Despite being based in a prison, in undertaking this study, I was not only interested in the creation and maintenance of masculinities within the prison space but also—unlike a lot of prison research—on how matters of class and gender intersect with key spaces both prior to and post incarceration.

1.1   Aims and Objectives

Largely led by Connell's (1995, 2000) hegemonic masculinity framework—particularly her relational concept of protest masculinities as well as the Teesside School's work on transitions (Johnston et al. 2000; MacDonald and Marsh 2005; Webster et al. 2004), the overarching aim of this study has been to explore the classed and gendered trajectories of a group of UK male prisoners and to examine if, and to what extent, significant cultural and institutional spaces were complicit in the construction and reinforcement of their versions of protest masculinities. In this study, my key objectives have been: to investigate if, and how class and gender intersect in the configuration of versions of protest masculinities; to assess the extent to which, and ways in which, investments in versions of protest masculinities lead informants to contribute to their own economic marginalisation, incarceration and continued disadvantage; and to explore the respondents' gender trajectories across key sites including neighbourhoods, schooling/education, working lives and prison, showing how these interconnect to create and maintain pathways to incarceration.

1.2   Structure of the Book

In Chapter 2 (Theorising Marginalised Masculinities), I set out the theoretical framework that underpins this study. I chart the rise of critical men's studies and introduce and critically evaluate Connell's (1995, 2000) theory of hegemonic masculinity and relational concept of protest masculinity.

Then in Chapter 3 (Economic Change: Post Industrial Masculinities), I review the existing scholarship on how boys and men navigate post-industrial masculinities. I chart the rich plethora of research on working-class masculinity, schooling and attainment. This is followed by an evaluation of (youth) transitions literature. In this evaluation I draw on the Teesside School's—and other—research that investigates how, in heavily deindustrialised regions in conditions of extreme poverty, young people navigate varying and alternative transitions to adulthood. After that, I explore the paucity of work that undertakes a specifically gender-focused analysis of criminal and prison masculinities. I conclude the chapter by showing how this study adds to existing research through a gendered analysis of how these key sites interconnect in creating and maintaining marginalised masculinities.

Chapter 4 (Background and Methods: Epistemological Privilege?) offers a sense of place and contextualises the study by briefly charting Hull's industrial legacy. I introduce Hull Local Prison—the site of my research—explaining its role in the prison estate and why I have chosen to focus upon it for the purposes of my research. In the following section, I discuss the qualitative strategies that I have employed for data gathering and analysis. I then go on to argue that, contrary to the many claims of epistemological privilege of "insider" positionality, my role as an ex-con prison researcher presented many challenges and often felt like a burden. After this, I outline how data for the project were gathered through the method of life history interviews, explaining why I used this approach—as well as the limitations of doing so.

In Chapter 5 ("Local Lads: Pathways to Prison"), I document the respondents' pre-prison backgrounds, mapping their pathways to incarceration. To understand the participants' biographies of exclusion it is necessary to explore the spaces in which they learned to become men. I chart how early masculinities were learned, performed, rejected or reinforced on the streets of their deprived neighbourhoods. I then explore the men's offending trajectories, highlighting the progressive and transitional nature of their criminal careers. I then consider how most of the men advanced from masculine posturing and adrenaline "buzz" crimes to criminal masculinities predicted upon being "grafters" or big "earners". I then highlight the prevalence—and role—of violence in "doing" street versions of protest masculinity.

In Chapter 6 ("(Non)Working Lives"), I explore how masculine investments made under the adverse conditions of childhood and adolescence not only seriously disrupted the men's entry into local labour markets, but also compromised their ability to sustain long-term employment. I argue that the criminal careers and early incarceration that fractured the school-to-work transitions of these respondents positioned them at the extreme end of the demographic of undereducated men who were found to be most adversely affected by widespread economic restructuring.

In experiencing difficulties in trying to turn away from the monetary rewards and visceral pleasure that are linked to criminal lifestyles, respondents significantly furthered their own marginalisation as young adults. Following this discussion, I look at how biographical scars—including street-worn bodies, long criminal records and an ex-con status—erode already-limited options in a changing labour market that is reliant on integrity and honesty—as well as "doing deference". I end the chapter with an analysis of the role that prison education and training opportunities play in supporting respondents to meet the challenges of changing workplaces once they have been released from prison.

In Chapter 7 ("Boys to 'Cons': Youth-to-Adult Transitions in Penal Spaces"), I trace how street-based protest masculinities were first imported into the penal space and adapted in relation to existing prison masculine cultures. I argue that earlier gendered experiences on the streets, in "care" and in both mainstream and alternative schooling spaces proved to be better preparation for serving time than for the changing workplace for these men. I then suggest that in the criminal justice system, transitions to adulthood—for many respondents—were institutionally imposed through uncompromising age-based markers. At the age of 18, for instance, most of these men made the transition into impoverished and violent young adult penal spaces that exacerbated—rather than challenged—troubling masculine performances. Reaching "full con" status at the age of 21 significantly changed—to the relief of some of the respondents—what constituted respected prison masculinities.

REFERENCES

Alexander, C. (2000). *The Asian gang: Ethnicity, identity, masculinity*. Oxford: Berg.

Allen, R., Bibby, D., & Parameshwaran, M. (2015). *Missing talent: Raising the aspirations and achievement of the 7,000 highly able pupils who fall behind at secondary school*. London: Sutton Trust.

Anderson, E. (1999). *Code of the street: Decency, violence, and the moral life of the inner city*. New York and London: W. W. Norton.

Ball, S. J. (2003). *Class strategies and the education market: The middle classes and social advantage*. London: Routledge.

Barker, G. (2005). *Dying to be men: Youth, masculinity and social exclusion: Youth and masculinity and social exclusion*. London: Routledge.

Bourgois, P. (2003). *In search of respect: Selling crack in El Barrio*. Cambridge: Cambridge University Press.

Brunton-Smith, I., & Hopkins, K. (2013). *The factors associated with proven re-offending following release from prison: Findings from Waves 1 to 3 of SPCR: Results from the Surveying Prisoner Crime Reduction (SPCR) longitudinal cohort study of prisoners*. London: Ministry of Justice.

Carlsson, C. (2013). Masculinities, persistence, and desistance. *Criminology, 51*(3), 661–693. https://doi.org/10.1111/1745-9125.12016.

Clemmer, D. (1958). *The prison community*. New York: Holt, Rinehart & Winston.

Coates, S. (2016). *Unlocking potential: A review of education in prison*. London: Ministry of Justice.

Cockburn, C., & Oaklek, A. (2013). The cost of masculine crime. *Open Democracy*. https://www.opendemocracy.net/5050/ann-oakley-cynthia-cockburn/cost-of-masculine-crime. Accessed 26 February 2015.

Collier, R. (1998). *Masculinities, crime and criminology: Men, heterosexuality and the criminal(ised) other*. London: Sage.

Connell, R. (1995). *Masculinities*. Cambridge: Polity.

Connell, R. (2000). *The men and the boys*. Cambridge: Polity.

Corrigan, P. (1979). *Schooling the smash street kids*. London: Palgrave Macmillan.

Crewe, B. (2009). *The prisoner society: Power, adaptation and social life in an English prison*. Oxford: Oxford University Press.

de Viggiani, N. (2012). Trying to be something you are not: Masculine performances within a prison setting. *Men and Masculinities, 15*(3), 271–291. https://doi.org/10.1177/1097184X12448464.

DeKeseredy, W. S., & Schwartz, M. D. (2005). Masculinities and interpersonal violence. In M. S. Kimmel, J. Hearn, & R. Connell (Eds.), *Handbook of studies on men and masculinities* (pp. 353–366). London: Sage.

Evans, G. (2006). *Educational failure and working class white children in Britain*. Basingstoke: Palgrave Macmillan.

Evans, T., & Wallace, P. (2008). A prison within a prison? The masculinity narratives of male prisoners. *Men and Masculinities, 10,* 484–507. https://doi.org/10.1177/1097184X06291903.

Frosh, S., Phoenix, A., & Pattman, R. (2002). *Young masculinities: Understanding boys in contemporary society.* Basingstoke: Palgrave.

Gunter, A. (2010). *Growing up bad? Black youth, "road" culture and badness in an East London neighbourhood.* London: The Tufnell Press.

House of Commons Educational Committee. (2014). *Underachievement in education by white working class children* (First Report of Session 2014–15). London: The Stationery Office.

Irwin, J., & Cressey. D. R. (1962). Thieves, convicts and the inmate culture. *Social Problems, 10,* 142–155. https://doi.org/10.2307/799047, https://www.jstor.org/stable/799047.

Jewkes, Y. (2002). *Captive audience: Media, masculinity, and power in prisons.* Cullompton: Willan.

Jewkes, Y. (2005). *Men behind bars: Men and masculinities, 8,* 44–63. https://doi.org/10.1177/1097184X03257452.

Jewkes, Y. (2012). Autoethnography and emotion as intellectual resources doing prison research differently. *Qualitative Inquiry, 18*(1), 63–75. https://doi.org/10.1177/1077800411428942.

Johnston, L., MacDonald, R., Mason, P., Ridley, L., & Webster, C. (2000). *Snakes and ladders: Young people, transitions and social exclusion.* Bristol: Policy Press.

Kennedy, E. (2013). *Children and young people in custody 2012–13.* London: HM Inspectorate of Prisons and Youth Justice Board.

Mac an Ghaill, M. (1994). *The making of men: Masculinities, sexualities and schooling.* Buckingham: Open University Press.

MacDonald, R., & Marsh, J. (2005). *Disconnected youth? Growing up in Britain's poor neighbourhoods.* Basingstoke: Palgrave Macmillan.

Maycock, M., & Hunt, K. (Eds.). (2018). *New perspectives on prison masculinities.* London: Palgrave Macmillan.

McAra, L., & McVie, S. (2013). Delivering justice for children and young people: Key messages from the Edinburgh Study of Youth Transitions and Crime. In A. Dockley (Ed.), *Justice for young people: Papers by Winners of the Research Medal 2013* (pp. 3–14). Howard League for Penal Reform. https://d19ylpo4aovc7m.cloudfront.net/fileadmin/howard_league/user/online_publications/Justice_for_young_people_web.pdf.

McDowell, L. (2003). *Redundant masculinities? Employment change and white working class youth.* Oxford: Blackwell.

McDowell, L. (2014). The sexual contract: Youth, masculinity and the uncertain promise of waged work in Austerity Britain. *Australian Feminist Studies, 29*(79), 31–49. https://doi.org/10.1080/08164649.2014.901281.

McDowell, L., & Bonner-Thompson, C. (2020). The other side of coastal towns: Young men's precarious lives on the margins of England. *Environment and*

Planning A: Economy and Space, 52(5), 916–932. https://doi.org/10.1177/0308518X19887968.

McDowell, L., Rootham, E., & Hardgrove, A. (2014). Politics, anti-politics, quiescence and radical unpolitics: Young men's political participation in an "ordinary" English town. *Journal of Youth Studies, 17*(1), 42–62. https://doi.org/10.1080/13676261.2013.825709.

Messerschmidt, J. W. (1994). Schooling, masculinities and youth crime by white boys. In T. Newburn & E. A. Stanko (Eds.), *Just boys doing business? Men, masculinities and crime* (pp. 81–99). London: Routledge.

Messerschmidt, J. W. (1997). *Crime as structured action: Gender, race, class and crime in the making.* Thousand Oaks, CA and London: Sage.

Messerschmidt, J. W., & Tomsen, S. (2018). Masculinities and crime. In W. S. DeKeseredy & M. Dragiewicz (Eds.), *Routledge handbook of critical criminology* (2nd ed., pp. 83–95). London, U.K.: Routledge.

Ministry of Justice. (2018). *Education and employment strategy.* London: Ministry of Justice.

Mullins, C. W. (2006). *Holding your square: Masculinities, streetlife, and violence.* Cullompton: Willan.

Nayak, A. (2006). Displaced masculinities: Chavs, youth and class in the post-industrial city. *Sociology, 40*(5), 813–831. https://doi.org/10.1177/0038038506067508.

O'Donnell, M., & Sharpe, S. (2000). *Uncertain masculinities: Youth, ethnicity, and class in contemporary Britain.* London: Routledge.

Phillips, C. (2012). *The multicultural prison: Ethnicity, masculinity, and social relations among prisoners.* Oxford: Oxford University Press.

Reay, D. (2018). *Miseducation: Inequality, education and the working classes.* Bristol: Policy Press.

Roberts, S. (2018). *Young working-class men in transition.* London: Routledge.

Sabo, D., Kupers, T., & London, W. (Eds.). (2001). *Prison masculinities.* Philadelphia, PA: Temple University Press.

Sturge, G. (2020). *Prison population statistics.* House of Commons Library. http://researchbriefings.files.parliament.uk/documents/SN04334/SN04334.pdf. Accessed 1 June 2017.

Sykes, G. (2007). *The society of captives: A study of a maximum security prison.* Princeton, NJ: Princeton University Press.

Webster, C., Simpson, D., & MacDonald, R. (2004). *Poor transitions: Social exclusion and young adults.* Bristol: Policy Press.

Willis, P. (1977). *Learning to labor: How working class kids get working class jobs.* Farnborough, England: Saxon House.

Winlow, S. (2001). *Badfellas: Crime, tradition and new masculinities.* Oxford: Berg.

Winlow, S. (2004). Masculinities and crime. *Criminal Justice Matters, 55*(1), 18–19. https://doi.org/10.1080/09627250408553590.

CHAPTER 2

Theorising Marginalised Masculinities

This chapter explores early debates surrounding gender, showing how—in the 1980s—these culminated in more sophisticated theories of masculinity. These were, in part, fuelled by—and in turn fuelled—an explosion of ethnographies of men and masculinities. The momentum, breadth and scope of this scholarship, that has been described by White-head (2002, p. 2) as being "simply staggering", is what this study is built on. As part of this work, I introduce and critically evaluate Raewyn Connell's (1995, 2000) theory of hegemonic masculinity and the relational concept of protest masculinity. Connell's work is often cited as being the major driver behind the surge of interest in men and masculinity and it has key relevance here, in that it constitutes the core conceptual framework that underpins this study.

2.1 Theorising Masculinities

The highly influential—but heavily contested—theory of hegemonic masculinity has had a significant impact on the flourishing growth in the critical study of men and masculinities. Before unpacking the main tenets and limitations of hegemonic masculinity, it is worth charting the emergence of masculinity studies. Early scholarship on gender—especially psychoanalytic approaches that emerged at the beginning of the twentieth century and sex role theory that took off as a dominant schema in the

© The Author(s) 2021
D. Maguire, *Male, Failed, Jailed,*
Palgrave Studies in Prisons and Penology,
https://doi.org/10.1007/978-3-030-61059-3_2

1950s—were based on a binary model of masculinity–femininity that positioned woman as being the inferior "emotional" or "expressive" "other" against the "rational" or "instrumental" man (Whitehead 2002).

It had been assumed that sex roles were deeply rooted in biological discourses and presented as being the cultural elaborations of the male and female sexes. Thus, from this perspective, being a man or a woman meant to act from a generalised set of expectations attached to a given sex. In most cultural contexts there were two roles, or scripts, of male and female (Connell 1995). "Masculinity" and "femininity" were understood as internalised sex roles taught through the process of socialisation.

Western feminism, in the latter decades of the last century, challenged sex role theory by exposing how women were tied to roles of subordination, while male roles benefited from privileges that were inherent within patriarchy (Segal 2007). Men—and male culture—came under critical scrutiny in ways that had never been previously seen. Influenced by the growing feminist critique of patriarchy, male writers too—though still drawing on sex role theory in what is described as the "first wave" in the sociology of masculinity (Whitehead and Barrett 2001)—highlighted the way in which socialisation into dominant masculine ideology was damaging to men's relationships with women, their children and their health (Segal 2007).

Such scholarship laid the foundation to question masculinity as the natural expression of sex and to recognise that sex roles were constrictive and costly to both men and women (see Brannon 1976; Pleck 1976, 1981). In the late 1980s as men's studies emerged under the "second wave" of masculinities scholarship, sex role theory came in for substantive critiques. With its demise, more critical and progressive theorising on men and masculinities surfaced.

With more advanced social constructionist approaches to masculinity, less emphasis was placed on the cost to men that had resulted in previous sex role perspectives. Instead, greater attention was afforded to the centrality of power and dominant ways of being a man (Segal 2007; Whitehead 2002). In these theoretical developments, the notion of a plurality of masculinities was introduced, out of which the concept of hegemonic masculinity would later emerge as a "politically, yet contested, powerful concept" (Whitehead and Barrett 2001, p. 15) as I will show in more detail later on in the chapter.

Still under the label of "social constructionism", the "third wave" in the sociology of masculinity has drawn from post-structuralism, using

Foucauldian ideas to propose that men's sense of identity is constructed through and maintained by dominant discursive practices (Whitehead and Barrett 2001). This approach rejects commonly accepted binary divisions such as the traditional male—female, man—woman, masculine—feminine, heterosexual—homosexual, black—white distinctions, arguing that they oversimplify gender inequality and only serve to reproduce the power axis between the sexes (see Butler 1990; Collier 1998; MacInnes 1998).

From this perspective "identity" and "self" are not given states but, rather, are discursively and "reflexively" configured. The body—socially constructed through powerful discourse—is simply a site of interaction for competing political and strategic interests (Butler 1990; Shilling 2003). A leading theorist in this area Judith Butler (1990) has argued—based on the concept of performativity—that there is no true sex; gender only comes into being through a set of socially regulated and repeated performances that reinforce and reproduce "heteronormativity". Performances of gender "imitate" dominant cultural representations of what it is to be a woman or a man. These fictitious representations are not politically innocent; they fuel the illusion of a natural (hetero)sexuality and gender identity. Through continuous reiteration, they bring gendered subjects into being (Butler 1990).

Connell (1995) cautions against seeing gender only as a performance; she warns against privileging the symbolic dimension of social practices over all other factors. Gender, she argues, is of real material meaning in the context of childbirth/rearing, violence, the accumulation of wealth and so on. Constructionist approaches are unified in their proposal that masculinity is socially created and reproduced through interactions between people, language and cultural discourses.

Gender is understood not as being a fixed natural phenomenon but, rather as something that is historically and culturally specific. It is something that we do (West and Zimmerman 1987)—something that has to be earned (Edley and Wetherell 1997), through a set of "performative acts" (Butler 1990). It is defined as much through what it is not as it is in positive terms (Jefferson 2002). From this perspective, masculine identities are seen as being gendered practices that are relational, contradictory and multiple. Depending on their particular social positions, men configure their masculinities in a plurality of fashions (Butler 1990; Connell 1995, 2000; Connell and Messerschmidt 2005; Edley and Wetherell 1997; West and Zimmerman 1987; Whitehead 2002).

2.2   Critical Men's Studies

Under the umbrella term of social constructionism, the rapid and continuing growth in critical studies of men has seen the interrogation of men as men across wide-ranging experiences and sites. Much of this scholarship reveals how masculinity—as a powerful, violent, controlling and destructive force—is created, maintained, celebrated and legitimatised in the context of cultural practices and the core institutions of Western societies. Michael Messner's (1990, 1995) influential research has shown how organised sports, for instance, are major arenas for the creation and promotion of violent—and, often, racialised masculinities (see also Messner and Sabo 1990).

Other researchers, meanwhile, have looked at how the pressures of trying to live up to a dominant masculine ideal can negatively impact men's health (Courtenay 2000; O'Brien et al. 2005; Watson 2000). The role of the male body in the creation and performance of "hard" masculinities has been addressed (Gill et al. 2005; Mosse 1998). Moreover, a large number of studies have explored the cultural representations of "macho" masculinities in film and media (Beynon 2002; Gilmore 2007; Jackson 1991) as well as work on the cultural politics of the black body in advertising (Jackson 1994). Other insightful explorations have focused on the intersection of masculinity and race (Hooks 2003; Majors and Billson 1993), ethnicity (Alexander 2000) and religion (Archer 2001; Gerami 2003; Hopkins 2007).

There is also an increasing body of scholarship by geographers in which they highlight the role of space and place in the creation of masculinities (Berg 1994; Berg and Longhurst 2003; Gorman-Murray and Hopkins 2014; Hopkins and Noble 2009; Van Hoven and Hörschelmann 2005). Such research has unveiled how intra-male violence (Archer 1994; DeKeseredy and Schwartz 2005; Hall 2002; Kenway and Fitzclarence 1997; Messner 1990), homophobia (D. Plummer 1999; Kimmel 2004; K. Plummer 2001), hate crime (Tomsen and Mason 2001) and, sometimes, the murder of gay men (Kimmel and Mahler 2003) relate to the dominant masculine ideology and strategies for performing idealised notions of manhood.

Other research on men has uncovered the ways in which domestic and sexual violence against women are deeply rooted in patriarchal and sexist societies where the core component of masculine identity is considered to be the domination and control of the opposite sex (Flood and Pease

2009; Hearn 1998; Messerschmidt 2000; Schwartz and DeKeseredy 1997). A considerable number of studies have explored the interplay between masculinities and schooling (Corrigan 1979; Evans 2006; Frosh et al. 2001; Mac an Ghaill 1994; Reay 2002, 2004; Skelton 2001; Willis 1977). Likewise important research has considered the subject of masculinities in the changing workplace (Hardgrove et al. 2015; McDowell 2003; Nayak 2003a).

In this large and rapidly expanding body of scholarship on men, there are two surprising areas of deficit as things stand. Currently, the links between masculinity and crime have not been adequately explored— despite the fact that most offenders and prisoners are men. There is also a dearth of ethnographic work that explores masculinities and incarceration.

However, there are some notable exceptions of instances where researchers have explored the interplay between masculinity and crime (Collier 1998; Hood-Williams 2001; Messerschmidt 1993, 1997; Messerschmidt and Tomsen 2018; Tomsen 2008; Winlow 2001). The body of relevant literature is growing, especially in the UK, regarding prison masculinities (Crewe 2009, 2014; Drake 2011; Evans and Wallace 2008; Jewkes 2002, 2005; Maycock and Hunt 2018; Phillips 2012). What is important here, however, is not how the informants' marginalised masculinities were created in one particular site; rather, it is the cyclical interrelations between cultural representations of masculinity, place, schooling, employment, crime and incarceration that are significant. It is in this particular regard that this study contributes to a developing field of scholarship.

2.3   Hegemonic Masculinity

The shift from unitary sex role theory to a plurality of masculinities— that has led to almost four decades of a sustained body of global critical scholarship on men—owes much to Connell's theory of hegemonic masculinity. Connell appropriated the concept of hegemony from Antonio Gramsci's (1971) analysis of class relations: an idea that denotes the cultural dynamic by which one class sees subordination by the dominant class as being "natural".

Connell has used this term in the context of masculinity and defines hegemonic masculinity as being a "configuration of gender practice which embodies the currently accepted answer to the problem of the legitimacy of patriarchy, which guarantees (or is taken to guarantee) the dominant position of men and the subordination of women" (Connell 1995, p. 77). She suggests that the version of masculinity that is hegemonic in any given pattern of gender relations is concerned with maintaining hierarchically organised power relations between men and women, and between men (Beasley 2008). In essence, she recognises that all masculinities are not created equal. Indeed, she addresses the multiplicity of masculinities by differentiating between the hegemonic masculine ideal of the racially superior, economically successful and visibly heterosexual white men who occupy positions at the summit of the hierarchy and—at the bottom of the hierarchy—the subordinated or marginalised masculinities of homosexual, ethnic minority and working-class men (Connell 1995).

Connell is careful to point out that most men never fully live up to the hegemonic ideal. Nevertheless in their endeavour to do so, they are complicit in the "hegemonic project" (1995, p. 79). Although many men may not exhibit all the characteristics of hegemonic masculinity, most will implicitly (or explicitly) endorse its core ideals and reap benefits from the patriarchal gender system that it legitimises and maintains.

The strength of Connell's theory is multifaceted. It lies not only in Connell's recognition that gender relations are configured in ways that justify the positioning of men as being the dominant gender but also in the way in which it captures the plurality of masculinities—significantly, the ways in which men are hierarchically stratified within society depending on race, class, age, sexual identity and so on (Connell 2000). Furthermore, there is an especially important dimension of this proposed hierarchy between men and women—and the hierarchy among men—upon which I draw in later chapters. It is that, although it is widely accepted that men in general benefit materially, socially and politically from their position as the dominant gender—advantages that have been described by Connell as the "patriarchal dividend"—these benefits are not distributed equally among all men. Marginalised men, as well as women, pay a price for the maintenance of an unequal gender order (Connell 1995; McDowell 2003).

2.4   Protest Masculinity

Connell's (1989, 1995) own empirical research on men from impoverished urban environments has shown that marginalised or subordinated masculinities will often be expressed or resisted through the form of what she terms "protest masculinity". The gendered performances of the participants in this study closely resemble the protest masculine identities shown in the work of Connell's and others (Walker 2006). It is, as such, worth exploring this identity of "protest masculinity" in a bit more detail. Connell's notion of protest masculinity builds on earlier psychoanalytical and functionalist writing on gender. Early writing on masculine protest, for instance, has been attributed to leading psychoanalyst Alfred Adler (1978) who proposed that it is what transpires when society overvalues masculinity. Those who engage in forms of masculine protest "attest to the subjective 'fact' that masculinity is 'prized' and 'superior' according to cultural standards" (cited in Mosak and Maniacci 2013, p. 104).

These men, Adler claimed, act in an overly masculine way—like "real men"—because, subjectively, they want to feel superior. Those who feel deficient in any way will either withdraw or will, more frequently, over-compensate in their masculine performance. A leading sociologist of the period, Talcott Parsons (1964), claimed that masculine protest results are most likely to originate from single-parent, female-headed households in which adolescent boys lack a father figure from whom they could learn to construct appropriate gender identities. Without such guidance, these young people invest in "bad boy" forms of masculinity, positioning themselves against everything that they consider to be "feminine". Most "bad boys", he claimed, grow out of their protest identities as they reach adulthood (Parsons 1964; Walker 2006).

Connell's (1989, 1995) use of the term "protest masculinity", as Walker (2006) has observed, is intrinsically linked to one's class position. The consequences of early "bad boy" forms of protest and limited resources make it much more difficult for poorer men to alter their masculine performances upon reaching adulthood than it is for their middle-class counterparts to do so. Connell (1995) has noted that, in western industrialised societies, large numbers of working-class young men are growing up without any expectation of securing stable employment: a key marker of successful adult masculinity. As a result, most of these men are shaping their identities as a response to class deprivation.

Cycles of casual work and long periods of unemployment cast many men into impoverished lifestyles. In these conditions, the project of protest masculinity is cultivated throughout the transition to adulthood. According to Connell, forms of protest masculinity develop out of situations where the claims to power that are so central to hegemonic masculinity are constantly negated by economic and cultural weaknesses.

In response to their relative powerlessness, men in this milieu use whatever resources are available to them to construct their own versions of masculinity: ones that usually involve hypermasculine, aggressive displays of violence and criminal behaviour (ibid.).

Cycles of casual work and long periods of unemployment cast many men into impoverished lifestyles. In these conditions, the project of protest masculinity is cultivated throughout the transition to adulthood. According to Connell, forms of protest masculinity develop out of situations where the claims to power that are so central to hegemonic masculinity are constantly negated by economic and cultural weaknesses. In response to their relative powerlessness, men in this milieu use whatever resources are available to them to construct their own versions of masculinity: ones that usually involve hypermasculine, aggressive displays of violence and criminal behaviour (ibid.).

Often, these protest identities are exhibited through a "juxtaposition of overt misogyny, compulsory heterosexuality and homophobia" (Connell 1995, p. 115). Those who adopt such identities are greatly concerned with "face work" whereby a great deal of effort is put into keeping up a front. This marginalised masculine identity is, therefore, one that both rejects and resists hegemonic masculinity on the one hand, while picking up themes of "hegemonic masculinity and rework[ing] them in a context of poverty" on the other (Connell 1995, p. 114). A core feature of protest masculinity is that it "divides the group [of workless working-class and poor men] from the rest of the working class" (Connell 1995; Walker 2006, p. 17). The main consequence of this, however—one that has been only too clearly demonstrated by the lives of the men that have been documented in this study—is that this performance ultimately leads nowhere. Protest masculinity, according to Connell, "looks like a cul-de-sac" (ibid., p. 117).

2.5   CHALLENGING HEGEMONIC MASCULINITY

Hegemonic masculinity has come under some criticism. There is, it has been claimed, too much conceptual "slippage" (Flood 2002; Beasley 2008) or, as Mike Donaldson (1993) has asserted, it covers too much and, therefore, not enough. A major issue that has been raised is the idea that the concept of hegemonic masculinity negates the significance of internal processes or the role of the psyche in (male) identity (Gadd 2003; Hood-Williams 2001; Jefferson 2002),

For Collier (1998), the idea reduces the complexity and nuances of what men actually do to simplistic and static typologies that only tend to emphasise the negative traits of manhood. Similarly, other scholars have argued about who—if anyone—embodies hegemonic masculinity (Demetriou 2001; Donaldson 1993). With so few men actually living up to the ideal—and because of the lack of substance in models of hegemonic masculinity who have been portrayed in films and other media, it is difficult, according to Whitehead (2002) and Donaldson (1993), to know what it actually looks like in practice.

2.5.1   Inclusive (Softer) Masculinities

The contemporary relevance of hegemonic masculinity has been questioned by some scholars, who argue that contemporary masculinities are more complex, "softer" and more open in terms of sexuality (Anderson 2009; McCormack 2012). Roberts (2014) has contended that the most symbolically important distinction between men in accordance with Connell's theory of hegemonic masculinity is sexuality, "with subordination occurring not only in terms of [the] oppression of homosexual boys, but in the gender policing of heterosexual boys and men" (p. 10).

Some recent research—that focused primarily upon middle-class male, sixth-form pupils and university students—showed that (young) men's attitudes towards homosexuality have "softened" or have become much more progressive. Configurations of masculinities are not, it would seem, as dependent upon homophobia and the aggressive enforcing of heterosexuality as they once were (Anderson 2009; McCormack 2012). In recognition of this shift, these researchers have been developing what they call an "Inclusive Masculinity Framework" (IMF) (ibid.).

Some scholars, like Roberts (2018), have extended the IMF to demonstrate other shifts in the configuration of working-class masculinities. Set against a tide of earlier research (McDowell 2003; Hardgrove et al. 2015; Nayak 2006), Roberts blended IMF with Bourdieu's theory of habitus to make sense of how working-class men are learning to adopt deference and configure the 'softer' types of masculinities that are needed in order to work in service-based, feminised labour markets. This was not, though, reflected in the experiences of the men in this study who—as I show later, in the empirical part of the book—were much more closely aligned to Connell's masculine protest forms of identity than the inclusive gender performances of McCormack's and Anderson's (middle-class) pupils/university students and Roberts' (2018) shop retail workers.

2.5.2   Reconfiguring Hegemonic Masculinity

In response to their critics, Connell (2000)—together with her long-term collaborator James Messerschmidt (Connell and Messerschmidt 2005)—reconfigured the concept of hegemonic masculinity, outlining how it might be appropriately applied in an empirical way (Messerschmidt 2012). In doing so, they bolstered their theory's already-strong analytical potential for helping researchers to understand their informants' gendered trajectories. A key aspect that Connell and Messerschmidt emphasised in their reworking of the concept—but was, notably, also one that has always been at the root of Connell's work—was that the subordinated and marginalised masculinities upon which the hegemonic form is dependent are not fixed.

To base a critique on this notion, as "inclusive masculinity" tends to do, fails to fully account for the "historicity of gender and ignores the massive evidence of change in social definitions of masculinity" (Connell and Messerschmidt 2005, p. 838). A major shift in their reappraisal is the emphasis that they place on the geographies of masculinities. They insist that, by analysing "empirically existing hegemonic masculinities", we will be able to gain broader understandings of the power relations between the genders—and between men—at the local, regional and global levels (ibid., p. 849).

This study contributes to these debates on men and masculinities by analysing the hegemonic masculinity at a local level. This involves exploring the informants' construction of masculinity in the "arenas of face-to-face interaction of families, organizations, and immediate communities" (Connell and Messerschmidt 2005, p. 849). The revision of the concept to include spatial differences captures variations in the forms of hegemonic and marginalised masculinities that exist in different localities, sites and spaces.

In a related and important response to the conceptual "slippage" critiques, Messerschmidt (2012) has offered some clarity by suggesting that a type of masculinity might be "dominant"... the most "celebrated ... in a specific social setting [neighbourhood or locality]; ... exercising power over people and events–'calling the shots' and 'running the show'" (p. 72). However, as Messerschmidt points out, it is not necessarily hegemonic unless it contributes to legitimising "hierarchical gender relations between men and women, between masculinity and femininity, and among men" (p. 73).

A commitment to seeking to understand how the informants navigated (marginalised) masculine trajectories within the confines of their regions, neighbourhoods and institutional spaces lies at the heart of this book. I have made use of Connell's theory of hegemonic masculinity with an awareness of its limitations. Nonetheless, it remains a suitable primary framework for this endeavour. Connell's theory continues to be, as Andrew Gorman-Murray and Peter Hopkins (2014) have noted, among the most "informative and powerful tools for explaining gender dynamics and power" (p. 7).

Having charted the rise of critical studies of men—and highlighted some of the key debates and theories that have stemmed from this large (and still rapidly growing) body of work—I now turn to the notion of a contemporary crisis of masculinity.

2.6   Masculine Crisis

Roberts (2014) has noted that—although the last four decades of critical research on men have exposed the hierarchal operation of power and differences among multiple masculinities—public debates, especially in the mainstream media and contexts of political/policy discourse, are dominated by claims of a crisis in masculinity. Segal (2007), commenting on this post-millennial scrutiny of men and masculinity, noted that the western world was surprised to discover that men experience gender troubles too. Boys' low levels of academic attainment, coupled with men's high rates of unemployment, crime, incarceration and suicide, have fuelled male "crisis-talk" since the start of the 1990s.

Political, academic and social commentaries on the troubles that are faced by *some* boys and men under the banner of a "crisis in masculinity" fail to account for the serious criticisms of this discourse by many of its opponents at the height of the masculinity crisis moral panic (Beynon 2002; Segal 2007; Whitehead 2002). Talks of a "crisis in masculinity" it has been argued, simply mark a step backwards to essentialising discourses that position men as a single, large, homogenous, ahistorical group who remain undifferentiated by class, race, ethnicity or place (Whitehead 2002).

A close look at male crisis-talk shows that it is working-class men/boys—not men per se—who are experiencing difficulties as a result of the seismic economic and societal changes that have occurred over recent decades. In the following sections and empirical chapters of this study, I chart the research that compellingly shows that it is mainly (young) men from poor neighbourhoods who are academically "under-achieving" (Nuttall and Doherty 2014). Such individuals are over three times more likely than their female counterparts to be permanently excluded from school (Graham et al. 2019).

It is these same undereducated young men who are finding themselves unemployable in an increasingly "feminised" labour market. If they do manage to secure work, it is usually in unstable and economically exploitative positions (McDowell and Bonner-Thompson 2020; McDowell et al. 2014; Nayak 2006; Shildrick and MacDonald 2007). These are the very same socially disadvantaged men/boys who are considerably more likely than their middle class peers to be convicted of committing crimes (DeKeseredy and Schwartz 2005; Newburn 2016).

It is the boys and men who come from poor neighbourhoods who make up the majority of the UK prison population (Crewe 2009; Jewkes 2005): a group of individuals that, for the last century has been over 90% male (Ministry of Justice 2012). Crime statistics and research have consistently shown that it is men who come from the poorest communities who are the most likely to violently attack others—or be attacked—and to be the victims of homicide (Ellis 2019; Office for National Statistics 2018), to abuse drugs (Seddon 2006) and alcohol (De Visser and Smith 2007) and have a far higher mortality rate when compared to other men who come from other class backgrounds and less deprived neighbourhoods (Steel et al. 2018).

Political commentaries and popular press coverage that purport a crisis in masculinity only serve to obscure or render invisible the structural inequalities that blight the lives of poor white—and certain ethnic minority men. Contrary to the aforementioned homogenising discourses of masculinity, one of the main objectives of this book is to explore how locality or place intersects with other social categories—such as class and gender—in the hierarchal (re)production of marginalised and protest masculinities. As McDowell and Massey noted two decades ago: "what it means to be masculine in the Fens is not the same as what it means in Lancashire" (Massey 1994, p. 178).

2.7 Conclusion

In this chapter, I have mapped early debates surrounding gender. I have shown how, in the 1980s, these culminated in the formation of more sophisticated theories of masculinity and the emergence of critical men's studies. I chart how Connell's highly influential—but heavily contested—theory of hegemonic masculinity has significantly contributed to the burgeoning of critical studies of men as a field of enquiry.

While acknowledging some of the limitations that have been levelled at Connell's hegemonic masculinity and her relational concept of protest masculinity, I contend that the strength of her framework—the one that I have chosen to adopt for this study—is that it recognises the plurality of masculinities and, significantly, the ways in which men are hierarchically stratified in accordance with their race, class, age, sexual identity and so on. The additional value of this framework lies in its recognition of hegemonic masculinities that have been empirically proven to exist at the local, regional and global level.

References

Adler, A. (1978). Masculine protest and a critique of Freud. In H. Ansbacher & R. Ansbacher (Eds.), *Cooperation between the sexes*. New York: Anchor.

Alexander, C. (2000). *The Asian gang: Ethnicity, identity, masculinity*. Oxford: Berg.

Anderson, E. (2009). *Inclusive masculinity: The changing nature of masculinities*. London: Routledge.

Archer, J. (1994). *Male violence*. London: Routledge.

Archer, L. (2001). 'Muslim brothers, black lads, traditional Asians': British Muslim young men's constructions of race, religion and masculinity. *Feminism & Psychology, 11*(1), 79–105. https://doi.org/10.1177/095935350101 1001005.

Beasley, C. (2008). Rethinking hegemonic masculinity in a globalizing world. *Men and Masculinities, 11*(1), 86–103. https://doi.org/10.1177/109718 4X08315102.

Berg, L. D. (1994). Masculinity, place and a binary discourse of "theory" and "empirical investigation" in the human geography of Aotearoa/New Zealand. *Gender, Place and Culture: A Journal of Feminist Geography, 1*(2), 245–260. https://doi.org/10.1080/09663699408721212.

Berg, L. D., & Longhurst, R. (2003). Placing masculinities and geography. *Gender, Place and Culture, 10*(4), 351–360. https://doi.org/10.1080/096 6369032000153322.

Beynon, J. (2002). *Masculinities and culture*. London: McGraw-Hill Education.

Brannon, R. (1976). The male sex role: Our culture's blueprint for manhood, what it's done for us lately. In B. Robert & D. D. Sarah (Eds.), *The forty-nine percent majority: The male sex role*. Boston: Addison Wesley Publishing Company.

Butler, J. (1990). *Gender trouble and the subversion of identity*. New York and London: Routledge.

Collier, R. (1998). *Masculinities, crime and criminology: Men, heterosexuality and the criminal(ised) other*. London: Sage.

Connell, R. (1989). Cool guys, swots and wimps: The interplay of masculinity and education. *Oxford Review of Education, 15*(3). https://doi.org/10.1080/0305498890150309.

Connell, R. (1995). *Masculinities*. Cambridge: Polity.

Connell, R. (2000). *The men and the boys*. Cambridge: Polity.

Connell, R., & Messerschmidt, J. W. (2005). Hegemonic masculinity rethinking the concept. *Gender & Society, 19*(6), 829–859. https://doi.org/10.1177/0891243205278639.

Corrigan, P. (1979). *Schooling the smash street kids*. London: Palgrave Macmillan.

Courtenay, W. H. (2000). Constructions of masculinity and their influence on men's well-being: A theory of gender and health. *Social Science & Medicine, 50*(10), 1385–1401. https://doi.org/10.1016/S0277-9536(99)00390-1.

Crewe, B. (2009). *The prisoner society: Power, adaptation and social life in an English prison*. Oxford: Oxford University Press.

Crewe, B. (2014). Not looking hard enough masculinity, emotion, and prison research. *Qualitative Inquiry, 20*(4), 392–403. https://doi.org/10.1177/1077800413515829.

De Visser, R. O., & Smith, J. A. (2007). Alcohol consumption and masculine identity among young men. *Psychology & Health, 22*(5), 595–614. https://doi.org/10.1080/14768320600941772.

DeKeseredy, W. S., & Schwartz, M. D. (2005). Masculinities and interpersonal violence. In M. S. Kimmel, J. Hearn, & R. Connell (Eds.), *Handbook of studies on men and masculinities* (pp. 353–366). London: Sage.

Demetriou, D. Z. (2001). Connell's concept of hegemonic masculinity: A critique. *Theory and Society, 30*(3), 337–361. https://doi.org/10.1023/A:1017596718715.

Donaldson, M. (1993). What is hegemonic masculinity? *Theory and Society, 22*(5), 643–657. https://doi.org/10.1007/BF00993540.

Drake, D. (2011). The "dangerous other" in maximum-security prisons. *Criminology and Criminal Justice, 11*(4), 367–382. https://doi.org/10.1177/1748895811408836.

Edley, N., & Wetherell, M. (1997). Jockeying for position: The construction of masculine identities. *Discourse & Society, 8*(2), 203–217. https://doi.org/10.1177/0957926597008002004.

Ellis, A.J. (2019). A de-civilizing reversal or system normal? Rising lethal violence in post-recession austerity United Kingdom. *The British Journal of Criminology, 59*(4), 862–878. https://doi.org/10.1093/bjc/azz001.

Evans, G. (2006). *Educational failure and working class white children in Britain*. Basingstoke: Palgrave Macmillan.

Evans, T., & Wallace, P. (2008). A prison within a prison? The masculinity narratives of male prisoners. *Men and Masculinities, 10,* 484–507. https://doi.org/10.1177/1097184X06291903.

Flood, M. (2002). Between men and masculinity: An assessment of the term "masculinity" in recent scholarship. In S. Pearce & V. Muller (Eds.), *Manning the next millennium: Studies in masculinities*. Perth: Black Swan Press.

Flood, M., & Pease, B. (2009). Factors influencing attitudes to violence against women. *Trauma, Violence, & Abuse, 10*(2), 125–142. https://doi.org/10.1177/1524838009334131.

Frosh, S., Phoenix, A., & Pattman, R. (2002). *Young masculinities: Understanding boys in contemporary society*. Basingstoke: Palgrave.

Gadd, D. (2003). Reading between the lines: Subjectivity and men's violence. *Men and Masculinities, 5*(4), 333–354. https://doi.org/10.1177/1097184X02250838.

Gerami, S. (2003). Mullahs, martyrs, and men conceptualizing masculinity in the Islamic Republic of Iran. *Men and Masculinities, 5*(3), 257–274. https://doi.org/10.1177/1097184X02238526.

Gill, R., Henwood, K., & McLean, C. (2005). Body projects and the regulation of normative masculinity. *Body & Society, 11*(1), 37–62. https://doi.org/10.1177/1357034X05049849.

Gilmore, R. W. (2007). *Golden gulag: Prisons, surplus, crisis, and opposition in globalizing California*. Berkeley and London: University of California Press.

Gorman-Murray, A., & Hopkins, P. (2014). *Masculinities and place*. Farnham: Ashgate.

Graham, B., White, C., Edwards, A., Potter, S., & Street, C. (2019). *School exclusion: A literature review on the continued disproportionate exclusion of certain children*. London: Department for Education.

Gramsci, A. (1971). *Selections from the prison notebooks of Antonio Gramsci*. New York: International.

Hall, S. (2002). Daubing the drudges of fury: Men, violence and the piety of the "hegemonic masculinity" thesis. *Theoretical Criminology, 6*(1), 35–61. https://doi.org/10.1177/136248060200600102.

Hardgrove, A., McDowell, L., & Rootham, E. (2015). Precarious lives, precarious labour: Family support and young men's transitions to work in the UK.

Journal of Youth Studies, 18(8), 1–20. https://doi.org/10.1080/13676261. 2015.1020933.

Hearn, J. (1998). *The violences of men: How men talk about and how agencies respond to men's violence to women.* Thousand Oaks, CA: Sage.

Hood-Williams, J. (2001). Gender, masculinities and crime: From structures to psyches. *Theoretical Criminology, 5*(1), 37–60. https://doi.org/10.1177/1362480601005001003.

Hooks, B. (2003). *We real cool: Black men and masculinity.* New York: Routledge.

Hopkins, P. (2007). Young people, masculinities, religion and race: New social geographies. *Progress in Human Geography, 31*(2), 163–177. https://doi.org/10.1177/0309132507075362.

Hopkins, P., & Noble, G. (2009). Masculinities in place: Situated identities, relations and intersectionality. *Social & Cultural Geography, 10*(8), 811–819. https://doi.org/10.1080/14649360903305817.

Jackson, P. (1991). The cultural politics of masculinity: Towards a social geography. *Transactions of the Institute of British Geographers, 16*(2), 199–213. https://doi.org/10.2307/622614.

Jackson, P. (1994). Black male: Advertising and the cultural politics of masculinity. *Gender, Place & Culture, 1*(1), 49–59. https://doi.org/10.1080/09663699408721200.

Jefferson, T. (2002). Subordinating hegemonic masculinity. *Theoretical Criminology, 6*(1), 63–88. https://doi.org/10.1177/136248060200600103.

Jewkes, Y. (2002). *Captive audience: Media, masculinity, and power in prisons.* Cullompton: Willan.

Jewkes, Y. (2005). *Men behind bars: Men and masculinities, 8,* 44–63. https://doi.org/10.1177/1097184X03257452.

Kenway, J., & Fitzclarence, L. (1997). Masculinity, violence and schooling: Challenging 'poisonous pedagogies'. *Gender and Education, 9*(1), 117–134. https://doi.org/10.1080/09540259721493.

Kimmel, M. (2004). Masculinity as homophobia: Fear, shame, and silence in the construction of gender identity. In P. S. Rothenberg (Ed.), *Race, class, and gender in the United States: An integrated study* (pp. 81–93). New York: Worth.

Kimmel, M., & Mahler, M. (2003). Adolescent masculinity, homophobia, and violence random school shootings, 1982–2001. *American Behavioral Scientist, 46*(10), 1439–1458. https://doi.org/10.1177/0002764203046010010.

Mac an Ghaill, M. (1994). *The making of men: Masculinities, sexualities and schooling.* Buckingham: Open University Press.

MacInnes, J. (1998). *The end of masculinity: The confusion of sexual genesis and sexual difference in modern society.* Buckingham: Open University Press.

Majors, R., & Billson, J. M. (1993). *Cool pose: The dilemmas of black manhood in America* (Reprint ed.). New York: Touchstone.

Massey, D. (1994). *Space, place and gender.* Cambridge: Polity.

Maycock, M., & Hunt, K. (Eds.). (2018). *New perspectives on prison masculinities.* London: Palgrave Macmillan.

McCormack, M. (2012). *The declining significance of homophobia: How teenage boys are redefining masculinity and heterosexuality.* New York and Oxford: Oxford University Press.

McDowell, L. (2003). *Redundant masculinities? Employment change and white working class youth.* Oxford: Blackwell.

McDowell, L., & Bonner-Thompson, C. (2020). The other side of coastal towns: Young men's precarious lives on the margins of England. *Environment and Planning A: Economy and Space, 52*(5), 916–932. https://doi.org/10.1177/0308518X19887968.

McDowell, L., Rootham, E., & Hardgrove, A. (2014). Precarious work, protest masculinity and communal regulation: South Asian young men in Luton, UK. *Work, Employment & Society, 28*(6), 847–864. https://doi.org/10.1177/0950017013510757.

Messerschmidt, J. W. (1993). *Masculinities and crime: Critique and reconceptualization of theory.* Lanham, Md.: Rowman & Littlefield.

Messerschmidt, J. W. (1997). *Crime as structured action: Gender, race, class and crime in the making.* Thousand Oaks, CA and London: Sage.

Messerschmidt, J. W. (2000). Becoming "real men" adolescent masculinity challenges and sexual violence. *Men and Masculinities, 2*(3), 286–307. https://doi.org/10.1177/1097184X00002003003.

Messerschmidt, J. W. (2012). Engendering gendered knowledge: Assessing the academic appropriation of hegemonic masculinity. *Men and Masculinities, 15*(1), 56–76. https://doi.org/10.1177/1097184X11428384.

Messerschmidt, J. W., & Tomsen, S. (2018). Masculinities and crime. In W. S. DeKeseredy & M. Dragiewicz (Eds.), *Routledge handbook of critical criminology* (2nd ed., pp. 83–95). London, U.K.: Routledge.

Messner, M. A. (1990). When bodies are weapons: Masculinity and violence in sport. *International Review for the Sociology of Sport, 25*(3), 203–220. https://doi.org/10.1177/101269029002500303.

Messner, M. A. (1995). *Power at play: Sports and the problem of masculinity* (Reissue ed.). Boston: Beacon Press.

Messner, M. A., & Sabo, D. F. (1990). *Sport, men, and the gender order: Critical feminist perspectives.* Champaign, IL: Human Kinetics.

Ministry of Justice. (2012). *Prison population figures: 2011.* Available at https://www.gov.uk/government/statistics/prison-population-2011. Accessed 12 December 2014.

Mosak, H., & Maniacci, M. (2013). *Primer of Adlerian psychology: The analytic— Behavioural—Cognitive psychology of Alfred Adler*. Philadelphia and London: Routledge.

Mosse, G. L. (1998). *The image of man: The creation of modern masculinity*. New York: Oxford University Press.

Nayak, A. (2003a). "Boyz to Men": Masculinities, schooling and labour transitions in de-industrial times. *Educational Review, 55*(2), 147–159. https://doi.org/10.1080/0013191032000072191.

Nayak, A. (2003b). Last of the 'Real Geordies'? White masculinities and the subcultural response to deindustrialisation. *Environment and Planning D: Society and Space, 21*(1), 7–26. https://doi.org/10.1068/d44j.

Nayak, A. (2006). Displaced masculinities: Chavs, youth and class in the post-industrial city. *Sociology, 40*(5), 813–831. https://doi.org/10.1177/003803 8506067508.

Newburn, T. (2016). Social disadvantage, crime, and punishment. In H. Dean & L. Platt (Eds.), *Social advantage and disadvantage* (pp. 322–345). Oxford: Oxford University Press.

Nuttall, A., & Doherty, J. (2014). Disaffected boys and the achievement gap: "the wallpaper effect" and what is hidden by a focus on school results. *Urban Review, 46*, 800–815. https://doi.org/10.1007/s11256-014-0303-8.

O'Brien, R., Hunt, K., & Hart, G. (2005). 'It's caveman stuff, but that is to a certain extent how guys still operate': Men's accounts of masculinity and help seeking. *Social Science & Medicine, 61*(3), 503–516.

Office for National Statistics. (2018). A summary of violent crime from the year ending March 2017 Crime Survey for England and Wales and police recorded crime.

Parsons, T. (1964). *Essays in sociological theory* (2nd ed.). London: Collier Macmillan.

Phillips, C. (2012). *The multicultural prison: Ethnicity, masculinity, and social relations among prisoners*. Oxford: Oxford University Press.

Pleck, J. H. (1976). The male sex role: Definitions, problems, and sources of change. *Journal of Social Issues, 32*(3), 155–164. https://doi.org/10.1111/j.1540-4560.1976.tb02604.x.

Pleck, J. H. (1981). *The myth of masculinity*. Cambridge, MA: MIT Press.

Plummer, D. (1999). *One of the boys: Masculinity, homophobia, and modern manhood*. New York: Routledge.

Plummer, K. (2001). *Documents of life 2: An invitation to critical humanism*. London: Sage.

Reay, D. (2002). Shaun's story: Troubling discourses of white working-class masculinities. *Gender and Education, 14*(3), 221–234. https://doi.org/10.1080/0954025022000010695.

Reay, D. (2004). "Mostly roughs and toughs": Social class, race and representation in inner city schooling. *Sociology, 38*(5), 1005–1023. https://doi.org/10.1177/0038038504047183.

Roberts, S. (2014). Introduction: Masculinities in transition: Change, continuity, crisis? In S. Roberts (Ed.), *Debating modern masculinities: Change, continuity, crisis?* Basingstoke: Palgrave Macmillan.

Roberts, S. (2018). *Young working-class men in transition.* London: Routledge.

Schwartz, M. D., & DeKeseredy, W. S. (1997). *Sexual assault on the college campus: The role of male peer support.* Thousand Oaks, CA: London Sage.

Seddon, T. (2006). Drugs, crime and social exclusion: Social context and social theory in British drugs—Crime research. *British Journal of Criminology, 46*(4), 680–703. https://doi.org/10.1093/bjc/azi079.

Segal, L. (2007). *Slow motion: Changing masculinities, changing men* (3rd ed.). Basingstoke: Palgrave Macmillan.

Shildrick, T., & MacDonald, R. (2007). Biographies of exclusion: Poor work and poor transitions. *International Journal of Lifelong Education, 26*(5), 589–604. https://doi.org/10.1080/02601370701559672.

Shilling, C. (2003). *The body and social theory* (2nd ed.). Theory, Culture & Society. London: Sage.

Skelton, C. (2001). *Schooling the boys: Masculinities and primary education.* Buckingham: Open University Press.

Steel, N., Ford, J. A., Newton, J. N., Davis, A. C. J., Vos, T., Naghavi, M., et al. (2018). Health in the countries of the UK and 150 English local authority areas 1990–2016: A Systematic Analysis for the Global Burden of Disease Study 2016. *The Lancet, 392,* 1647–1661. https://doi.org/10.1016/S0140-6736(18)32207-4.

Tomsen, S. (2008). *Crime, criminal justice and masculinities.* Aldershot: Ashgate.

Tomsen, S., & Mason, G. (2001). Engendering homophobia: Violence, sexuality and gender conformity. *Journal of Sociology, 37*(3), 257–273. https://doi.org/10.1177/144078301128756337.

Van Hoven, B., & Hörschelmann, K. (2005). *Spaces of masculinities.* London: Routledge.

Walker, G. W. (2006). Disciplining protest masculinity. *Men and masculinities, 9*(1), 5–22. https://doi.org/10.1177/1097184X05284217.

Watson, J. (2000). *Male bodies: Health, culture and identity.* Buckingham: Open University Press.

West, C., & Zimmerman, D. H. (1987). Doing gender. *Gender & Society, 1*(2), 125–151. https://doi.org/10.1177/0891243287001002002.

Whitehead, S. (2002). *Men and masculinities: Key themes and new directions.* Cambridge: Polity.

Whitehead, S., & Barrett, F. J. (Eds.). (2001). *The masculinities reader*. Oxford: Polity.

Willis, P. (1977). *Learning to labor: How working class kids get working class jobs*. Farnborough, England: Saxon House.

Winlow, S. (2001). *Badfellas: Crime, tradition and new masculinities*. Oxford: Berg.

CHAPTER 3

Economic Change: Post-industrial Masculinities

In this chapter, I review the existing scholarship on how boys and men navigate post-industrial masculinities. First, I look at the debates surrounding economic changes in the UK, exploring how these impact gender relations and gendered identities at national, regional and local levels. I then set out the main discussions on working-class masculinity, schooling and attainment. In the early 1990s, as deindustrialisation began to bite in many areas—and with working-class boys largely struggling to make what was once an almost guaranteed post-schooling transition to the workplace—widespread "panic" emerged surrounding boys' levels of "underachievement". This has led to a surge of social, political and academic interest in the schooling experiences of boys. Following this, I explore the youth transitions literature. Of particular relevance to this study is some of the work that has been undertaken by the Teesside School to investigate how young people navigate alternative and varying post-schooling transitions to adulthood under similar economic conditions. I then go on to outline the key debates surrounding questions of masculinity and crime, showing that, for some men—when legitimate avenues to manhood, such as employment, are in short supply—crime serves as an easily accessible and potent resource for "doing masculinity". I finish by reviewing the scholarship on men, masculinity and incarceration, with a focus on recent and emerging prison masculinities literature in the UK.

© The Author(s) 2021   33
D. Maguire, *Male, Failed, Jailed*,
Palgrave Studies in Prisons and Penology,
https://doi.org/10.1007/978-3-030-61059-3_3

3.1   NATIONAL LEVEL

The rapid onset of deindustrialisation in the UK from the late 1960s onwards has been well-documented. However, to provide a broader picture of how the national industrial landscape impacts social relations and, thus, the creation of marginalised identities, it is worth briefly recapping on the speed and extent of this process. Since the 1960s, all advanced economies have experienced a shift away from manufacturing towards service-based economies. The UK, though, was one of the most extreme cases. Deindustrialisation started earlier, moving faster and further than any of the other advanced economies (Tomlinson 2020). The UK experienced the biggest post-war deterioration in its manufacturing trade balance; no other advanced economy, as Rowthorn and Coutts have pointed out, moved from "surplus to deficit in such a spectacular fashion" (Rowthorn and Coutts 2013, p. 5). In 1957, for instance, almost half of all workers (48%) were in industrial employment in the UK, by 2016 this had fallen to 15% (Tomlinson 2020). This decline in traditional heavy industry and manufacturing, together with the rise of the service economy, directly impacted the working lives of the men who have contributed to this study. By 2018, the service sector accounted for 80% of the UK's economy (Rhodes 2020). Data have shown that women are much more likely than men to be employed in service industries, with 92% of women working in service-based occupations in 2011—compared with 71% of men for the same period (Office for National Statistics 2013).

In contemporary UK labour markets, the high rates of unemployment among (young) undereducated working-class men are—in large part—the consequences of this economic restructuring. The shift from conventional "masculine" heavy manual work to a "feminised" service sector that is increasingly dependent on a temporary, part-time, low-paid and insecure labour force or poor work (Brown and Scase 1991) has severely affected these men. Increasingly, they face unemployment—or find that they have to become "women workers", expected to work in caring- and hospitality-based occupations (McDowell 2014). In illustrating the extent of this economic shift to feminised work, McDowell (2014) notes that—out of Britain's workforce of almost 26 million people—three million are in occupations that involve direct contact with bodies. Another three million work in low-paid jobs that involve interactions with customers, including cafes, bar work and security. All but the last category, McDowell has argued, represent typically feminised jobs.

Research both in the UK and in the US has shown that it is under-educated working-class men who are especially vulnerable in neoliberal labour markets that are characterised by this type of feminised poor work (Bourgois 2003; McDowell 2014; McDowell and Bonner-Thompson 2020). As I demonstrate through my own findings in Chapter 4, the type of masculine identities that enable young men to survive in tough estates and school spaces only serve to further exclude them from labour markets that are reliant on the feminised attributes of "docility and deference" (McDowell 2003, p. 829). Not only do many men from working-class backgrounds often lack the educational and social skills that are needed to navigate these workspaces, they also add to their own disqualification from employment opportunities through gendered performances that see conceding to customer demands and deferring to (often female) managerial authority as an affront to their already well-established (protest) masculinities (Bourgois 2003; McDowell et al. 2014; Walker 2006). Contemporary labour markets have changed from the time when, as Paul Willis (1977) vividly demonstrated, doing little else but "havin' a laff" at school, having strong bodies and exhibiting a willingness to work were sufficient for life on the shop floor.

Recent research has shown that it is not just attitudes and outdated gender performances that contribute to (young) working-class men's rates of exclusion from the contemporary workplace; it is, also, how they look. Hardgrove et al. (2015), for instance, have found that young men who are heavily tattooed and/or have piercings—or have a general "transgressive" appearance—are even less attractive candidates to employers who already prefer to employ women. Women who occupy the same class positions as these young men tend to be preferred by many employers because they are regarded as having the ideal attributes for lower-end service work. They are, in essence, seen as being less likely to resist managerial demands and to pose a risk of workplace disruption (Hardgrove et al. 2015; McDowell 2014; Nayak 2006).

Encountering both structural and personal barriers to employment, growing numbers of men from working-class and deprived backgrounds are struggling to meet both their own and socio-cultural expectations of the acceptable attributes of masculinity on several fronts. Many young men are finding themselves increasingly reliant on their families—and the more employable women, such as their working mothers and partners—for food, clothes and shelter (Hardgrove et al. 2015; Shildrick and MacDonald 2007). The informants for this study—many of whom had bodies that bear the ink and scars of their years of having to inhabit violent street spaces—were heavily reliant on their family members, especially their mothers. However, their experiences of the local labour markets, as I show in Chapter 6, were not simply ones of exclusion. Some of the men with whom I spoke in the context of this study talked of their interesting and diverse histories of employment—while others had no professional experience at all.

3.2   Regional

Deindustrialisation and the rise of the service sector have had a major impact on many aspects of social/gender relations throughout the UK. As I demonstrate in the later empirical chapters of this book, the more adverse effects of economic restructuring vary significantly in geographical terms. Many of the cities and towns in the northern regions that were hit the hardest by such changes are still dealing with the legacy of deindustrialisation today.

Cities and towns in the North East and the North West that were dependent on heavy industry are currently enduring some of the highest rates of unemployment. Indeed, they continue to be at the top of many measures of deprivation (see Noble et al. 2019). Consistently, Manchester, Liverpool, Sunderland, Middlesbrough and Kingston Upon Hull suffer some of the highest rates of unemployment. This ongoing unemployment crisis—and the associated poverty-related consequences—has seen life expectancy for men in the North West and North East dropping to being among the lowest in the UK. Between 2016 and 2018, the life expectancy rates for men in these regions were 78.3 and 77.9 years respectively—compared with 80.7 for men in the South East and 79.3 on average across the UK (Office for National Statistics 2019a). In 2018, the North East had the highest male suicide rate in England, followed by Yorkshire and Humber in the third place (Office for National Statistics 2019b). These bleak geographical variations continue with the North East and the North West suffering the highest mortality rates for drug misuse in the 10 years to 2018. The Office for National Statistics reported that the drug-related mortality rates in these northern regions were more than double those for Greater London in 2018 (Office for National Statistics 2019c).

Depressing as these figures are, it is not all grim in the North. Parts of Liverpool and Manchester—as well as the "poster child" for the new north, Newcastle (Short 2015)—among others, have been fighting their way back. The Centre for Cities 2015 Outlook reported that, between 2013 and 2014, Newcastle was the eighth most successful city in terms of rates of job growth. Hull, however—which I shall discuss in more detail in the following chapter—was 59th out of the 63 cities that were ranked on the basis of job growth (Centre for Cities 2015).

Much of the growth in Liverpool, Manchester and Newcastle has been brought about by considerable investment in the cultural sectors, including internationally renowned museums and galleries such as Manchester's Lowry, Tate Liverpool and Newcastle's Baltic. Related developments in these post-industrial places have seen the rise of a strong hospitality sector, including cafes, restaurants and flourishing night-time economies of bars and clubs—albeit ones that often offer low-wage employment opportunities. The current cuts in local authority funding, however, raise questions about the sustainability of this growth.

A number of notable studies have explored the ways in which (young) men create and adapt their classed and gendered identities in post-industrial economies in the northern regions of England. A large part of this work has focused on the North East. Geographer Anoop Nayak's (2003a, b, 2006) research has centred on white working-class identity in Newcastle, sharing many parallels with McDowell's (2003) work discussed earlier, he explores the ways in which place intersects with class and ethnicity to determine varying performances of masculinities among the same class.

Nayak found that, for one group of lads from his study—the "Real Geordies"—alternative routes to manhood were found in the new culturally based economy that has been built around bars, clubs and hospitality. This new, thriving cultural and night-time economy has not only been a source of employment for many but for going out, too; drinking, clubbing and partying has played a major role in their expressions of coming-of-age masculinities. Nayak notes that the Real Geordies clung on to some aspects of their white, industrial, masculine heritage through their affiliations with the local football club, territorial loyalties and physical humour.

Not everyone, though—as Nayak found—had the economic resources to participate in the drinking cultures and other leisure transitions that revolved around the new cultural spaces in the city. Those who were excluded, known locally as "Charvers", included those young men who came from families that had experienced long-term intergenerational unemployment. Like the other young men who had been interviewed by McDowell et al. (2014), they, too, struggled to earn a legitimate wage through serving. As such, they turned to the streets as a space for both leisure and cultural expressions. Nayak (2006) notes that, for the "Charvers", their masculine performances were built around whatever was available in their impoverished communities. Empty or abandoned buildings, for instance, were commissioned for illegal raves. Fighting, petty crime and the consumption of alcohol and drugs constituted daily activities.

Although the "Real Geordies" exhibited fear and anxiety of the "Charvers'" hardness, Nayak found that they would overtly denigrate their style and assume that they were criminals as part of an instrumental process whereby the culturally inferior "Charver" label was used as a platform by the "Real Geordies" by way of asserting the latter's perceived, superior, hegemonic, working-class, "respectable" masculinities. The "Real Geordies" portrayal of the "Charvers", Nayak claims, says a great deal about "class insecurities and attempts at clinging on tooth and nail to the last vestiges of white respectability in the post-industrial moment" (2006, p. 825).

Other research regarding post-industrial northern regions has shown how some men have adapted and sustained their revered (or feared) masculine performances through violence, drug dealing and/or the use of their bodies to provide security and to maintain order as "bouncers" in the night-time economy (Ellis 2016; Winlow 2001). In his ethnographic study of men and violence, Ellis (2016) charted how, in disadvantaged northern regions, men who have resisted or struggled to adjust to economic and cultural change—and with the scarcity of well-paid work—have formed their masculine identities by means of violence.

For some men, as a result of their brutalisation and trauma at the hands of other men—often their fathers—violence becomes a learned response to self-preservation (Ellis et al. 2017). In highly competitive neighbourhoods, with a paucity of resources, controlled violence generates status, enables dominance over other men, warns off threats and provides a means of economic gain (Ellis 2016). As Winlow (2001) discovered through his earlier research into men's experiences in Sunderland, the valued working-class masculine attributes of bodily strength, hardness and the ability/willingness to both confront and perpetrate violence have been packaged as saleable and valued commodities in the night-time economy. Winlow and Ellis, in their respective studies, have shown how economic change has provided some working-class men with entrepreneurial opportunities. Primarily, these are opportunities to invest in their physicality, hardness and violence. However, this—as I explore in more detail in a later section—often draws from and feeds into criminal networks that are built around lifestyles of drugs, violence and intimidation.

Other more comprehensive and longitudinal studies of mainly white working-class young adults in heavily deindustrialised and impoverished neighbourhoods in the North East include those that have been undertaken by Teesside University's Youth Research Unit: the Teesside School (Johnston et al. 2000; MacDonald and Marsh 2005; Webster et al. 2004). Their work provides excellent insights into varying youth-to-adult transitions among the same class group in the UK.

These studies show that undereducated young people in post-industrial regions in the North East are competing with adults in their own neighbourhoods for similar types of "poor work" as aforementioned. A concerning finding was the lack of progression in this type of work. Research subjects were still in the same low-level types of employment in their late twenties that they had been in at the age of 17 (Webster et al. 2004). With an endless supply of willing local labour, it was clear that working lives were highly precarious. Young people who found employment often worked under punitive managers who, too often, quickly followed up on continuous threats to fire their employees. The researchers reported that the difficulty that was faced by many young people was not so much obtaining a job but, rather, keeping it. Equally bleakly, they found that many of these young people who initially engaged in further education and training were, years later, negotiating the same "cyclical precarious types of poor work" (Webster et al. 2004, p. 10) as those who had undertaken little to no education or training.

The Teesside researchers have indicated that not all of the young people who have been involved in their studies have been willing or able to continuously negotiate transitions in the context of poor work conditions, with low pay, overly authoritarian managers/supervisors and no viable route of job progression (Johnston et al. 2000; Webster et al. 2004). They found—as I discuss in more detail in a later section—that their young participants consequently sought out alternative pathways or leisure, drug and criminal "careers".

From these studies that have explored transitions into poor forms of work, it is clear that it is the young men who leave school as soon they are able to do so—with few or no educational credentials—who face the biggest challenges. There is a long tradition of research that has convincingly shown schooling to be one of the most powerful spaces in the construction and reproduction of early marginalised or protest masculinities.

3.3   SCHOOLING WORKING-CLASS MASCULINITIES

3.3.1   Failing Boys

Interest in the education and schooling of working-class boys in the UK has a long tradition, from Paul Willis' (1977) *Learning to Labour* and Paul Corrigan's (1979) *Schooling the Smash Street Kids*. Both authors have shown how the rejection of the formal curriculum and school authority generates high cultural value and was a way of being one of the "lads". The authors of these early studies recognised the importance of schooling in creating and reproducing revered forms of working-class masculinity; that regardless of their levels of attainment young men would secure roles on the "shop floor" and be fully engaged in the labour market. Towards the end of the twentieth century, as deindustrialisation began to bite in many areas, working-class boys started to struggle to make what was once an almost guaranteed post-schooling transition to the workplace. This economic shift, coupled with the introduction of school performance league tables in 1992, saw interest in the academic attainment of boys extend beyond the academy. Politicians, policymakers, journalists and social commentators expressed concern and generated "panic" about so-called academic "underachievement" and the underemployment of boys (see Griffin 2000 for a comprehensive review of these debates).

In the main, anxieties were based around the assumption—as outlined by the then Secretary of State for Education, David Blunkett—that boys' troubles and their low self-esteem had resulted from schools encouraging "too much equality" and "assertive aggressiveness' in girls" (cited in Segal 2007, p. xx). The implication of these debates was that feminism and equal opportunities had gone too far—that "males were the new disadvantaged" (Francis 1999, p. 357) and that the focus should now turn to addressing the needs of boys.

Anxieties about boys' levels of academic attainment and schooling stemmed from—and contributed to—the broader commentary around masculine "crisis" discourse. As Willis (1977) and Corrigan (1979) revealed decades earlier, and many others have demonstrated since, commentaries on the educational "underachievement" of many working-class and certain ethnic minority boys are nothing new (Evans 2006; Nuttall and Doherty 2014; Reay 2002). Their "alienation from study in school has always accompanied the assertion of a reactive form of rebellious bravado" (Segal 2007, p. xx).

3.3.2 Schooling Masculinity

In what Marcus Weaver-Hightower (2003) has termed the "boy turn", many Western industrialised countries—especially those dealing with discourses around failing boys and masculinity crises—have seen, during the 1990s and early millennium, an outpouring of research and publications about masculinity and schooling. As Mairtin Mac an Ghaill and Chris Haywood (2012) have suggested, such research has identified schools as being cultural arenas wherein masculinity becomes an important concept in describing issues such as underachievement, sex education, peer group cultures, language use, sexual violence and pedagogy.

For Connell (1989), this research lens into school is vital because the school is one of the—if not the—most potent influences in the formation of masculinities. Schools are, she has argued, "masculinity making" sites that do not just adapt to exciting gender configurations but are active in constructing particular forms of masculinity and femininity. From this large body of research into masculinity and schooling, including studies that have explored the intersection of ethnicity (Archer 2007; Evans 2006; Khattab and Modhood 2018) and race (Archer 2003; Sewell 1997; Wright, Maylor et al. 2016), the core consensus was that social class and gender are the most potent forces that determine an individual's level of educational attainment.

Much of this research has centred on the construction of working-class masculinities. In doing so, it has brought to the fore the structural forces that have served to create the "crisis" behind the failing boys' discourses. Such studies have shown how working-class masculine culture, and the gender identities that many of their respondents aspired to, had changed little from those of the 1970s. Like earlier research, most of these studies have revealed that working-class masculinity continues to be formed by "battering against the school's authority" (Connell 1989, p. 301). In contrast, the hegemonic masculinity of middle-class pupils is constructed through rationality and academic achievement (Frosh et al. 2002). Consistently, in this scholarship, working-class masculinities have been described as being both dominant and aggressive—any difference is perceived as weakness and makes one a target for ridicule—and a macho image, based on rebellion against school authority and a belief that schoolwork is for "wimps" and effeminate boys (Evans 2006; Francis 2006; Mac an Ghaill 2019; Reay 2002), was most common.

In his influential ethnographic study on boys and schooling, Mac an Ghaill (1994) has argued that the "laddish" or "macho" characteristics of working-class masculinity cannot simply be understood in terms of individual choice. Rather, it is a collective project "operating at the level of the institution and the organisation of peer group relations" (p. 53). Mac an Ghaill found that male peer groups within schools are usually organised around matters of class, sexual identities, sporting prowess and antagonistic attitudes towards the school's authority and one's own academic work. In his empirical work, the group that Mac an Ghaill named "macho lads" were drawn to each other as a result of their shared, negative outlooks towards the school and its teachers. Masculine currency could be gained through the "three Fs": fighting, fucking and football. This group, as seen in many other studies, associated academic work with an inferior effeminacy, referring to boys who chose to do school work as "dickhead achievers" (ibid., p. 59).

Much of this research on masculinity and education has been criticised for the assumption that all working-class boys are hypermasculine thugs who have no desire to learn (Delamont 2000). What is often not recognised is the fact that, even within some of this work, many working-class boys do engage with schooling and learning (Ingram 2011; R. Roberts 2012). Early research, for instance, has identified "earholes" (Willis 1977), "achievers" (Mac an Ghaill 1994) and—more recently—"boffins" (Francis 2009) and "geeks" (Ward 2014). Consistently acknowledged in many of these studies are the extremely difficult environments and many barriers that working-class boys who want to engage in the learning process find themselves having to face. Diane Reay (2002) found that Shaun, a working-class boy in her case study, displayed impressive enthusiasm and overriding determination to be educated. She highlighted how, in the context of a poorly resourced "sink" school that served the catchment for Shaun's tough neighbourhood, he invested "super human effort" (p. 228) so that he could realise his own desire to learn.

In her research regarding white working-class students in London, Evans (2006) highlights the challenges that many of her young male pupils faced in reconciling their identities over multiple sites, including their homes, the streets and their school. The finely refined hard-masculinities that were needed to be able to navigate the streets of their estates and informal school spaces were in constant conflict with the formal structures of the school and the institutional setting of the class-room. This estate culture of masculinity eventually led to the removal, for many, from mainstream schooling. It was equally concerning, though, she noted, that the masculine performances of the few had a detrimental impact on the majority and took up a great deal of school time and limited resources. An exploration of how the participants in my own study used the informal spaces of schools to reinforce their existing street masculinities—and their rejection or refusal to adapt to the more formal disciplined spaces of school—proved, as I outline in Chapter 5, interesting and for many marked a defining period in their marginalised gendered trajectories.

This resistance to schooling and the poor academic attainment of white working-class boys—that has been identified in scholarship over recent decades—has become a subject of widespread political and policy concern. In June 2013, Ofsted—in their report, "Unseen Children: Access and Achievement 20 Years On"—highlighted the fact that white British chil-dren who were eligible for free school meals were the lowest-performing group at the age of 16, with less than a third of them (31%) gaining five or more GCSEs at grades A*–C (Ofsted 2013a). White British pupils account for two-thirds of formal school students—and so this lowest-performing group was a large one. The sheer magnitude of this issue made it difficult not to acknowledge the relationship between social class, ethnicity and educational attainment. Just a month after Ofsted published concerns about the "real and persistent" underachievement of white working-class boys, the Select Committee for Education launched an enquiry and documented the outcome in their 2014 report, "Under-achievement in Education by White Working-Class Children" (House of Commons Educational Committee 2014).

Confirming earlier findings, white British boys were identified as being the lowest-performing cohort in the country. The difference in attainment between them and their "less deprived" peers is wider than for any other group. Both of these reports recognised the fact that, although some of the widest gaps in attainment are between white British boys and everyone else, girls from this group are also significantly "underachieving" (ibid., see also Allen et al. 2015).

3.3.3   *"Poverty of Expectation"*

A dominant theme that has emerged from the official narratives of under-achieving white boys is that they, and their parents, have lacked aspiration and confidence. During one of the periodical flare-ups of panic regarding white working-class boys' levels of attainment in 2014, the then head of Ofsted, Sir Michael Wilshaw, noted that the "poverty of expectation"—in particular, the low expectations of others—has a greater impact on rates of educational achievement than material poverty (House of Commons Educational Committee 2014, p. 29). As research into masculinity and schooling shows, the causes behind working-class underachievement are much more complex and various than the oversimplified poverty of aspira-tions or expectations discourses would suggest. Roberts and Evans (2012) point out that policymakers like to cite low aspiration as being the cause of most of the challenges that are faced by working-class communities. He has urged policymakers to look at what lies behind the low aspira-tion discourse and how it links to neoliberal ideology that equates "good qualifications with a good job".

Roberts and Evans (2012) have noted that, as long as aspiration remains so tightly linked to notions of educational and occupational success, working-class students will always be defined as having low aspira-tions. Francis (2006) has posited that there is much evidence of high levels of aspiration in working-class families. What they lack, she has argued, is the prerequisite knowledge of how to operationalise that aspiration effec-tively so as to achieve the best outcomes for their children. Money makes the difference—but so does, she has claimed, knowing the rules of the game.

3.3.4   *Underperforming Schools*

To focus on individuals who come from homes that ostensibly lack aspira-tion distracts us from a major dimension of the underachievement debate: namely, the structural role that schools play in reproducing low rates of attainment among working-class students. Roberts (2018) has pointed out that a major factor that contributes to the under attainment of working-class boys is the inadequate schools they attend. These schools are, in most cases, simply under-resourced to meet the learning needs of boys from poor backgrounds. It has been long established in the sociology of education literature, for instance, that young people's educational experiences and outcomes are profoundly shaped by the place or localities of schools and their pupils (Ball 2003; Blokland and Savage 2001; Reay and Lucey 2000).

For decades, Ofsted's annual reports have highlighted the fact that the consistently worst-performing local education authorities (LEA) are mainly in the northern regions of England. The majority of so-called "stuck schools"—those that have not been judged as being any good since 2006—are located mostly in northern deindustrialised regions (Ofsted 2020). Hull's LEA, responsible for the schooling of most of the participants in this study, has a long track record of being one the worst-performing. In 2013, it was ranked 129th out of 150 authorities (Ofsted 2013b). In January 2020, there were no sign of improvement, with the *Hull Daily Mail* reporting that Ofsted had found that every school in Hull and East Yorkshire either "required improvement" or was "inadequate" (Riley 2020).

Research into working-class boys' resistance to compulsory forms of education has emphasised the importance of the role that local schools and wider place-based social relations play in the construction of young marginalised masculinities. These debates have raised questions that I have explored with the participants and discuss in Chapter 5. The participants' experiences vividly chart which immediate and longer-term post-schooling options exist in deeply impoverished and deindustrialised regions for young men who have little to no educational credentials.

3.4   Youth Transitions

The Teesside School's key studies (Johnston et al. 2000; MacDonald and Marsh 2005; Webster et al. 2004) have used the concept of "transition" to explore how young respondents—who are often described as being "hard to reach"—navigate post-schooling pathways to adulthood in the context of severe socio-economic deprivation. According to Tracy Shildrick and Robert MacDonald (2007), transitions are the pathways that young people take after they have completed their compulsory schooling as they enter the labour market. They also include the housing and family situations that individuals must negotiate as part of this journey to adulthood. In studying youth transitions, they have claimed, they are not only "observing the snakes and ladders" of individual biographies but they are also exposing the ways in which similar divisions and hierarchies in society are reproduced and maintained (MacDonald et al. 2001).

Shildrick et al. (2009) and others accept that economic developments over recent decades have had a significant impact on post-schooling trajectories for many young people—not just those who are at the higher end of the poverty spectrum (Roberts 2011). This has led to transitions being described as "long", "broken", "extended", "protracted", "uneasy" and "fractured" (Shildrick and MacDonald 2007, p. 590). Young people's increased levels of reliance on their parents for longer periods, for example—and delays in attaining other signifiers of adulthood, such as having an income that sustains independent living and housing tenancy/ownership—are less accessible for many in austerity Britain than they were in previous generations (Hardgrove et al. 2015). For many low-income young people who leave the parental/family home, the main housing transition that demarcates adult status is increasingly difficult to effect due to a profound lack of appropriate social housing and allocation policies that exclude the young (Clapham et al. 2014; Crane et al. 2014).

Educated young adults, too, are finding that the transitions to adulthood are becoming less predictable (Calvert 2010; Heath and Calvert 2013). Many young professionals who do manage to find employment face uncertainty in a growing knowledge-based economy that is built on temporary/short-term contracts. It has been suggested that the recent emergence of this precarious professional group—with the longer-standing precarious poor—constitutes a new class: the "precariat" (McDowell 2014; Standing 2011). If not class, what does unite many of these young people in the UK is the fact that temporary contracts, erratic income streams and periods without work—coupled with increasingly limited independent housing options—suggest a widespread struggle across the spectrum, albeit under different conditions, in terms of trying to meet the traditional markers of adulthood.

The relevance of highlighting challenges in navigating standard routes to adulthood for those who have previous work experience as well as educated young people lies in the fact that the process of doing so foregrounds an even more significant question: what, then, for undereducated men? What are the options for those who may have long criminal records and little to no legitimate work experience—many of whom carry the visible scars of their time in institutions and on the streets?

As I show in Chapters 5 and 6, alternative transitions from school to unemployment and/or prison are all too easy and increasingly common in the austere world of insecure work and neoliberal governments. This is not to dismiss or to detract from the point that, across class divides, significant barriers limit avenues to adulthood. However, I argue in the following sections that it is the poorest—who are at the sharpest end of economic change—for whom the cost is the greatest. It is for them that the transitions are the most protracted and are most likely to be, ultimately, unsuccessful.

3.4.1   Challenging Transitions

A consistent criticism of older—and some recent—transition studies is the overemphasis on school-to-work trajectories at the cost of capturing young people's more varied and longer-term experiences of growing up (Furlong et al. 2011; Wyn et al. 2017). Steven Roberts (2011) has noted that the transition discourse is too dualistic. Young people are typically either seen as being unemployed "sinkers" or employed "swimmers", "fast track" (those who leave education with few or no credentials) or "slow track" (those who gain qualifications, staying on in education or going into FE/training). Far too little focus, he has argued, has been given to those who fall between these "lines of dualism": the "missing middle" (p. 22). A major charge is that, in post-industrial societies, the transition model fails to account for the complex, multiple and individualised paths that young people take.

Some of these challenges to transition studies are part of a much broader debate throughout the social sciences stemming from theories of individualisation and reflexivity. Ulrich Beck (1992, 2000)—one of the leading thinkers in these discussions—has suggested that, in late modernity, or what he terms "risk" societies, categories such as class, gender and ethnicity have lost much of their analytical purchase. They are, he has argued, now merely "zombie categories" that are no longer up to the task of explaining youth trajectories in the twenty-first century (Beck and Beck-Gernsheim 2001). Highly contested in youth studies, Beck's concept of "choice biographies" posits that, in late capitalist societies, greater access to knowledge has meant that individuals are much more reflective. This has contributed, he has argued, to affording more choice when we are shaping our futures (Beck 1992, 2000). Consequently, routes to adulthood are significantly less structurally constrained and less predictable (ibid.).

This loosening of structure and this emphasis on agency in explaining young people's biographies have been fiercely opposed in youth studies (for an overview and contrasting exchange on Beck's individualisation theory of "choice biographies" and its application in youth studies, see S. Roberts 2010, 2012; Woodman 2009, 2010). Indeed, as can be seen across social science research—as well as in what follows in this book—so-called "zombie" categories are very much alive in the real world and continue to play a significant role in the informants' disadvantaged biographies.

Despite some difficulties with which the concept of "transition" has been associated, if used reflexively, it can—as Shildrick and MacDonald (2007) have argued—be a powerful tool. It can reveal, in contrast to individualised or "choice" discourse, the structural barriers that shape youth transitions. The limitations of some earlier transition studies, they have conceded, were that they overly focused on school-to-work careers and failed to consider other important aspects of youth experience.

In seeking to fully understand disadvantaged biographies, account needs to be taken of the "local peer networks, of the cultures and identities of 'the street', and of the value placed on becoming/being a young man with a particular style of resilient, 'hard' masculinity" (MacDonald et al. 2001, paragraph 4.16). To capture their research subjects' full exclusionary biographies, they expand the concept of transitions to include alternative routes of criminal, drug-using and leisure "careers"—along with the more traditional school-to-work, family and housing pathways (Johnston et al. 2000; MacDonald and Marsh 2002, 2005; MacDonald and Shildrick 2007; Webster et al. 2004).

3.4.2   *"Alternative Careers"*

In focusing on the interrelationships between these well-established and "alternative careers" in youth transitions, MacDonald et al. (2005) and Tracy Shildrick et al. (2009) found that many of their young research subjects were highly dependent on, and locked into, their communities (also see McDowell 2003; Sayer 2005). Their local and family connections, for example, meant that they often qualified for and sought social housing in the same areas in which they had lived as children. They discovered, too, that—for many of their research subjects—living close to other family members, once they had transitioned to independent living, was part of a strategy of survival. There was often a mutual dependency between family and friends in navigating the challenges of being poor in impoverished neighbourhoods.

Of notable relevance to this study—and highlighting the many similarities with my informants, as I show in Chapter 5—is the previous work in which the links between leisure, drug and criminal careers have been explored (MacDonald and Marsh 2002; MacDonald and Shildrick 2007; also see Webster et al. 2004). MacDonald and Shildrick (2007) discovered that a large majority of their research subjects had, during their early teens, spent a great deal of their spare time "in the company of peers in the public spaces of their home estates" (ibid., p. 342). So much street leisure time, they highlight, was due to a lack of financial resources for other activities such as the cinema or bowling. However, for their research subjects, spending time on the streets was often spoken about in positive terms; for many, once they reached young adulthood and found jobs and forms of training, their leisure transitions shifted from street-based to commercialised alcohol-based leisure pursuits.

Sharing parallels with Nayak's (2006) description of "Charvers" as previously discussed, MacDonald and Shildrick (2007) have highlighted the fact that many of the young unemployed men in their sample deviated from this main pattern of pursuing a "leisure career". This group lacked funds and were, therefore, excluded from the "clubs and pubs" that most other young men of their age were enjoying. From a young age, the main issue for these men was the challenge of filling "tedious" time. Most of this group had avoided formal education and spent the days when they should have been in school on the streets of their neighbourhoods. This street space leisure time continued post-school and past their teens.

MacDonald and Shildrick (2007) have been careful to point out that widespread street socialising was not synonymous with delinquency. However, for several of their unemployed men, it provided a space for early drug exploration and delinquency and provided an alternative to regular employment or training. They found that those with sustained criminal careers suggested that street-based youth culture facilitated their transitions into crime—although, even then, the authors have been careful to suggest that this is not inevitable and that some who displayed high-risk factors at early stages stuck "stubbornly" to conventional transitions. In later years, criminal careers or networks provided a sense of security and income for some; even those who were not directly affiliated with criminal networks knew who was and where to go for cheap stolen goods or illegal substances.

Other work that has explored street spaces and their connections to transitions into education, work and/or crime includes Anthony Gunter's and Paul Watt's (2009) study of a small, multi-ethnic, East London neighbourhood. They found that varying transitions were created through the interaction of paid employment and leisure cultures and identified three divergent—but by no means fixed—routes: grafting (manual dirty work); college (preparation for "clean" service-based employment) and alternative "working on road" (low-level criminal conduct). Grafter culture, they claimed, takes over from "road culture" in some of the (mainly white) men's post-schooling routes. London's relatively buoyant construction sector facilitates—albeit increasingly insecure—"traditional 'learning to labour' masculine transitions" (p. 526) for those who have access to neighbourhood employment networks and who "possess [a] positive attitude to dirty, hard graft" (p. 526). The construction sector, for these men, offered no job security. Those who pursued the "grafter" transitions were regularly between jobs and got by, the authors have noted, by "ducking and diving" around the estate.

The vast majority of the young people in their study—especially young black men—pursued college studies: the second transition. Those who elected to follow this route bought into the neoliberal discourses of "opting in" (Roberts and Evans 2012) and enrolled in full-time education in the hope of gaining credentials for "clean" service work. For these young men, though, this transition was fraught with pitfalls—ones that were similar to those with which compulsory education can be associated—and many ended up dropping out. For this group to successfully engage in the "alien" spaces of further/higher education and "clean" service sector work, they would have to learn to distance themselves from familiar "road culture and its attendant bodily 'habitus' of speech and style" (p. 527).

Like MacDonald and Shildrick (2007), Gunter and Watt (2009) found that all of their young research subjects were consumers of road cultural life. Only a small number of men, whom they described as the "Arm House Crew", pursued day-in-day-out alternative transitions of "life on road" (p. 525) that involved "badness", "characterised by 'spectacular' hyper-aggressive/hyper-masculine modes of behaviour, incorporating violent and petty crime, fraud or personal identity theft, and low-level drug dealing" (p. 525). The "Arm House Crew" resisted the discourse of "equality and opportunity through learning and earned respect on their 'own terms'" (p. 527).

Consistently recognised in much of this work on transitions is the paradoxical situation whereby the strategies that are employed in order to navigate impoverished neighbourhoods—and the social capital that is earned during this process—only serve to further isolate young people from already-limited opportunities, thereby perpetuating marginalisation and reproducing class-based inequalities. However, as shown in this transition scholarship, some men who have been brought up and live in these poor neighbourhoods may, to some extent, contribute to their own exclusion.

Their marginalisation, however, is exacerbated by the neoliberal agenda that has created considerable structural challenges for those who seek to find and sustain legitimate routes to manhood. Simon Winlow (2004) has warned that young men in marginal neighbourhoods—who are not in education, who face exclusion from the formal economy and who lack the material means to have and to support a family—consequently lack the core bounds of social control and, as such, are less constrained by societal norms. In these conditions, crime and violence will, for many, offer an accessible and attractive route to achieving and sustaining respected "underclass" masculine identities.

3.5   Masculinities and Crime

Notwithstanding the over-focus of criminal justice agencies on detecting and prosecuting poor and minority males, it is statistically evident—from the high levels that have been recorded and the numbers of reported offences—that a real and pervasive social phenomenon of disproportionate male criminality exists (Tomsen 2008). International data, that have been captured over several decades, indicate that—throughout industrialised societies—men account for almost 100% of all recorded crimes (DeKeseredy and Schwartz 2005).

Alongside sex, youth is presented as being the strongest predictor of offending (Collier 1998; Messerschmidt 2001). Richard Collier (1998) has noted the "spectacular" flaw of criminology is evident in the discipline's failure to explore this core fact through an analysis of gender. Men commit most crimes—but the failure to explicitly explore this phenomenon through gendered analyses has opened up fertile ground for regressive and unopposed essentialising discourses that attribute male criminality as being an inherent and pre-social drive of all men (Collier 1998; Winlow 2004). Until recently, some of the more established scholarship that seeks to explain—including robbery, homicide, and spouse violence—has been drawn from essentialist biological and evolutionary approaches that have viewed offending as being a consequence of defective male (female) identities (see Anderson and Bushman 2002; Archer 1994; Daly and Wilson 1988).

3.5.1   Masculine Turn

Analyses of the links between masculinity and crime started to emerge in some of the early feminist scholarship that was produced in disciplines other than criminology (which followed later) (Collier 1998). Sharing some parallels with the evolutionary work cited above, however, masculinity was viewed as being one coherent gender. Men's crimes and (domestic-, sexual and intra-male-) forms of violence were understood as being determined by an individual's position in the class structure and/or other structural systems of dominance, characterised as patriarchy (see Daly and Chesney-Lind 1988; Gelsthorpe and Morris 1990; Hood-Williams 2001; Smart 1977 for an overview of this early criminological feminist scholarship). On the whole, this traditional criminological scholarship has been concerned with the study and control of "dangerous" forms of masculinity—especially working-class male delinquency—but has failed to take into account the links between criminality and the socially varied strategies that men employ in order to attain power and status (Collier 1998; Tomsen 2008). It was not until the start of the 1990s that researchers, building on earlier feminist work and drawing on the more sophisticated theoretical approaches that had been developed in critical men's studies, began to explicitly address the subject of masculinities and crime.

In what Collier (2004) has hailed as the "masculine turn", key criminological texts emerged that emphasised relations between different masculinities and identified the causes and patterns of most acts of crime—as well as critically highlighting the broader workings of policing, courts and prisons (Messerschmidt 1993; Newburn and Stanko 1994; Tomsen 2008). Messerschmidt (1993)—a key contributor to this scholarship—has examined the connections between gender, violence and crime through a structured action approach that recognises differences according to class, race, ethnicity, sexuality and age. Masculinities, for Messerschmidt, are linked to struggles for power that occur between men and women and among groups of men. Within this framework he developed the idea of gender as a "situational accomplishment" and of crime (and violence) as a means of "doing gender". For Messerschmidt, men will "situationally accomplish masculinity in response to their social structured circumstances...and crime can serve as a suitable resource for doing masculinity within the specific context of the street" (ibid., p. 113) when conventional or legitimate avenues to masculinity are in short supply. Following Messerschmidt, Heath Copes and Andy Hochstetler (2003)—in a study that explores the situational construction of masculinity among American street thieves—have found that acquisitive crimes such as robbery and burglary help men to accumulate the material resources that they need in order to be able to present a respected form of street masculinity. Many of these men, they have claimed, use the proceeds of their crimes to build street credibility via the purchase of clothes, cars, drugs and the pursuit of sexual conquests.

In the UK, Beatrix Campbell (1993) has linked the decline of car manufacturing in Oxford—a location in which the industry used to employ large numbers of working-class male school leavers—to the criminality and antisocial behaviour of many of the white men who live on the surrounding estates. Campbell has highlighted how the process of stealing cars and driving them at high speeds around their local housing estates—together with their intimidation of those who objected to them doing so—was important to the young men in terms of their sense of themselves as being daring risk-takers, enforcers and real men (also see Corbett 2003). Similarly, research on young working-class men in Australia (Cunneen 1995) and Canada (O'Connor and Kelly 2006) has identified similar patterns of economic and vehicle crime wherein risk-taking and driving prowess have been regarded as means of performing protest masculinity.

Other studies that explore the interplay of masculinity and crime in post-industrial regions in the UK have focused on the "night-time economy". The night-time formal economy offers legitimate income for hard-masculine bodies who can provide security services as aforementioned (Monaghan 2002; Winlow 2001; Ellis 2016). As these studies have shown, this type of work is often a platform where feared and respected masculinities are reproduced through a cyclical system of excessive violence and entrepreneurship that centres on protection, drug dealing and stolen goods.

3.5.2   Masculinity and Violent Crime

The many manifestations of violence and the role that they play in legitimising constructions of masculinity have been convincingly identified and explored throughout the social sciences over recent decades (see Ellis 2016, 2019; Ellis et al. 2017; Gadd 2003; Kimmel and Mahler 2003; Polk 1994; Segal 2007; Toch 1992). However, because of its close resonance with the informants' gendered trajectories, it is worth reiterating Messerschmidt's (1997) claim that intrapersonal male violence serves as a direct and potent situational resource for the construction of masculinity among marginalised men because of its strong association with hegemonic masculinity. Messerschmidt's assertion echoes Connell's (1995) empirical findings concerning protest masculinity—characterised by hypermasculine aggressive displays and violent crime as responses to economic and cultural weakness—as I discussed in detail in the opening section of this chapter. Gary Barker (2005), in his comparative study of young males in the Caribbean, Nigeria, Africa, America and Brazil, has suggested that this is the case across many cultures. He has shown how young men who have limited or no access to work—in societies in which employment is the defining feature of masculinity—invest heavily in protest masculinity where their cultural expectations of machismo have found expression, often through serious gang violence, on the streets.

Similarly, Mullins' (2006) work has shown how violence has been readily employed as a resource with which one may prove one's masculinity. Interestingly, his research found that after proving they were capable of doing gender this way, many felt trapped or tied into it as a resource in maintaining future gender identities. Katz (1988) has highlighted that, once violent or criminal identities have been established, they must be continually backed up or one risks losing credibility in the few places, like the street or the prison, where it is most needed. It is in these spaces, Copes and Hochstetler (2003) have observed, that "pretenders" who provoke situations that they cannot actually handle face serious denigration (p. 288), usually, finding themselves on the receiving end of insults that are loaded with feminine connotations. In some cases, this may even lead to homicide (Polk 1994). Kenneth Polk's (1994) influential study of men who kill, for example, highlighted typical "masculine scenarios" that lead to homicide often evolved from minor disputes relating to perceived acts of disrespect and an affront to personal honour.

Winlow (2004) claimed that although this work on multiple masculinities adds to gendered analysis of men, it inadvertently overshadows the critical focus on the ways in which the men have generated economic gains, social status and visceral pleasure from performances of violent masculinity. Violence tends to be utilised as a resource in these ways—mostly by men who come from certain harsh social, economic and cultural backdrops (Ellis 2016; Winlow 2004). This scholarship is careful to point out that not all men who lack social and economic resources are prone to violence. Many different men, from across the class spectrum, experience the thrill that comes with successfully transgressing some aspects of the law. However, the thrill and respect that come with (violent) offending tend to appeal to lower-class men for many of the reasons that have already been discussed. Importantly, this means that the likelihood of perpetrating—or being a victim of—violence is much greater for lower-class men; consequently, this likelihood pervades many aspects of their daily lives (Ellis 2019). Under these conditions, Winlow (2004) has argued, "lower working-class boys" learn, at an early stage, the "emotive nature of physical combat" and learn a "variety of scripts enabling successful negotiation of potentially violent situations" (p. 18). As Gunter (2008) found in his research into the experiences of young black men who came from an impoverished estate in London, the safest way of avoiding being a victim of adrenalin-based violence or attacks by those who seek to acquire masculine capital by means of violent acts is, ironically, through successful performances of the same aggressive masculinity (see also Ellis et al. 2017).

3.6   Prison Masculinities

Considering men commit the majority of crime and account for over 90% of the prison population at any one time in the UK, there is a surprising dearth of research that explores the "doing" of masculinity in UK prison spaces. This is not to argue that there is a lack of research on prison but, rather, as Joe Sim (1994) has pointed out, existing research concentrates too much on "men as prisoners rather than prisoners as men" (p. 101). Before going on to highlight recent scholarship that focuses more explicitly on masculinity and imprisonment, I want to take first introduce a number of early and widely cited sociological studies on men in prison. Although, in this classic work, gender is not explicitly drawn upon as an analytical framework, the significant relevance for this study stems from its focus on prison subcultures that implicitly identify hierarchised masculinities and, consequently, recognise the role of the prison space in creating and sustaining dominant and subordinated masculinities.

3.6.1   Early Sociology of Prisons

Early key studies mainly took place in the US and posited that prison culture or prison societies, that in turn shape and influence masculine identities/hierarchies, were created and maintained through adaptation strategies to the conditions of the carceral space. One of the earliest and more influential of these prison studies is Donald Clemmer's (1958) *The Prison Community*. Although it is now over 70 years old, this work still—as I show in Chapters 7 and 8—offers interesting insights that are relevant to my informants' prisoner identities. Clemmer was primarily interested in the culture of prison and how structural and social relationships generated class stratification or what might be understood today as prison masculine hierarchies. Using the dominant functionalist framework of the time, he introduced the concept of prisonisation, which he explained as the assimilation process that occurs when inmates accept the "folkways, mores, and customs, and general culture of the penitentiary" (Clemmer 1958, p. 299). For him, every prisoner—depending on the length of their sentence and factors such as outside support/contact—will internalise and accept prison culture to some extent and will experience varying degrees of prisonisation. As part of this process, "inmates" adjust to their environments and, in order to "survive", they practice expected modes of behaviour that they understand as constituting the "inmate code". Having evolved over many years, and being known to every prisoner, this collective code mainly centres on the concept of inmate loyalty when dealing with each other, the policing of taboo (sex) crimes and the prohibition of colluding with officers or volunteering information about other criminals. Although in practice many men in prison breach this code, it is seen as being effective at controlling and organising prisoners.

Clemmer, in his exploration of prison culture, found that—although aspects of the penitentiary were extremely atomised—it was a highly stratified environment. Inmates were positioned or classed depending on their adherence to the code, the ways in which they carried themselves and how others perceived them—including officers. He listed three distinct typologies or classes based on the informally dominant and the dominated. The most revered masculinity—what he termed the "elite" class—comprised intelligent, sophisticated, urbanised prisoners. Close to the bottom of the hierarchy was the type of denigrated or subordinated masculinity with which a "hoosier", the "objectionable"—a stupid person, officer or "stool pigeon" (informer)—would be associated. The lowest prisoners of all in terms of status were the sex offenders.

Clemmer's work, although highly regarded, has been criticised on several fronts. The main criticism that has been levelled at his work is that he failed to explain the origins of the prison culture that has structured prisoner society and on which his concept of prisonisation is based (Wheeler 1961). These challenges have given rise to two of the most prominent theories in penology, known as the deprivation model and the importation thesis.

The sociologist Sykes (2007)—in his landmark study, *Society of Captives*—proposed the use of the deprivation model. Like Clemmer, he accepted that culture originates from behind the prison walls. However, where he departs from Clemmer is in his assertion that the process of prisonisation originates from the "pains of imprisonment" that are born out of the deprivations with which inmates have to cope upon incarceration. Sykes proposed five forms of deprivations: the deprivation of liberty, the deprivation of autonomy, the deprivation of goods and services, the deprivation of heterosexual relations and the deprivation of security. Each prisoner responds to and negotiates the depravations and pains of their incarceration in different ways. Sykes, like Clemmer, has shown how this leads to "argot roles" or hierarchal identities/masculinities. The "rats", for instance, ease the pain of incarceration by their acts of informing; the "gorillas" exert control through acts of violence. Sykes has claimed that the social cohesion of prison is sustained by a particular type of revered masculinity: the "real man". This is the prisoner who "pulls his own time", "confronts his captors with neither subservience or aggression", "embodies the inmate's version of decorum" (p. 102) and has the respect of both prisoners and staff.

Irwin's and Cressy's (1962) importation thesis challenges the idea that behaviour classified as being part of prison culture was solely created as a response to imprisonment. Instead, they have argued that identities are imported into the institution by the criminal who has been sentenced to a jail term. They have suggested that much more consideration needs to be given to the environmental values from which prisoners originate. They proposed that prison populations can be better understood as falling into three types of culture: "convict culture", "thieves" and "legitimate culture". The most respected prisoners are the "thieves" who, they argue, bring their status with them via their connections from outside the prison. Thieves are well aware of the rules of conduct and how to behave in prison—a long time before they ever actually receive a sentence. Once they are inside, the thieves are seen as being loyal adherents to a strict criminal code; they hold a special power and influence over the other prisoners.

3.6.2   "Prisoners as Men"

Pemberton (2013) has argued that, despite the implicit importance of masculine identities in early sociological work, a great deal of the penal, empirical enquiry and theorising that has followed has failed to explicitly explore the gendered nature of male prisoners. She has highlighted that prisons—as some of the last bastions of official gender segregation—are obvious sites for the investigation of the ways in which masculinities are constituted in the context of, and in opposition to, authoritative power. Similarly, in their explorations of the organisation of ethnicities (and masculinities) in UK prisons, Earl and Phillips (2012) have highlighted this omission when noting that it is still relatively unusual for penal spaces to appear in any of the increasing numbers of masculinity studies. They go further and note: "ever since Foucault, penal scholars have excelled in 'big picture' theorizing – but Foucault's 'docile bodies' have no gender; they have no faces and no places…[Prisoners] must be revealed from the shadows into which they have most literally been thrown" (p. 153).

In a less pessimistic tone than Pemberton's, Earl's and Philips', there is a scattering of existing research and a contemporary academic interest—that is growing at an encouraging rate—in the gendered nature of male prisoners. Writing predominantly from an American penal perspective, Sabo et al. (2001) published an edited collection on "prison masculinities" almost two decades ago in which they highlighted how masculinities in the overwhelming male space of the prisons have to be continuously worked and competed for, showing that they are organised around the adherence and policing of a universal prisoner/criminal code. Other interesting contributions to this collection centre on the interplay between sexuality, masculinity and incarceration. Stephen Donaldson (2001), for example, focused on how the "queens" and "punks" fuse masculinity and femininity in a particular form of performance that is based around passive homosexuality. He noted that the "other" role or denigration of this homosexual identity forms part of the strategy for the construction of "daddy" or manly prison masculinities. Terry Kupers (2005), an American psychologist, has drawn on his considerable experience of interviewing male prisoners to develop his idea of "toxic masculinity". It is an identity that he claims is the most revered by inmates and can be understood as being a combination of all of the socially destructive aspects of Connell's hegemonic masculinity, such as "misogyny, homophobia, greed, and violent domination" (2005, p. 716).

In the UK, Yvonne Jewkes' research (2005) into men who have experienced the English prison system found that proving one's male credentials on the streets—which, for many working-class young men, often leads to criminal behaviour and, consequently, incarceration—is itself a prerequisite of successfully adapting to life inside (2005, p. 51). She notes that, once inside, a man's masculinity is positioned not only in accordance with the crime allegedly committed but also in relation to how prisoners typically carry themselves in the prison space. Young male prisoners enter the prison and attempt to adhere to a particular type of "hard" protest masculinity—but most, she claims, are quickly dismissed as "wannabe gangsters" by the long-termers, often "lifers" and armed robbers, who are equally keen to maintain the revered and hypermasculine identity of the proper "villain". Jewkes found that men who are unable to live up to these masculine performances tend to adopt alternative types of masculinity—that of the skilled tradesman, scholar, or legal adviser—to counter their potential marginalisation. However, Jewkes has posited that an extreme construction of protest or hypermasculinity is the almost universal response to adapting to the lower working-class prison culture. This exaggerated version of manliness, she has suggested, is both a response to the pains of imprisonment identified by Sykes (2007) and related forms of resistance to the powerlessness with which the label of "prisoners" tends to be associated.

Ben Crewe (2009), another UK prison scholar, has shown how shifting power and social relations in the "neoliberal prison" have brought about changing prison masculine identities. He has argued that the modern prison, governed in accordance with managerialist principles, exercises power over prisoners in increasingly diffused ways that are, consequently, more and more difficult for prisoners to identify. The move away from officers arbitrarily imposing power over prisoners towards a centralised system instead—one that is based on formalised procedures for sanctioning and privileges—has meant that prison masculinity has become less reliant upon collective construction in opposition to the staff and prison authority as had previously been documented in classic penology work. This shift, coupled with what many of Crewe's respondents believed to be the changing culture of prisons—as a result of drug use and related offences—has seen the significant erosion of the prisoner/criminal code that was core to the older, preceding expressions of prison masculinities. These changes, he has argued, have meant that prisoners have become less inclined to express their masculinities through the overt, hypermasculine, violent displays that have been documented in other prison research.

Phillips' (2012) work on English prisons has focused in more depth on how gender intersects with other social categories in the construction of masculinities—as well as how they are formally and informally organised in the prison space. In what she has termed the "multicultural prison", Phillips has suggested that prison masculinities are much more complex than those that have been portrayed in a lot of UK penal research. She has argued that the growing incarceration of black and minority men has significantly dislodged the once-dominant position of white masculinity. Race, ethnicity and religion play major roles in changing prison masculine identities and hierarchies. "Blackness", Phillips has found, is a highly revered masculine identity among inmates of all ethnicities. Prisoners were found to be attracted to how masculinities associated with "blackness" were expressed through a particular style, music, food and expressions of loyalty and belonging to place. Phillips was careful to point out that, despite obvious strains, the prisons she has studied can in no way be regarded as being as violent or anywhere near as racially divided as those that can be found in the American system. She has contended that, over the years, some progress has been made in recognising diversity throughout the prison body.

This growing focus on the gender of men in prison has been reflected in Mathew Maycock's and Kate Hunt's (2018) edited collection, "New Perspectives on Prison Masculinities". Including a wide selection of penal scholars, many from the UK, this collection has covered both well-documented and lesser-explored forms of prison masculinities. Contributors have shown how prison masculinities are embodied and enacted through highly refined gym bodies. Other authors challenged the pervasive overrepresentation of hypermasculine prisoners; they have contended that evidence of "softer" masculinities configured through acts of intimacy and compassion to fellow inmates. The collection also includes chapters on prison masculinity and fatherhood. In a shift away from the usual, oversimplified portrayals of racialised, violent, gang-affiliated prison identities, one contributor explores the configuration of faith-based (black) masculinities.

Across all of this scholarship on prison masculinities, the common theme that emerges is that of the hierarchal organisation of men across prison spaces. Counterposed to the revered hypermasculine and violent men are the informers, the "poor copers", and—even lower down—the deviant "beast" masculinities. However, as I show in Chapters 7 and 8, informants' prison masculinities are much more multifaceted and complex than the simplified binary of dominant and subordinate gender performances would suggest. Furthermore, a great deal of research to date that has explored prison masculinities has focused on the experiences of men while they are inside the institution of the prison. In doing so they have failed to fully account for the ways in which locality or place might be implicated in prison identities/hierarchies. In Phillips' (2012) study, for example, the organisation of masculinities around multiple ethnicities—and the reverence for black masculinities—was indicative of the specific regional catchments that the prison serves. I show that, in contrast to "blackness", the "local" prison in my study housed those who were from the surrounding, mostly white, working-class neighbourhoods; "white hegemony" remained the revered masculinity.

3.7   Conclusion

In this chapter, I have critically reviewed the existing research into how boys and men situationally configure post-industrial masculinities across crucial sites. In doing so, I have outlined how economic change impacts gendered identities at national, regional and local levels. Having outlined the main scholarship on working-class masculinity, schooling and attainment, I offered an overview of (youth) transitions literature and explored the dearth of work that specifically employs a gender analyses of criminal and prison masculinities. The literature considered through this chapter provides a valuable insight into the configuration of masculinities over one or two sites. In the empirical chapters that follow I will offer a gendered analysis of how these sites interconnect in creating and maintaining marginalised masculinities. Before presenting these findings, I want to first outline the background to the study and the epistemological and methodological challenges it raised.

References

Allen, R., Bibby, D., & Parameshwaran, M. (2015). *Missing talent: Raising the aspirations and achievement of the 7,000 highly able pupils who fall behind at secondary school*. London: Sutton Trust.

Anderson, C., & Bushman, B. J. (2002). Human aggression. *Psychology, 53*(1), 27. https://doi.org/10.1146/annurev.psych.53.100901.135231.

Archer, J. (1994). *Male violence*. London: Routledge.

Archer, L. (2003). *Race, masculinity and schooling: Muslim boys and education*. Maidenhead: Open University Press.

Archer, L. (2007). *Understanding minority ethnic achievement: Race, gender, class and "success"*. Abingdon: Routledge.

Ball, S. J. (2003). *Class strategies and the education market: The middle classes and social advantage*. London: Routledge.

Barker, G. (2005). *Dying to be men: Youth, masculinity and social exclusion: Youth and masculinity and social exclusion*. London: Routledge.

Beck, U. (1992). *Risk society: Towards a new modernity*. London: Sage.

Beck, U. (2000). *Brave new world of work*. Cambridge: Polity.

Beck, U., & Beck-Gernsheim, E. (2001). *Individualization: Institutionalized individualism and its social and political consequences*. London: Sage.

Blokland, T., & Savage, M. (2001). Networks, class and place. *International Journal of Urban and Regional Research, 25*(2), 221–226. https://doi.org/10.1111/1468-2427.00308.

Bourgois, P. (2003). *In search of respect: Selling crack in El Barrio*. Cambridge: Cambridge University Press.

Brown, P., & Scase, R. (1991). *Poor work: Disadvantage and the division of labour*. Milton Keynes: Open University Press.

Calvert, E. (2010). *Young people's housing transitions in context*. ESRC Centre for Population Change Working Article 8. Centre for Population and Change.

Campbell, B. (1993). *Goliath: Britain's dangerous places/Beatrix Campbell*. London: Methuen.

Centre for Cities. (2015). *Cities outlook 2015*. London: Centre for Cities.

Clapham, D., Mackie, P., Orford, S., Thomas, I., & Buckley, K. (2014). The housing pathways of young people in the UK. *Environment and Planning A: Economy and Space, 46*(8), 2016–2031. https://doi.org/10.1068/a46273.

Collier, R. (1998). *Masculinities, crime and criminology: Men, heterosexuality and the criminal(ised) other*. London: Sage.

Collier, R. (2004). Masculinities and crime: Rethinking the "man question"? In C. Sumner (Ed.), *The Blackwell companion to criminology* (pp. 285–308). Hoboken: Blackwell Publishing Ltd.

Connell, R. (1989). Cool guys, swots and wimps: The interplay of masculinity and education. *Oxford Review of Education, 15*(3). https://doi.org/10.1080/0305498890150309.

Connell, R. (1995). *Masculinities*. Cambridge: Polity.

Copes, H., & Hochstetler, A. (2003). Situational construction of masculinity among male street thieves. *Journal of Contemporary Ethnography, 32*(3), 279–304. https://doi.org/10.1177/0891241603032003002.

Corbett, C. (2003). *Car crime*. Crime and Society Series. Cullompton: Willan.

Corrigan, P. (1979). *Schooling the smash street kids*. London: Palgrave Macmillan.

Crane, M., Warnes, A. M., Barnes, J., & Coward, S. (2014). The resettlement of homeless young people: Their experiences and housing outcomes. *Social Policy and Society, 13*(02), 161–176. https://doi.org/10.1017/S1474746413000468.

Crewe, B. (2009). *The prisoner society: Power, adaptation and social life in an English prison*. Oxford: Oxford University Press.

Cunneen, C. (1995). *Juvenile justice: An Australian perspective*. Melbourne and Oxford: Oxford University Press.

Daly, K., & Chesney-Lind, M. (1988). Feminism and criminology. *Justice Quarterly, 5*(4), 497–538. https://doi.org/10.1080/07418828800089871.

Daly, M., & Wilson, M. (1988). *Homicide*. New York: Aldine.

DeKeseredy, W. S., & Schwartz, M. D. (2005). Masculinities and interpersonal violence. In M. S. Kimmel, J. Hearn, & R. Connell (Eds.), *Handbook of studies on men and masculinities* (pp. 353–366). London: Sage.

Delamont, S. (2000). The anomalous beasts: Hooligans and the sociology of education. *Sociology, 34*(1), 95–111. https://doi.org/10.1177/S0038038500000079.

Donaldson, S. (2001). A million jokers, punks, and queens. In D. F. Sabo, T. A. Kupers, & W. J. London (Eds.), *Prison masculinities* (pp. 118–126). Philadelphia: Temple University Press.

Earle, R., & Phillips, C. (2012). Digesting men? Ethnicity, gender and food: Perspectives from a "prison ethnography". *Theoretical Criminology, 16*(2), 141–156. https://doi.org/10.1177/1362480612441121.

Ellis, A. J. (2016). *Men, masculinities and violence: An ethnographic study*. London: Routledge.

Ellis, A. J. (2019). A de-civilizing reversal or system normal? Rising lethal violence in post-recession austerity United Kingdom. *The British Journal of Criminology, 59*(4), 862–878. https://doi.org/10.1093/bjc/azz001.

Ellis, A., Winlow, S., & Hall, S. (2017). 'Throughout my life I've had people walk all over me': Trauma in the lives of violent men. *The Sociological Review*, 65(4), 699–713. https://doi.org/10.1177/0038026117695486.

Evans, G. (2006). *Educational failure and working class white children in Britain*. Basingstoke: Palgrave Macmillan.

Francis, B. (1999). Lads, lasses and (new) labour: 14–16-year-old students' responses to the 'laddish behaviour and boys' underachievement' debate. *British Journal of Sociology of Education*, 20(3), 355–371. https://doi.org/10.1080/01425699995317.

Francis, B. (2006). Heroes or zeroes? The discursive positioning of "underachieving boys" in English neo-liberal education policy. *Journal of Education Policy*, 21(2), 187–200. https://doi.org/10.1080/02680930500500278.

Francis, B. (2009). The role of The Boffin as abject other in gendered performances of school achievement. *The Sociological Review*, 57(4), 645–669. https://doi.org/10.1111/j.1467-954X.2009.01866.x.

Frosh, S., Phoenix, A., & Pattman, R. (2002). *Young masculinities: Understanding boys in contemporary society*. Basingstoke: Palgrave.

Furlong, A., Woodman, D., & Wyn, J. (2011). Changing times, changing perspectives: Reconciling "transition" and "cultural" perspectives on youth and young adulthood. *Journal of Sociology*, 47(4), 355–370. https://doi.org/10.1177/1440783311420787.

Gadd, D. (2003). Reading between the lines: Subjectivity and men's violence. *Men and Masculinities*, 5(4), 333–354. https://doi.org/10.1177/1097184X02250838.

Gelsthorpe, L., & Morris, A. (1990). *Feminist perspectives in criminology*. New Directions in Criminology Series. Milton Keynes: Open University Press.

Griffin, C. (2000). Discourses of crisis and loss: Analysing the "boys" underachievement' debate. *Journal of Youth Studies*, 3(2). https://doi.org/10.1080/713684373.

Gunter, A. (2008). Growing up bad: Black youth, 'road' culture and badness in an East London neighbourhood. *Crime, Media, Culture*, 4(3), 349–366. https://doi.org/10.1177/1741659008096371.

Gunter, A., & Watt, P. (2009). Grafting, going to college and working on road: Youth transitions and cultures in an East London neighbourhood. *Journal of Youth Studies*, 12(5), 515–529. https://doi.org/10.1080/13676260903083364.

Hardgrove, A., McDowell, L., & Rootham, E. (2015). Precarious lives, precarious labour: Family support and young men's transitions to work in the UK. *Journal of Youth Studies*, 18(8), 1–20. https://doi.org/10.1080/13676261.2015.1020933.

Heath, S., & Calvert, E. (2013). Gifts, loans and intergenerational support for young adults. *Sociology, 47*(6), 1120–1135. https://doi.org/10.1177/003 8038512455736.

Hood-Williams, J. (2001). Gender, masculinities and crime: From structures to psyches. *Theoretical Criminology, 5*(1), 37–60. https://doi.org/10.1177/1362480601005001003.

House of Commons Educational Committee. (2014). *Underachievement in education by white working class children* (First Report of Session 2014–15). London: The Stationery Office.

Ingram, N. (2011). Within school and beyond the gate: The complexities of being educationally successful and working class. *Sociology, 45*(2), 287–302. https://doi.org/10.1177/0038038510394017.

Irwin, J., & Cressey. D. R. (1962). Thieves, convicts and the inmate culture. *Social Problems, 10*, 142–155. https://doi.org/10.2307/799047, https://www.jstor.org/stable/799047.

Jewkes, Y. (2005). *Men Behind Bars: Men and Masculinities, 8*, 44–63. https://doi.org/10.1177/1097184X03257452.

Johnston, L., MacDonald, R., Mason, P., Ridley, L., & Webster, C. (2000). *Snakes and ladders: Young people, transitions and social exclusion.* Bristol: Policy Press.

Katz, J. (1988). *Seductions of crime: Moral and sensual attractions in doing evil.* New York: Basic Books.

Khattab, N., & Modood,T. (2018). Accounting for British Muslim's educational attainment: Gender differences and the impact of expectations. *British Journal of Sociology of Education, 39*(2), 242–259. https://doi.org/10.1080/01425692.2017.1304203.

Kimmel, M., & Mahler, M. (2003). Adolescent masculinity, homophobia, and violence random school shootings, 1982–2001. *American Behavioral Scientist, 46*(10), 1439–1458. https://doi.org/10.1177/0002764203046010010.

Kupers, T. A. (2005). Toxic masculinity as a barrier to mental health treatment in prison. *Journal of Clinical Psychology, 61*(6), 713–724. https://doi.org/10.1002/jclp.20105.

Mac an Ghaill, M. (1994). *The making of men: Masculinities, sexualities and schooling.* Buckingham: Open University Press.

Mac an Ghaill, M. (2019). Reconfiguring masculinities and education. *Routledge International Handbook of Masculinity Studies.*

Mac an Ghaill, M., & Haywood, C. (2012). The queer in masculinity: Schooling, boys, and identity formation. In J. C. Landreau & N. M. Rodriguez (Eds.), *Queer masculinities* (pp. 69–84). Explorations of Educational Purpose. Netherlands: Springer.

MacDonald, R., & Marsh, J. (2002). Crossing the Rubicon: Youth transitions, poverty, drugs and social exclusion. *International Journal of Drug Policy, 13*(1), 27–38. https://doi.org/10.1016/S0955-3959(02)00004-X.

MacDonald, R., & Marsh, J. (2005). *Disconnected youth? Growing up in Britain's poor neighbourhoods.* Basingstoke: Palgrave Macmillan.

MacDonald, R., Mason, P., Shildrick, T., Webster, C., Johnston, L., & Ridley, L. (2001). Snakes & ladders: In defence of studies of youth transition. *Sociological Research Online, 5*(4), 1–13.

MacDonald, R., & Shildrick, T. (2007). Street corner society: Leisure careers, youth (sub)culture and social exclusion. *Leisure Studies, 26*(3), 339–355. https://doi.org/10.1080/02614360600834826.

MacDonald, R., Shildrick, T., Webster, C., & Simpson, D. (2005). Growing up in poor neighbourhoods: The significance of class and place in the extended transitions of "socially excluded" young adults. *Sociology, 39*(5), 873–891. https://doi.org/10.1177/0038038505058370.

Maycock, M., & Hunt, K. (Eds.). (2018). *New perspectives on prison masculinities.* London: Palgrave Macmillan.

McDowell, L. (2003). *Redundant masculinities? Employment change and white working class youth.* Oxford: Blackwell.

McDowell, L. (2014). The sexual contract: Youth, masculinity and the uncertain promise of waged work in Austerity Britain. *Australian Feminist Studies, 29*(79), 31–49. https://doi.org/10.1080/08164649.2014.901281.

McDowell, L., & Bonner-Thompson, C. (2020). The other side of coastal towns: Young men's precarious lives on the margins of England. *Environment and Planning A: Economy and Space, 52*(5), 916–932. https://doi.org/10.1177/0308518X19887968.

McDowell, L., Rootham, E., & Hardgrove, A. (2014). Precarious work, protest masculinity and communal regulation: South Asian young men in Luton, UK. *Work, Employment & Society, 28*(6), 847–864. https://doi.org/10.1177/0950017013510757.

Messerschmidt, J. W. (1993). *Masculinities and crime: Critique and reconceptualization of theory.* Lanham, Md.: Rowman & Littlefield.

Messerschmidt, J. W. (1997). *Crime as structured action: Gender, race, class and crime in the making.* Thousand Oaks, CA and London: Sage.

Messerschmidt, J. W. (2001). Masculinities, crime and prison. In D. Sabo, T. Kupers, & W. London (Eds.), *Prison masculinities.* Philadelphia, PA: Temple University Press.

Monaghan, L. F. (2002). Hard men, shop boys and others: Embodying competence in a masculinist occupation. *The Sociological Review, 50*(3), 334–355. https://doi.org/10.1111/1467-954X.00386.

Mullins, C. W. (2006). *Holding your square: Masculinities, streetlife, and violence.* Cullompton: Willan.

Nayak, A. (2003a). "Boyz to Men": Masculinities, schooling and labour transitions in de-industrial times. *Educational Review, 55*(2), 147–159. https://doi.org/10.1080/0013191032000072191.

Nayak, A. (2003b). Last of the 'Real Geordies'? White masculinities and the subcultural response to deindustrialisation. *Environment and Planning D: Society and Space, 21*(1), 7–26. https://doi.org/10.1068/d44j.

Nayak, A. (2006). Displaced masculinities: Chavs, youth and class in the post-industrial city. *Sociology, 40*(5), 813–831. https://doi.org/10.1177/0038038506067508.

Newburn, T., & Stanko, E. A. (1994). *Just boys doing business? Men, masculinities and crime.* London: Routledge.

Noble, S., McLennan, D., Noble, M., Plunkett, E., Gutacker, N., Silk, M., & Wright, G. (2019). *The English Indices of Deprivation 2019* (Research Report). Ministry of Housing, Communities and Local Government.

Nuttall, A., & Doherty, J. (2014). Disaffected boys and the achievement gap: "The wallpaper effect" and what is hidden by a focus on school results. *Urban Review, 46*, 800–815. https://doi.org/10.1007/s11256-014-0303-8.

O'Connor, C., & Kelly, K. (2006). Auto theft and youth culture: A nexus of masculinities, femininities and car culture. *Journal of Youth Studies, 9*(3), 247–267.

Office for National Statistics. (2013). *170 years of industrial change across England and Wales.*

Office for National Statistics. (2019a). Health state life expectancies, UK: 2016 to 2018.

Office for National Statistics. (2019b). Suicides in the UK: 2018 registrations.

Office for National Statistics. (2019c). Deaths related to drug poisoning in England and Wales: 2018 registrations.

Office for Standards in Education. (2013a). *Unseen children: Access and achievement 20 years on.* London.

Office for Standards in Education. (2013b). *Her Majesty's chief inspector of education, children's services and skills annual report 2012/13.* Schools.

Office for Standards in Education. (2020). *The annual report of Her Majesty's Chief Inspector of Education, Children's Services and Skills 2018/19.* London: Ofsted.

Pemberton, S. (2013). Enforcing gender: The constitution of sex and gender in prison regimes. *Signs, 39*(1), 151–175. https://doi.org/10.1086/670828.

Phillips, C. (2012). *The multicultural prison: Ethnicity, masculinity, and social relations among prisoners.* Oxford: Oxford University Press.

Polk, K. (1994). *When men kill: Scenarios of masculine violence.* Cambridge: Cambridge University Press.

Reay, D. (2002). Shaun's story: Troubling discourses of white working-class masculinities. *Gender and Education, 14*(3), 221–234. https://doi.org/10.1080/0954025022000010695.

Reay, D., & Lucey, H. (2000). "I don't really like it here but I don't want to be anywhere else': Children and inner city council estates. *Antipode, 32*(4), 410–428. https://doi.org/10.1111/1467-8330.00144.

Rhodes, C. (2020). *Manufacturing: Statistics and policy.* London: House of Commons.

Riley, A. (2020, January 6). Every school in Hull and East Yorkshire ordered to improve by Ofsted. *Hull Daily Mail.*

Roberts, S. (2010). Misrepresenting "choice biographies"? A reply to Woodman. *Journal of Youth Studies, 13*(1), 137–149. https://doi.org/10.1080/13676260903233720.

Roberts, S. (2011). Beyond "NEET" and "tidy" pathways: Considering the "missing middle" of youth transition studies. *Journal of Youth Studies, 14*(1), 21–39. https://doi.org/10.1080/13676261.2010.489604.

Roberts, R. (2012). "I just got on with it": The educational experiences of ordinary, yet overlooked, boys. *British Journal of Sociology of Education, 33*(2), 203–221. https://doi.org/10.1080/01425692.2011.649832.

Roberts, S. (2012). One step forward, one step Beck: A contribution to the ongoing conceptual debate in youth studies. *Journal of Youth Studies, 15*(3), 389–401. https://doi.org/10.1080/13676261.2012.663896.

Roberts, S. (2018). *Young working-class men in transition.* London: Routledge.

Roberts, S., & Evans, S. (2012). Aspirations' and imagined futures: Choices, aspirations and economic hardship in working class student experience. In W. Atkinson, S. Roberts, & M. Savage (Eds.), *Class inequality in austerity Britain: Power, difference and suffering* (pp. 70–89). Palgrave.

Rowthorn, R., & Coutts, K. (2013). *De-industrialisation and the balance of payments in advanced economies* (Future of Manufacturing Project: Evidence Paper 31). London: Foresight, Government Office for Science.

Sabo, D., Kupers, T., & London, W. (Eds.). (2001). *Prison masculinities.* Philadelphia, PA: Temple University Press.

Sayer, R. (2005). *The moral significance of class.* Cambridge: Cambridge University Press.

Segal, L. (2007). *Slow motion: Changing masculinities, changing men* (3rd ed.). Basingstoke: Palgrave Macmillan.

Sewell, T. (1997). *Black masculinities and schooling: How black boys survive modern schooling.* Stoke-on-Trent: Trentham.

Shildrick, T., Blackman, S., & MacDonald, R. (2009). Young people, class and place. *Journal of Youth Studies, 12*(5), 457–465. https://doi.org/10.1080/13676260903114136.

Shildrick, T., & MacDonald, R. (2007). Biographies of exclusion: Poor work and poor transitions. *International Journal of Lifelong Education, 26*(5), 589–604. https://doi.org/10.1080/02601370701559672.

Short, M. J. (2015). City rivalries: How Newcastle became a "poster child" for the new North. *The Guardian.* Available at http://www.theguardian.com/cit ies/2015/mar/20/newcastle-poster-child-north-sunderland-rivals. Accessed 11 June 2015.

Sim, J. (1994). Tougher than the rest? Men in prison. In T. Newburn & E. A. Stanko (Eds.), *Just boys doing business? Men, masculinities and crime.* London: Routledge.

Smart, C. (1977). *Women, crime, and criminology: A feminist critique.* London: Routledge.

Standing, G. (2011). *The precariat: The new dangerous class.* London: Bloomsbury Academic.

Sykes, G. (2007). *The society of captives: A study of a maximum security prison.* Princeton, NJ: Princeton University Press.

Toch, H. (1992). *Violent men: An inquiry into the psychology of violence.* Washington, DC: American Psychological Association.

Tomlinson, J. (2020). De-industrialization: Strengths and weaknesses as a key concept for understanding post-war British history. *Urban History,* 1–21. https://doi.org/10.1017/S0963926819000221.

Tomsen, S. (2008). *Crime, criminal justice and masculinities.* Aldershot: Ashgate.

Walker, G. W. (2006). Disciplining protest masculinity. *Men and Masculinities, 9*(1), 5–22. https://doi.org/10.1177/1097184X05284217.

Ward, M. (2014). "I'm a geek I am": Academic achievement and the performance of a studious working-class masculinity. *Gender and Education, 26*(7), 709–725. https://doi.org/10.1080/09540253.2014.953918.

Weaver-Hightower, M. (2003). The "boy turn" in research on gender and education. *Review of Educational Research, 73*(4), 471–498. https://doi.org/10.3102/00346543073004471.

Webster, C., Simpson, D., & MacDonald, R. (2004). *Poor transitions: Social exclusion and young adults.* Bristol: Policy Press.

Wheeler, S. (1961). Socialization in correctional communities. *American Sociological Review, 26,* 697–712. https://doi.org/10.2307/2090199.

Willis, P. (1977). *Learning to labor: How working class kids get working class jobs.* Farnborough, England: Saxon House.

Winlow, S. (2001). *Badfellas: Crime, tradition and new masculinities.* Oxford: Berg.

Winlow, S. (2004). Masculinities and crime. *Criminal Justice Matters, 55*(1), 18–19. https://doi.org/10.1080/09627250408553590.

Woodman, D. (2009). The mysterious case of the pervasive choice biography: Ulrich Beck, structure/agency, and the middling state of theory in the sociology of youth. *Journal of Youth Studies, 12*(3), 243–256. https://doi.org/10.1080/13676260902807227.

Woodman, D. (2010). Class, individualisation and tracing processes of inequality in a changing world: A reply to Steven Roberts. *Journal of Youth Studies, 13*(6), 737–746. https://doi.org/10.1080/13676261.2010.506533.

Wright, S., Crewe, B., & Hulley, S. (2016). Suppression, denial, sublimation: Defending against the initial pains of very long life sentences. *Theoretical Criminology, 21*(2), 225–246. https://doi.org/10.1177/1362480616643581.

Wright, C., Maylor, U., & Becker, S. (2016). Young black males: Resilience and the use of capital to transform school 'failure'. *Critical Studies in Education, 57* (1), 21–34. https://doi.org/10.1080/17508487.2016.1117005.

Wyn, J., Cuervo, H., Crofts, J., & Woodman, D. (2017). Gendered transitions from education to work: The mysterious relationship between the fields of education and work. *Journal of Sociology, 53*(2), 492–506. https://doi.org/10.1177/1440783317700736.

Background and Methods: Epistemological Privilege?

4.1 Introduction

In this chapter, I contextualise the study by describing the sense of place in which the respondents navigated their gendered identities. Moreover, I discuss the complexities of my positionality as an "ex-con" researcher and justify the methods that I chose to use while undertaking this research. In the opening section, I map Hull's industrial heritage as a city that went from a thriving industrial "golden age"—when it was the UK's third-largest port—to, at the time at which I undertook my research, between 2011 and 2015, languishing at the bottom of almost every UK indicator of wealth.

Most of the men in this study proudly claimed to have been "born and bred" in Hull, having spent "all of their lives" in and around the city's local authority housing estates. Their ability to earn a living, legitimate or otherwise, was closely linked to their localities. This was one of the main factors that served to "trap" them in place and contributed, as I show in the next chapter, to their early pathways to prison. Then, I introduce Hull Local Prison—the site, or field, of my research—explaining its role in the prison estate and why I chose it for the purposes of this study. Next, I go on to critically evaluate my "insider" status, arguing that—contrary to the content of much scholarship that associates epistemological privilege with "insider" status—an ex-prisoner identity presents significant challenges.

© The Author(s) 2021
D. Maguire, *Male, Failed, Jailed*,
Palgrave Studies in Prisons and Penology,
https://doi.org/10.1007/978-3-030-61059-3_4

After this, I outline how I gathered data for the project by conducting life history interviews, explaining why I used this approach as well as the limitations of doing so.

4.2   Place of Research: "I Grew Up on an Estate in Hull… I Just Took the Wrong Road"

Hull's advantageous geographical position—with its rivers and estuary systems that allow easy access to the North Sea and Northern Europe's once-lucrative trade routes—is what led to its ascendency as one of Europe's biggest and busiest ports (Gillett and MacMahon 1989). The city has prospered through the industries with which its port is associated, like shipbuilding and importing timber. Because of its relatively close proximity to the "Silver Pits" (fish-rich parts of the North Sea), fishing and associated industries are what has generated most of its wealth (ibid.). Following the Icelandic "cod wars" of the 1970s (see Jonsson 1982), Hull's fishing industry spiralled into rapid decline. The disappearance of the fishing industry inevitably had a devastating impact on the surrounding fishing ancillary trades such as processing, packing and smoking plants—and specialist haulage and transportation companies. While reeling from the collapse of the deep-water trawler industry, the 1970s saw the onset of soaring unemployment in other areas and sectors. Hull's dockers, for instance, were losing their jobs in significant numbers as a result of automation that saw the introduction of heavy-lifting machinery and more sophisticated storage and shipping systems (Gillett and MacMahon 1989). By the 1980s, like almost everywhere else in the UK, Hull's modest manufacturing sector had profoundly suffered under Thatcher's neoliberal agenda. The city experienced exceptionally high levels of unemployment during that decade's recession—and the following one in the early 1990s.

Census data from 1981 to 2001 show that Hull suffered disproportionately in the aftermath of the recessions. The city was especially vulnerable in the 2008 crash, being one of the hardest-hit places in England (Dolphin 2009). This can partly be explained by the decades of neglect on the part of the central government as well as the city's failure to adequately diversify so as to benefit from its geographical assets, including the deep water of the Humber and the city's proximity to the North Sea (Lee 2010).

Hull, as I highlight in Chapter 3, continues to be at the wrong end of measures for health, education and economic success. The Centre for Cities' most recent "Cities Outlook" (Enenkel et al. 2020) shows that, in 2018, Hull had one of the lowest numbers of businesses—and the lowest start-up rate. The same Outlook reports that, in November 2019, Hull had one of the highest numbers of unemployment benefit claimants. A government-commissioned review of education qualifications in England found that the working-age population of Hull holds lower qualifications than most other places, with 66% of individuals holding qualifications to level two and above. Only 22% have higher education qualifications. These statistics fall well below the national averages of 74% and 37% respectively (DfE 2017). According to The English Indices of Deprivation (MoHC&LG 2019), the City has been one of the top 5 areas that have persistently been the most deprived across historic iterations of the Indices.

As the research drew to a close in early 2015, however, Hull and the surrounding areas had begun an ambitious programme of economic diversification. I noted an air of optimism among probation staff and others who were involved in supporting the employability of prisoners, believing that the city was on the cusp of a new industrial era. "Green Port Hull" captured how millions of pounds were being invested to tap into Hull's (and East Riding of Yorkshire's) advantageous geography for offshore energy; the city has been hailed as a future "world-class centre" for renewable energy (see greenporthull.co.uk). Leading the way, Siemens had chosen Hull as the location for over £300 million of investment into the manufacture, assembly and servicing of wind turbine blades. In 2017 Hull was chosen as the City of Culture, bringing investment and contributing to the creation of nearly 800 new jobs in the cultural and visitors economy (Bianchini et al. 2019).

It is unlikely that the men who participated in this study, or many of their peers from the surrounding council housing estates, will see any short- or medium-term improvements to their prospects or economic status in the contexts of cultural sectors that demand deference and social/cultural capital or a specialised energy industry that primarily requires highly skilled workers. "Trapped" in Hull's poorest neighbourhoods and impoverished institutions, the only city that is visible to these men is the one that most indicators show as being a "late capitalist dystopia of poverty, worklessness and deprivation" (Featherstone 2013, p. 184).

4.3   FIELD: LOCAL PRISON

Hull prison was an appropriate location for this research because, as a "local"[1] its catchment covers some of heaviest deindustrialised northern regions. The City of Hull is home to one of Europe's largest expanses of local authority housing that spreads across two main council estates. A Victorian prison, Hull is situated in a relatively central location in the city and was first opened in 1870, housing both men and women. At the time of conducting my research, its official function as a category B local prison meant, as with other locals, that it accepted those within a particular catchment who had been detained either before or directly after their conviction. In this local capacity, the prison is responsible for sentenced and remanded adult males and young offenders from the Crown Court areas for Hull, York and Grimsby, as well as various magistrates' courts across the region. It has an operational capacity of around 1000 and deals with a highly transient population of remand and short-sentenced prisoners.

Hull prison, like others with a similar allocation of prisoners, manages a large turnover of men. At the time of the study, about a third of those held were serving a sentence of four years or more for serious offences. On average this prison receives anywhere between 3200 and 3600 new receptions a year. A 2009 report jointly compiled by National Treatment Agency (National Treatment Agency 2009) and Hull prison highlights that during this period over 80% of their inmates came from within a 50 mile radius of the prison and that over 50% of those released in this time were released into the city of Hull. Hull's role as the main city feeding the prison is certainly reflected in this study as over two-thirds of the 30 men interviewed all lived in the city before their incarceration and nearly all of them proudly declared that they were "born and bred" in and around the two main local authority housing estates. It is the prison's archetypal status, with a high turnover of males from surrounding deprived estates, serving sentences for all nature of offences, that qualifies Hull local as a suitable site for the purposes of this research.

I have outlined why I chose Hull and the local prison for study. As I show in Chapter 5, many respondents spent their formative years

---

[1]A local prison holds offenders on remand who have been sent to them by their local courts. Once sentenced, and depending on the categorisation and sentence plan, the offenders may serve their sentence at the local or high security, training or open prison.

there and, consequently, transitioned from being boys to men in those surroundings. Starting with positionality and how my role as an "insider" impacted on the research process, I want to use the remaining sections of this chapter to discuss the methodological complexities of the study and to introduce the qualitative strategies that I adopted when collecting the data.

4.4   EPISTEMOLOGICAL PRIVILEGE?
"GOD NUTTERS OR FUCKING GRASSES"

In qualitative research, the importance of the social characteristics of the researcher and their relationship to those they study is the essence of the "insider/outsider" debate (see Berger 2013; Chavez 2008; Earle 2016; Griffith 1998; Merton 1972; Wakeman 2014). An "insider" is someone whose biography (gender, race, class, sexual orientation and experiences, etc.) gives them a lived familiarity with the group that is being researched. This tacit knowledge informs the research process in ways that are not available to the "outsider". Recent decades have seen insider perspectives increasingly contributing to criminological knowledge. From the early 1990s in the US and later in the UK, a growing movement of "convict scholars" has emerged who draw on their own experiences of imprisonment to offer a "provocative" and alternative lens to the study of criminology and criminal justice (see Earle 2016; Ross and Richards 2003). An influential convict criminologist from the UK, Rod Earle, has claimed that "lived experience of imprisonment can extend the boundaries of the criminological imagination and foster novel approaches to criminological practice..." (Earle 2018, pp. 1499–1514). Similarly, the criminologist Steve Wakeman (2014) has asserted that his own criminal history as a drug user and dealer has enabled him to provide a "clear and progressive account of heroin addiction" (p. 705), stating that the "biographical congruence between my participants and myself afforded me something of a privileged position in the field" (ibid., p. 711). This claim of "epistemological privilege" for the "insider" permeates emancipatory scholarship and rests on common-sense notions that a biography provides sufficient grounds for sharing knowledge (Griffith 1998).

Alternatively, the "outsider" doctrine—which is the traditional perspective of objectivist sociology—focuses not on the advantages of a common identity but on "the corrupting influence of group loyalties on human understanding" (Merton cited in Griffin 1998, p. 362). The feminist scholar Chavez (2008) has argued that insider/outsider positionality is better understood as operating on a spectrum rather than in opposition. At one end of the continuum is the "total insider": a researcher who shares multiple characteristics of ethnicity, class and knowledge of the same institutions, social environments and social groups with their informants.

Secondly, Chavez has introduced the notion of the "partial insider": a researcher who shares one or several characteristics with—but remains relatively detached from—their participants. Robert Merton (1972), in his often-cited analysis of the sociology of knowledge, had argued that—whether an outsider or an insider—both categories can be associated with distinct assets and liabilities. The "detachment" of the outsider allows them to see that which others take for granted. Too much social distance, however, can mean that misunderstandings are likely to occur (Miller and Glassner 1997).

The extensive and tacit knowledge the insider brings to the research produces a different understanding of the experiences of the group being studied. However, too strong a claim to insiderism would inherently limit sociological research; the researcher would only be able to attempt to understand the groups to which he or she belongs (Merton 1972). Griffith (1998), paralleling Chavez's (2008) claims about full or partial insider, has taken care to note that—while the researcher and the participant might share one facet of their identities—there will always be other aspects that differ.

For me, the process of negotiating the realities of insider positionality was much more complex than Chavez (2008), Griffith (1998) and others have suggested. While some aspects of my identity would have, at one stage, been strikingly similar to the informants'—growing up on a deprived estate, having experienced exclusion from school, criminality, drug use and incarceration—a university education, professional career, age, locality and almost two decades of freedom are just some of the structural differences that now separate me from the informants.

Perhaps more importantly—as I argue in the next section—far from being privileged, I suggest that the experience of researching the prison as a field is, for an ex-"convict", unique in that it imposes limitations that will not be experienced by others—whether insiders or outsiders—in other research contexts. For the reasons that I have indicated above—ones that will become clearer as this discussion progresses—I ultimately decided that my history had more potential to hinder rather than benefit the research process. As such, I hoped to undertake this study as an academic, first and foremost. I soon discovered that it was naive of me to think that I had any autonomy in making this decision, at least with regard to my interactions with officials. I was, however, able to retain some control over my positionality with the informants.

4.4.1 Getting In: Access

Having reviewed the literature regarding insider positionality, it is clear that it is widely accepted that—because of the advantages or privileges that it affords—it is almost a given that researchers who share similar lived experiences with their participants will embrace, with reflexivity, this position (Berger 2013; Earle 2018; Chavez 2008; Wakeman 2014; Griffith 1998). The main advantages that are often highlighted include the assumptions that "insiders" will have smoother access to the field, will have more legitimacy among participants and will enjoy easier assimilation. In my case, although access was initially granted informally as a result of a pre-existing relationship that I had with the governor—dating from my time as a prisoner—I, like all other researchers, still had to follow bureaucratic procedures and apply to the Ministry of Justice (MoJ) for security clearance. This presented the first major difficulty because the security officers who are attached to the prison are the ones who process the first stage of any applications. I was consequently forced to disclose my criminal history and periods of incarceration to this department.

Prison staff, as in any other institution, have learned to be curious as part of their roles. It later became evident that I—as a "friend of the boss" who was attempting to enter the establishment and had a long list of criminal convictions—was the subject of intrigue and gossip. I later discovered that these levels of curiosity about the ex-"convict" researcher had intensified when the Ministry of Justice, without explanation, deemed me to be too high risk and refused to grant me clearance to undertake the research. Fortunately, after some delay, significant stress and much correspondence between the governor and the senior managers of the Ministry of Justice, my access was granted—but with some limitations that I will highlight later. It is important to acknowledge, too, that the challenges and power struggles that researchers of both genders and various backgrounds encounter when entering prisons are well-documented; they are by no means unique to me. Prison scholars have suggested that— because of their perceived middle-class status, suspected left-wing liberal political views and gender—they have faced resentment and often sexist and misogynous ridicule from prison staff while endeavouring to undertake studies into the experiences of men and women in prisons (Cowburn 2007).

The important point, however, is that—from the moment that I had to disclose my history—I quickly became an "ex-con" first and a researcher second. It was this imposition of the insider status that presented some of the biggest challenges in the early days of the project. A significant drawback of being an ex-convict researcher was that, despite having the support of an influential gatekeeper, I was not—like many other "outsider" prison researchers/visitors—trusted with a set of keys or "unfettered" access to the prison. Instead, I was allocated an escort who—before the introduction of new working structures in 2013—was the old (long-serving) Principal Officer (PO).

Although—as I show later in the discussion—this would turn out to be a fortuitous arrangement, the early days of this relationship and the process of working out how best to manage this imposed insider status were both exhausting and distracting.

The first day being shown around the prison, for example, prison officers, after the PO escort introduced me as a researcher, would, in their attempts at being interested and helpful, put questions to me, including: "Have you ever been in a prison before"? "This is a segregation unit; do you know what happens here"? "You know you can't trust any of these lot in here?" In the reception area where men from the courts are received, one officer opened the file of the prisoner standing at a counter in front of us being processed. Pointing to the official court papers listing his offence of buggery of his seven-year-old child, the officer exclaimed: "this the kind we deal with daily"! Soon afterwards, my PO escort talked at length of his experiences of outwitting prisoners in order catch them out with drugs and other contraband, And for reasons I am still unsure the PO took me to the area in prison for (family)visits, where for a while I was left standing in close proximity to the resident drug sniffer dog and his handler, while he excused himself and left for a cigarette.

After the inner turmoil and stress that I had experienced in dealing with these issues—some very real, some possibly imagined or blown out of proportion—I decided that there were certain situations in which it would be best for me to disclose my history. It transpired that I only had to explain this to the PO escort—who told me that he was already aware of my history—and to one other officer who was his close colleague. I can only suppose that the security team had informed some of the staff.

Despite my early difficulties, we went on to establish a great relationship; I later learned that he was a highly respected officer by both prisoners and colleagues. This was, of course, helpful to the study. Unfortunately, this was not the case with all of the disciplinary staff, resulting in some extremely challenging times in the field. I had to remain constantly alert, for instance, in terms of how I chose to respond to the open and widespread denigration of prisoners and their families by a minority of officers who regularly referred to them as the "scum of the earth" and coming from "drug-addled, filthy estates".

4.4.2   Building Rapport

Another major privilege with which the insider status has been associated in scholarship is the assumption that it facilitates the establishment of a good rapport with participants. Davies (2015) has argued that, when he had only two weeks in the prison to undertake his study on the impact of short-term prison sentences, his insider status of being an ex-prisoner was extremely beneficial in that it enabled him to rapidly build rapport with the participants of his study. This was achieved through a "pre-interview discussion" that allowed for the "reciprocal information sharing of personal experiences" (p. 463). This resulted in his respondents seeing him as being an "equal"—someone who "understood their identity as prisoners" (p. 464)—and led to "an apparent level of openness" (p. 464).

From my experience, having worked with both serving and ex-prisoners over the course of a decade, I have found that it takes time and investment to build up trust and rapport with study participants, especially with individuals with whom you share similar backgrounds/trajectories. I felt that personal disclosures with respondents required much more than a discussion at the start of an in-depth interview about their own life histories. This was partly why I decided not to disclose my own experiences of crime, drugs and imprisonment.

This decision was soon vindicated when I asked a respondent what he thought about an ex-prisoner coming back into the establishment. In stark contrast to scholarly claims about insiders having the advantage of being able to form rapports easily, he responded: "seen loads of ex-prisoners come back into do inspirational talks and stuff and they are either god nutters or fucking grasses". He went on to say that "when you get talking to them, you can't trust them; they are not like proper prisoners. They might have done a silly sentence for fraud or drink driving or some crazy twat who murdered his wife, but they have not really done jail in the same way". Each prison researcher will, of course, encounter different challenges and individuals; this is just one example of what I experienced. Nevertheless, it was a view that—I would argue—could easily be changed over the course of more sustained interactions beyond a single research interview.

Another important point is that prisons, as I show in the following empirical chapters, are highly masculinised and hierarchical spaces. Male researchers—whether they are insiders or outsiders—who enter the prison will be positioned in accordance with this masculine hierarchy. Middle-class academics—who, on the outside, usually hold more cultural, social and economic capital—find themselves in a space in which their masculinity is much less openly valued and can even be a source of humour or ridicule (see Crewe 2014). A middle-class researcher is reliant on the informants to educate them about their world and their way of life. Arguably, the unknowing, male middle-class academic is of little threat to the informants; this might, perhaps, encourage a feeling of safety that encourages openness and more vulnerable masculine performances. In contrast, ex-convict researchers who choose to disclose their criminal credentials have to think carefully about where they might fit into this masculine hierarchy and how this might impact the data generated. Will the researcher's criminal history, for instance, overshadow that of their respondents or, instead, serve to win their approval? Will they have "done enough" or "too little" prison? When and where did they serve? How did I "do" jail?

4.4.3   Equalised Power Relations

Another ostensible advantage that has been attributed to insider positionality is the notion that the common characteristics that are shared by a researcher and their research subjects make for a more equal and legitimate relationship (Berger 2013; Chavez 2008; Davies 2015; Griffith 1998). I found, though, that a prison that holds incarcerated informants significantly challenges this claim. Unequal power relations could not have been more profoundly evident than when, at the end of an interview, an informant was escorted back to their cell while I either went for lunch in the staff mess—or, as an ex-prisoner, celebrated my release at the end of each day.

4.4.4 Covert Insider

It is difficult to fully document or even grasp what my history brought to the research process. ("Convict") Criminology and other "insider" (emancipatory) scholarship has certainly contributed to "giving voices to the voiceless" and enriching the social sciences with greater inclusion of more representative experiences (see Earle 2016; Ross and Richards 2003). It would be misleading to highlight just the challenges and fail to acknowledge that my insider status may have benefited the study at certain points.

It is impossible to fully dismiss my shared history with the respondents. Therefore, it is also difficult to deny that an insider's tacit knowledge has, to some extent, its own advantages—perhaps more so during the stages of conducting interviews, analysing data and writing up my findings. Despite attempts as covert insiders who try to "blend in" (May 2001), class and elements of our life histories are worn or embodied (Reay 2005; Skeggs 2004). Research participants, according to Holland and Scourfield (2000), will make assumptions about the rhetoric on masculinity that the interviewer requires—ones that are based purely on the interviewer's overt characteristics (class, ethnicity, gender, accent, etc.). This in itself may well enhance a study as it reveals something about the participant's dominant ideas of masculinity. I would strongly argue, however, that this does not amount to a position of privilege; playing the role of covert insider was incredibly hard-going and emotionally costly. One of the more difficult aspects was the need to strip the respondents of their experiences without offering anything in return, especially given my experiences of fighting substance misuse, fighting to achieve an education, withdrawing from crime and enduring the jobs that I held before becoming an academic.

In this section, I have suggested that the prison as a research site has the potential to negate or significantly undermine the so-called privileges and many advantages with which insider positionality is commonly associated. In the next part, I introduce the qualitative methods that I used in order to select the participants, collect data and conduct my analysis.

4.5   Methods

4.5.1   Participants

The study's core aim to investigate the classed and gendered trajectories of male prisoners from impoverished working-class neighbourhoods—required that I work with a purposive sample. This strategy permits a researcher to seek out participants who have particular characteristics that are central to the research process (Bryman 2012). I was interested in recent and future working lives and keen to explore experiences across more than one generation. As such, I actively sought to recruit a group of respondents who would cover a broad age range of between 18 and 45 years. I did not intentionally focus on any one ethnicity over another. Although it is currently experiencing some degree of cultural diversification, this region (and the prison population) was, at the time at which I conducted this study, still predominantly white. This was certainly reflected in the group of participants, with all except one of the participants (who identified as being mixed race) being white. On the whole, the type of offence for which an individual was serving time was not of great importance when I was deciding whom I ought to interview. However, I avoided those whose offences were mainly of a sexual nature wherever possible; such individuals already belong to a highly researched cohort. All prison terms/experience were equally valid, ranging from first timers to "persistent" offenders or long-termers and from popular prisoners to those who were struggling or "poor copers". The nature of the "local" prison means that the bulk of men who come through its gates are "revolving-door" prisoners who come from the locality and the surrounding areas. In the main, these are men who have committed mainly lower scale acquisitive and/or violent crimes. I interviewed thirty men from all areas of the prison who I had identified through a variety of means. Several officers had nominated individuals whom they felt would fit the required criteria. These participants then suggested friends—a method that is sometimes described as "snowball sampling" (Bryman 2012). I identified further volunteers over a period of months, having spent time observing and interacting with prisoners on the wings and in education classes and workshops. I have changed all of the respondents' names and any other identifiable forms of information to preserve their anonymity. Instead, I have used pseudonyms throughout the following chapters.

4.5.2 *Life History Interviews and Non-participant Observation*

I generated the bulk of the data by conducting in-depth life history interviews. The life history interview, according to Connell (1995), is a "first[-]class method" (p. 89)—not only because it produces data about an individual's actions as a human agent but also because life histories document the interactions between social structures, social movements and institutions (Connell 1995; Plummer 2001). For the most part, the interviews took place in the relatively comfortable and vacant staff offices on the respondents' respective wings. Interviews often ran for well over an hour and I recorded them for the purposes of later analysis.

Tim May (2001) has suggested that a disadvantage of recording interviews is that some participants may find the presence of an audio-recorder to be inhibiting and may not wish for their conversations to be documented. My own experience meant that I was aware that the participants would have already been interviewed on numerous occasions while they had been in police custody; indeed, in many cases, these recordings would have been used as evidence against them. My awareness of these issues meant that I was able to fully reassure the informants and to continually remind them of their confidentially and anonymity. In most cases, though, I seemed to be much more concerned than the informants were about protecting their anonymity; a common response that I encountered was: "I don't give a fuck anyway" (Billy). I collected other valuable data that have proven to be helpful to this study by observing the men engaging with the prison regime and going about their daily routines in the workshops, educational sessions and through their interactions with other prisoners. Quite unexpectedly—but fortuitously, as a result of a PO escort—I was able to spend a great deal of time with some of the prison's more senior staff members in their private space where they retire for breaks and relaxation. It was during these periods that officers dropped their guard slightly and, through observation and participation in some of their discussions, I was able to gain brief snapshots (Bryman 2012) of the senior officers' culture as well as insights into their masculine trajectories and performances.

4.5.3   Data Analysis

I thematically analysed my interview data, indexing and listing distinct collective themes under main headings that correspond to key sites in the formation of the participants' masculinities (streets, schooling, workplace, the local prison and so on). In undertaking my analysis, I have sought to uncover the elements that have contributed—both individually and collectively—to the "making and un-making of masculinity" in and against various structures, spaces, and institutions (Connell 1995, p. 91).

4.6   CONCLUSION

In this chapter, I have discussed the place of research and its relevance to this study, charting Hull's industrial rise, its decline and the profound impact of economic change on the area and many of its residents. I then introduced the site of the research—Hull's local prison—and explained how the role that it plays in the prison estate and the type of prisoners that it houses render it a suitable field for the purposes of my research aims. In discussing my positionality, I argued that the prison as a field negates many of the privileges that are often associated with insider positionality. In the final section of the chapter, I outlined the methods that I have employed in my data collection and analysis. In the subsequent part of this book, I discuss the men's life histories and how they relate to—or challenge—the previous research documented in Chapter 2. In these empirical chapters, I endeavour to present the informants' voices—as much as possible—to explore their classed and gendered trajectories across the main sites that I discuss. In the first of the empirical chapters that follow, my focus is on the role of the neighbourhood—as well as schooling—in pathways to prison.

REFERENCES

Berger, R. (2013). Now I see it, now I don't: Researcher's position and reflexivity in. *Qualitative Research, 15*(2), 219–234. https://doi.org/10.1177/146879 4112468475.
Bianchini, F., Bissett, V., Cavalleri, F., Grabher, B., Morpeth, N., Oanca, A., & Tommarchi, E. (2019). *Cultural transformations the impacts of Hull UK City of Culture 2017*. Culture, Place & Policy Institute, University of Hull.
Bryman, A. (2012). *Social research methods*. Oxford: Oxford University Press.

Chavez, C. (2008). Conceptualizing from the inside: Advantages, complications, and demands on insider positionality. *The Qualitative Report, 13*(3), 474–494. https://nsuworks.nova.edu/tqr/vol13/iss3/9.

Connell, R. (1995). *Masculinities*. Cambridge: Polity.

Cowburn, M. (2007). Men researching men in prison: The challenges for profeminist research. *The Howard Journal of Criminal Justice, 46,* 276–288. https://doi.org/10.1111/j.1468-2311.2007.00474.x.

Crewe, B. (2014). Not looking hard enough masculinity, emotion, and prison research. *Qualitative Inquiry, 20*(4), 392–403. https://doi.org/10.1177/1077800413515829.

Davies, W. (2015). Unique position: Dual identities as prison researcher and ex-prisoner. In D. H. Drake, R. Earle, & J. Sloan (Eds.), *The Palgrave handbook of prison ethnography*. London: Palgrave Macmillan. https://doi.org/10.1057/9781137403889_25.

Department for Education (DfE). (2017). *York, North Yorkshire, East Riding and Hull area review final report*. London.

Dolphin, T. (2009). *The impact of the recession on northern city regions*. Newcastle-upon-Tyne: IPPR North.

Earle, R. (2016). *Convict criminology—Inside and out*. Bristol: Policy Press.

Earle, R. (2018). Convict Criminology in England: Developments and dilemmas. *The British Journal of Criminology, 58*(6), 1499–1516. https://doi.org/10.1093/bjc/azy016.

Enenkel, K., Quinio,V., & Swinney, P.(2020). *Cities Outlook 2020. Holding our breath*. Centre for Cities.

Featherstone, M. (2013). Being-in-Hull, being-on-Bransholme: Socio-economic decline, regeneration and working-class experience on a peri-urban council estate. *City, 17*(2), 179–196. https://doi.org/10.1080/13604813.2013.765648.

Gillett, E., & MacMahon, K. A. (1989). *A history of Hull* (2nd and extended ed.). Hull: Hull University Press.

Griffith, A. I. (1998). Insider/outsider: Epistemological privilege and mothering work. *Human Studies, 21,* 361–376. https://doi.org/10.1023/A:1005421211078.

Holland, S., & Scourfield, J. B. (2000). Managing marginalised masculinities: Men and probation. *Journal of Gender Studies, 9*(2), 199–211. https://doi.org/10.1080/713677981.

Jonsson, H (1982). *Friends in conflict: Anglo-Icelandic cod wars and the law of the sea*. London: Hamden, Conn: C Hurst & Co Publishers Ltd.

Lee, N. (2010). *No city left behind? The geography of the recovery—And the implications for the coalition*. London: The Work Foundation.

May, T. (2001). *Social research: Issues, methods and process* (3rd ed.). Buckingham: Open University Press.

Merton, R. K. (1972). Insiders and outsiders: A chapter in the sociology of knowledge. *American Journal of Sociology, 78*(1), 9–47.

Miller, J., & Glassner, B. (1997). The "inside" and the "outside": Finding realities in interviews. In D. Silverman (Ed.), *Qualitative research: Theory, method and practice* (pp. 98–111). London: Sage.

Ministry of Housing, Communities and Local Government (MoHC&LG). (2019). *The English Indices of Deprivation 2019 (IoD2019)*. Statistical Release. London.

National Treatment Agency. (2009). *HMP Hull integrated drug treatment system: Treatment plan 2009/10.*

Plummer, D. C. (2001). The quest for modern manhood: Masculine stereotypes, peer culture and the social significance of homophobia. *Journal of Adolescence, 24*(1), 15–23. https://doi.org/10.1006/jado.2000.0370.

Reay, D. (2005). Beyond consciousness? The psychic landscape of social class. *Sociology, 39*(5), 911–928. https://doi.org/10.1177/0038038505058372.

Ross, J., & Richards, S. (Eds.). (2003). *Convict criminology*. Belmont: Wadsworth Publishing.

Skeggs, B. (2004). *Class, self, culture*. London: Routledge.

Wakeman, S. (2014). Fieldwork, biography and emotion doing criminological autoethnography. *The British Journal of Criminology, 54*(5), 705–721. https://doi.org/10.1093/bjc/azu039.

CHAPTER 5

Local Lads: Pathways to Prison

5.1 Introduction

This chapter starts from a position that the men in this study did not just find themselves imprisoned. Rather, their pathways to prison started many years before they received their first prison sentences. To begin to understand the biographies of these prisoners, then, it is necessary to explore the spaces in which they learned to become men. In this chapter, I show how the streets of their impoverished neighbourhoods were the primary arenas in which the respondents' early masculinities were learned, performed, rejected or reinforced. Illustrating the powerful role that institutions play in the creation and reproduction of marginalised masculinities, in this chapter, I then chart the respondents' masculine trajectories across the environments of schooling/education and local authority "care". Far from being comforting, positively nurturing spaces of growth and learning, I show that schools and "care" proved to be fertile environments for the further creation and performance of forms of protest masculinities. I argue that in "care" spaces—and in both mainstream and alternative learning environments—the problematic protest masculine performances that contributed to the respondents' initial exclusions were not only institutionally reinforced but were, in fact, significantly amplified as a means of navigating these sites.

© The Author(s) 2021
D. Maguire, *Male, Failed, Jailed*,
Palgrave Studies in Prisons and Penology,
https://doi.org/10.1007/978-3-030-61059-3_5

I then go on to show how, from these sites of extreme exclusion, primary criminal trajectories mostly emerged as a result of the masculine posturing that manifested itself as adrenaline-fuelled "buzz"-based crimes that usually took the form of vehicle theft. Highlighting the transitional nature of their criminal careers, the respondents' attributes—such as driving prowess, an ability to evade capture and a refusal to talk to the authorities—often led them up fast track routes to more established criminal peer groups. In the final section of this chapter I highlight just how central the role of violence is in configurations of protest masculinities. Indeed, as I foreground throughout this study the participant's propensities to commit—and/or be victims of violence were all-too-frequent occurrences in most of the men's lives.

5.2   Deprived Neighbourhoods

In order to understand the men's pre-prison gender trajectories, we need to start by exploring how their masculinities were constructed in the context of the deprived neighbourhoods in which they lived. The men in this study came from strikingly similar poor areas and shared—or were influenced by—a culture that stemmed from values learned as a means of navigating or surviving their council housing estates. One of the core codes of this value system was simply an understanding not to talk to anybody from "the authorities"—particularly the police or "outsiders". Billy, one of the most experienced and seemingly highly respected men of the group, put it quite simply by stating: "when you are out there, you don't talk to no one you don't know. Even most [of] the cunts you do know, you tell them fuck all". Other important principles to life and the culture of the criminal/street subgroups of the estate include not "taking from your own" or "shitting on your own doorstep" (Marcus) and "protecting your turf" against invasion by neighbouring groups. Some of the respondents suggested that—with everybody experiencing—the same struggles or being in the "same boat"—taking from your own is one of the lowest acts and anyone caught doing so was dealt with severely. Under closer scrutiny, this so-called self-policing constitutes more of an ideal than a reality. Street or prison codes were regularly breached according to the respondents; the men continuously complained that there were "too many informers on the estate" or that prison was full of "wrong uns".[1] Indeed, a number of the participants in this study were found to have breached the code either by stealing from/victimising "their own" and/or giving information to the authorities about their criminal counterparts. In some cases, as I discuss in more detail in Chapter 8, those who were accused or suspected of going against the code had to be segregated from mainstream prisoners for their own safety (see Maguire 2019).

It is important to emphasise here that estate cultures or these codes were significant in shaping the boyhood and young adult masculine identities of the men in this study. In their formative years, valued masculine capital was generated through the expression of territorial loyalty—by protecting your "turf" and projecting "hardness":

> ...a lot of it is about territory ...they step onto our territory, then we end up fighting with them, and if we step onto theirs, it's the same... (Paul)

> [D]ickheads from other areas would come to our estate looking to fight... I was known as being the hardest, they would come and ask for me and then we would fight it out....I would never back down, even if it was men and I was 14 or 15. I would never back down and err, yeah...I just thrived off it... (Billy)

Enforcing the value system of the (subsection) "estate" and living up to the expected masculine obligations that followed was an easily accessible resource for doing a particular type of protest masculinity. The testimonies of the respondents confirmed Messerschmidt's (1997) assertion that men who have little economic and cultural capital will draw on whatever resources are available to them to configure their own masculine identities.

The streets of their estates were the main sites in which masculine identities were performed, monitored, accepted or rejected by older peers or siblings. Most of the men who I interviewed recalled how they had lacked the necessary resources to undertake conventional leisure activities like their more affluent counterparts. Without the financial means and other forms of (social/cultural) capital, they had no reason or motivation to venture too far from their neighbourhoods. In the years

---

[1] An individual who goes against criminal or prison code by performing transgressive or violent acts such as robbing an elderly victim or giving information to the police or prison staff.

vital for shaping their masculine identities, they were stuck on impoverished housing estates or "trapped in place" (Connolly and Healy 2004; McDowell 2003). Boyhood years, across the cohort, were spent on the streets "fucking about" and "having a laugh"—usually in small "gangs" formed through the common identity of having "nothing to do and nowhere to go".

This "fucking about" on the streets—some from as young as nine years old—occurred mainly in all-male groups. A large part of the respondents' young lives were spent avoiding adult supervision or being abandoned by adults. Street elders were the "family" with whom they spent most of their time and, by being on the streets, they were able to avoid too much adult or authoritative interference. Parsons (1964), in his early influential work on protest masculinity, posited that a delinquent adolescence spent on the streets, school truancy and the avoidance of adult or authoritative gaze are unlikely routes to responsible and socially respectable manhood. In classic functionalist work on gender, protest masculinity is attributed to not having a father figure from whom to learn appropriate gender roles (Adler 1978; Broude 1990; Parsons 1964). For these respondents, it was the older male peers whose masculine identities they tried to emulate:

> I've got an older brother and I used to follow his path - and some of my mates have older brothers as well - and they used to follow their path and it was like we were all looking at our brothers. We wanted to be like them... (Harry)

> ...my brother, he hung around with all these people committing crime and all that kind of stuff. I wanted to be, like, in with them, and I'd talk to his mates and stuff like that, but he would be like "oh get away, get home"... by the time I got to 14 or 15 - their type of age - we'd gone past that, to the point where we were committing crime together... (Gibson)

Masculinities that have been forged through street-based relationships with older peers and through the reproduction of a particular aspect of estate culture in many cases resulted in individuals gaining greater levels of visibility and, consequently, being met with greater levels of authoritative surveillance/intervention.

5.3 "Care of Local Authority"

Sustained street presence and persistent criminal activities saw many of the respondents becoming well known to the police and social services at an early age. The connection between being in care and following pathways to prison have been well established in data (Laming 2016). Indeed, care was a common route to prison for almost a third of these respondents, with eight of them reporting that they had been placed or ordered into local authority "care". Participants with care "experience" reported having spent most of their time in residential children's homes as opposed to foster placements. Two disclosed that they had suffered sexual abuse in such contexts; a third stated they had endured physical abuse while they were in these institutions. None of the others who had been in the care system reported having experienced any form of abuse. However, they suggested that their experiences of social workers and of being in care had only compounded their mistrust and lack of respect for authority.

During these discussions, it was notable that none of the men interviewed had been taken into care while they were babies or toddlers. The two respondents—who were the youngest of the group—were taken into care when they were nine and ten years old. Others had been put into the care system when they reached their early teens at around 13 to 14 years. The oldest had been taken into care when he was just months away from his 16th birthday. "Being out of control" or "off the rails" were recurrently provided as explanations as to why the respondents had been ordered or placed into care:

> ...I was nine, and then I got placed in foster care. Like I say I was a bit ruthless and they couldn't cope with me. Well, my mum couldn't and my dad left when I was young. (Brian)

> [at boarding school] robbing and violence levels were getting a little worse... they came to pick me up and exclude me. After they excluded me, they told me I was going home - but then, when they got me in the car, they put me in with the teacher that I got on with, a female teacher, and then told me that I was going to a kids' home and not home. So I think that is where I went a bit out of control...(Lee)

This entire group felt that they had been taken into "care" not because of the failings of others, but because of their own behaviour. Reflecting on their time in the care system, the men in question described their experiences as ones that were not in any way stabilising: rather, they saw care as offering a space that was governed by few sanctions. It was a place where they could "go off the rails" with little concern or worry about the response from the authorities:

> ...they were passing me about from kids' home to kids' home and I couldn't understand why because I thought I was behaving. I did not give a fuck about what they thought they could do to me so I started to get really violent and then, when they put me in a special kids' home school for the day, I kicked off, hitting teachers. I was done for battery and affrays, assaults....I felt betrayed a lot, I did not know what was happening, I felt unloved - that was it, that is what was going through my head at the time. (Lee)

> I got put in a children's home and there's [sic] no consequences to any of your actions so you're not interested anymore...you are led astray by the other people that you are living with...a lot of people in care are not very bright so they don't go to school and they get to do what they want...I was more interested in being with them...I knew that, if I didn't go to school, there was nothing anyone could do to me anymore, like punishment wise, so I just didn't see the point...(Marcus)

The care system did not address the matter of what led to these individuals being taken away in the first instance. Instead it amplified the behaviour and made the situation much worse. These were "homes" with "staff"—or relationships that involved limited authority, sanctions or positive influences. When the men talked of their time in local authority care, they talked of being on the outskirts of their original communities—and of being part of a large group of other young people who had little fear of the consequences or sanctions from "staff". They understood, from an early stage, that the paid workers held little power over them—that, for those who were working in a "home", it was only a job to them. Being under the "care" of the local authority, they understood that there were statutory duties that the staff had to fulfil. When attending the police station, for example, as their appropriate adult, these adults would ideally advocate for the quick release of the respondent from police custody. A few of the "looked-after" respondents noted that, soon after being released from police custody, they would be out again—with the same people doing the same things. Indeed, many of the men who came from care environments were serving prison sentences by the age of 15 years.

Working-class masculinity is often constructed in opposition to authority (Charlesworth 2000; Connell 1995) and so the care staff provide a potent resource for protest. The respondents described the care home as being a space in which they configured masculinities without too many restrictions—where their engagement with activities relating to drinking, crime, violence and sexual conquests generated highly valued masculine currency among their peers. They reported being grouped together with others who admired or invested heavily in these symbols of protest masculinity. Young men like these, as Bourdieu suggests (1984), often "make a virtue of necessity"; in the space of the "care home", they amplify the characteristics that initially led to their troubles and exclusion.

Though some described the so-called freedom to "do what they want" while in local authority care, a closer analysis of these narratives suggests that being in care was an emotionally costly experience. Lee openly described how he felt "unloved". This had resulted, he claimed, in him not caring very much about anything. He recognised that this rejection had led to his overly aggressive behaviour towards the staff, teachers and others who were in positions of authority. Many of the respondents talked of wanting to be back "on the estate" and with their families. They talked about stealing cars to make their way back home or absconding from the home to be with their mothers. Geoff, however, felt differently:

> ...they moved me to [the country] and I lived with an old couple. They were *[sic]* quite nice...They were better than my real mum and dad. They didn't have many rules, but yet again I still carried on at school. I couldn't help it. I had to be the centre of attention in school. I ended up doing stupid stuff like fighting, being mischievous, so I ended up fucking that up...they ended up moving me back down to Doncaster into a children's home.

Researchers, advocacy and policy groups, and a wide range of social commentators have long raised concerns about how local authorities accommodate and facilitate opportunities for their looked-after children. Failings that have repeatedly been reported include low academic attainment, school exclusion, a lack of post-16 care options among this demographic and high rate of imprisonment (Fitzpatrick 2016). Alarmingly, just over half of people in prison have at some stage been in care (laming 2016). The care-experienced respondents in this study are the real lives behind the numbers. Their experiences of navigating institutional spaces—and the accompanying challenges of local authority "care"—compounded their masculine protest and accelerated their journeys towards prison.

5.4   SCHOOLING

Sociology of education scholarship convincingly shows that a particular version of working-class masculinity is constructed through battering against the school authority as well as a resistance to the formal curriculum. I found that the forms of resistance to compulsory education that were exhibited by these respondents were on the more extreme side and led to more adverse individual consequences than those that are often reported in scholarship on the subject. Only six of the respondents had completed their schooling at the official minimum leaving age; only three of those six achieved "ok" or "very low" grades in their leaving exams. The other three reached the end of their formal schooling with no recognisable qualifications at all. The remaining 24 interviewees experienced multiple exclusions and expulsions from both mainstream and alternative or "special" provision schools. School learning was not a priority. A great deal of energy was already being directed in just managing, adapting and finding strategies to deal with the everyday demands of their immediate living environments. Geoff, for example, linked his troubled school life to challenges at home and his difficult relationship with his stepfather:

> …I was always naughty in school because he used to hit me and I used to take my anger out at school. I used to show myself up at school and be the class clown and this went on until I was old enough to have a go back at him, which I did when I was 16… (Geoff)

In Isaac's case, too, it is clear that his home environment may have significantly contributed to his lack of regard or respect for the school's authority:

> …I chucked a chair at one [teacher] and, my form teacher really, he was a complete dickhead. I chucked a chair at him too and my dad come up and I think my dad battered him as well. (Isaac)

As indicated in the previous section, the care system proved to be hugely disruptive to the schooling of these participants. Those who had been in care recalled that it was simply not worth the effort of trying to settle or to build relationships because life back in "homes", as Lance suggests here, was unsettling, emotionally challenging and highly transitory:

> ...it was a bit messed up, being in care and all that, I think it had an impact on me when I was at school...I was in five or six care homes and one foster placement, I was always moving around quite a bit... (Lance)

5.4.1   Masculinities: Barriers to Learning

The men mostly reflected that, "at the time" they felt that schooling had very little to offer them; they only attended because they had to. Their parents or carers forced them to go to school only for the sake of avoiding prosecution. Several of the men suggested that there was a tacit understanding between them and their parents/carers that, once they had left for school, they were free to negotiate their attendance and participate in whatever way they chose—so long as the authorities were not alerted. A small minority of the men, however, challenged the low aspiration discourse that is often espoused in official accounts to explain the rates of academic failure among white working-class boys. Two informants, who lived at home, reported that their parents were "always on their case" trying to convince them of the importance of learning. Billy explained that his parents "wanted him to do well and they pushed him really hard". He went on to say that his brothers had gone to university and were doing well. He admitted that, unlike his brothers, he acquired a reputation for fighting; although it got him in with the "wrong crowd" and a lot of trouble, he—I noted earlier—"thrived off it". James also talked of his parental support and his parent's encouragement in his schooling and learning. His parents had emphasised the importance of "giving a hundred per cent", and "having respect for the teachers" was constantly reinforced at home. James was very good at sports and could have gone on to play rugby professionally. His parents were supportive of this and actively involved themselves in school events and, alongside his coaches, the various sports teams. James, like Billy, spoke about how his other siblings had gone onto university or were "getting trades behind them". As the discussion progresses into the succeeding empirical chapters, it will become evident that James' case stands out from those of the other respondents. It is important to note, here, that he explained that his rugby career ended when his love for football violence and drinking got in the way.

Others talked about how their parents had been supportive of their learning and schooling—but were not able to provide many details about the specific forms of support that they had experienced. As Skelton (2001) found in her research, on the whole, working-class parents are not without aspirations for their children. Often, they simply just do not have the necessary social capital or the same "feel for the game" as their middle-class counterparts. Out of all of the men, only James and Billy seemed to come from quite settled and economically stable home environments. Both of their fathers became self-employed after many years of working for other people. Even though, over time, both of their families progressed to secure owner-occupied family homes that were located on the periphery of the council housing estates, both Billy and James ended up in the same place as the other men: HMP Hull.

Compulsory schooling was, for most of the respondents, a forced inconvenience: an institution that offered little stimulation. As Evans (2006) found in her study of white working-class boys from South East London, many males found that a commitment to learning offered too little return for their futures. School, as some explained, just exposed some of their weaknesses and left many of them feeling inadequate and "thick":

> I wasn't always off school but I didn't get any qualifications because I was in [the] bottom groups...I always messed about. I was the clown, I was one of them - the one that made you laugh, that's what people used to say...(Jerry)

> ... I do find it hard, sometimes, to read and write. I'm all right with the writing; it is more of the reading. Like, I think, I thought, just give up on it... (Dwayne)

For nearly all the respondents, academic activities in the mainstream classroom did very little to engage them. Unlike middle-class boys, their masculinity was not constructed through an expression of academic knowledge. Rather, in contrast, their gender identities—as widely reported in other research—were expressed through resistance to and the rejection of the school's authority and book learning.

As Willis (1977) found decades earlier—and many others have since—having a "laff" or "fighting, fucking and football" (Mac an Ghaill 1994) have constituted the main pursuits of schooling for many of these men. Jerry's experiences and those of several other respondents indicate that being the class clown was one strategy for navigating schooling under an LEA that, since the introduction of league tables, has consistently been shown to be one of the country's worst-performing.

In an LEA catchment area that serves some of countries toughest council estates, being "school smart"—as Billy's notes below—goes against certain masculine ideals and carries the risk of rejection, ridicule and sometimes violence:

> ... [those who were] seen as clever in school or looked different... They would become victims, definitely... I dunno and maybe it was just me, but there weren't many clever kids in our classrooms, because it used to be sorted into sets. If you weren't very intelligent you was [*sic*] put with all the dumb kids. (Billy)

For some of these informants—as the following men's extracts suggest—their identities, levels of confidence and sense of masculinity were contingent upon their rejection of classroom learning as well as their demonstration of their adeptness at stealing and handling motor vehicles:

> ...I'd pinch motorbikes, you know superbikes, because I used to like riding motorbikes and I used to pinch motorbikes and go to the school grounds... (Charlie)

> ...doing our own things throughout the day, ...we were 14 years old and there was a big quarry with these big Bobcats and JCBs and we would just break in and drive them...(Lee)

The respondents' disruptive masculine trajectories had been set in motion—and had already gained a great deal of momentum—well before the young men were forced into their respective underperforming secondary schools. In their neighbourhoods it was the norm to see the older boys express a version of tough masculinity by driving at high speed in stolen vehicles, sometimes while being pursued by the police. These are the types of gender performances identified by Campbell (1993) across estates in other parts of the country. Looking to their elders, most of these men had already learned the revered symbols of a version of working-class estate masculinity before they had entered their teens. Several of the participants noted that they were as young as ten when they were first picked up by the police and escorted home off the streets:

> ...[at] the age of ten, I used to get took home in a police car, my mum and dad would go mad... I'd make up with my mum and dad and be allowed out the next day ...we'd all get together again and go and do summat and if I got took home again I'd stay in and be out again the next day and do the same again, just like a round circle. (Harry)

5.4.2   Schooling Hard Masculinities

When they did attend school, the respondents reported how important it was to project and maintain "hard" masculinities as a means of avoiding being targeted and exploited. As I discuss in more depth later on in the chapter, the ability to project a willingness and propensity to fight or to engage in other forms of violent conduct was an important self-preservation strategy that underpinned the respondents' daily interactions in almost every environment in which they found themselves. The school corridors or the yard were, for these men, no different from the streets on their estate; they still had to jostle to prove their fighting credentials and to create and maintain their reputations. To be seen as "soft" or weak heightened their risks of experiencing intimidation and exploitation. As such, these young men would go to great lengths—often ones that involved serious violence—to construct their own ideal version of a hard masculinity:

> .... I was the Cock [toughest] of my schools as well...I had a reputation, since I was 14 and it has stuck with me to this day...I had to do a few people in...maybe slash him up or do him in... (Charlie)

> ...proper fighting started when I was at school...I got kicked out at Year 7, for stabbing someone with a chisel, because he was bullying my sister... (Paul)

In some cases, as Aidan outlines below, schools were instrumental in encouraging this type of conduct and were, in fact, complicit in the construction of "hard" masculinity:

...it was a good old school. If you got into a row then they would put boxing gloves on you and stick you in a gym and you would have to sort it out that way...(Aidan)

Some of the men talked about how their school was not overly concerned with the "odd scuffle here and there". Their teachers, as Charlie explains, would often be heard saying such things as "sort this out in your own time" or "why don't you two fight it out after school or during lunch?" Billy notes below that some of the male staff were not averse to exhibiting their own versions of hard masculinity; if necessary, they, too, would not shy away from using force:

DM: What was it that you saw in a teacher that you respected?
Billy: There was one teacher, Mr ..., and another called Mr .... They was [sic] pretty tough teachers who used to train rugby, but also class teachers as well. There were sports teachers. I looked up to them and they didn't take no crap, either. Couldn't really mess about with these teachers, I mean they'd think nothing of giving you a proper slap - or at least they would then.

Just as a few teachers are reported to have used aggression, so too—as I noted earlier—did the men themselves (and in some cases their fathers) readily use violence against the school staff. In one particular case, Lee—who at the time of the study, was serving an indeterminate sentence for public protection (IPP)[2] for his role in an extremely violent crime—seriously threatened his head teacher because he wanted to join cooking classes. This was an aspect of the curriculum that he thoroughly enjoyed, despite its usual association with femininity. Lee's actions inevitably led to his permanent exclusion from mainstream education:

...I got kicked out because I started to get violent and that was over...I took a liking to cooking and the headmaster wouldn't let me do it and so I got violent with him and threatened to chop him up and use him as the ingredients...(Lee)

---

[2] Although they were abolished in 2012 and replaced with determinate and extended sentences, IPP sentences were indeterminate sentences, set at a minimum term, for those whose crimes did not merit a life sentence.

Most of the respondents had already transgressed the law and had little respect for police authority. It is clear that even the hardest of schools, serving the toughest estates in the region, were unable to contain or to challenge the protest masculine performances of many of these respondents; most of them were, consequently, excluded and/or expelled.

5.4.3   Alternative Provision

Over half of the participants were eventually deemed to be too disruptive and violent for mainstream education and were, consequently, placed in alternative learning environments by their respective local education authorities. Those who attended alternative learning sites or "exclusion centres" were aware that they had been categorised as being the "bad lad".

> I ended up getting kicked out my primary school and had to go to another one, just for bad behaviour and stuff like that, and then - when I went to secondary school - I ended up getting kicked out of that and then I had to go to this. It's like, it's like a bad boy school... (Gibson)

> ...I ended up in the exclusion centre because they couldn't cope with me. I got expelled three times, once for fighting and once for selling drugs and the other one was that one of the teachers ended up having a nervous breakdown because of...(Rob)

Some have suggested that their experiences of being out of mainstream schooling were positive because the new alterative learning environment actually felt more mature and less pressurised:

> ... I went to college basically and I did my Maths and English GCSE... I was in [a] much more adult environment - I had grown up in my mind, I didn't fight no more...it was all about getting my qualifications...working on the cars, I used to get top marks out of everybody, grown blokes,...I daresay I was one of the top in the class...(James)

> ...the exclusion centre, it was more relaxed and they knew my capabilities...obviously, you have to stick to the curriculum, but you could do interesting stuff like football legends and things like that. I'm into history and stuff like that. I like my history, especially the Royal family and stuff like that...(Rob)

These alternative learning spaces proved to be more successful at engaging the respondents in learning because, as James and Rob point out, parts of the curriculum were of interest to them. Furthermore, the experience of being among older learners meant that they felt less pressure to live up to "hard" masculinities.

5.4.4   School for "Bad Lads"

A common form of alternative educational provision for those who were involved with the care system or social services was a boarding school for "bad lads". The term "boarding school" conjures up images of pupils who attain high levels of academic achievement as well as ideas of structure, discipline and privilege. The state residential schools that these respondents attended, though, could not have been further removed from the elite institutions that are typically reserved for the children of the rich. The men recounted their experiences of an alternative learning space that was aimed more at containment and physically engaging "hard" masculinities:

> I was in boarding school at the age of 11 or 12, …I wasn't even, doing runners at first. I was behaving and everything…we would go canoeing, rock climbing…Then it would be "I can't be arsed, come on let's go and do a runner or whatever!" … I used to stay there for a full fortnight and come home for one weekend (Harry)…

> I was 14 when I started boarding school…it had a gym [where] you could do weights and boxing. We would go carting and everything but it was one of them where you had to stay away from home and I only would get to go home on a weekend, which for some reason I've never been bothered about that, it never fazed me, do you know, being away from home. It was alright, I enjoyed it…I just started running off a lot and running off with all the other lads, doing our own things throughout the day… (Lee)

With an alternative curriculum that centred on boxing, gym and outdoor activities of rock climbing and canoeing, boarding schools had some positive aspects according to those who attended them—a space, so evidently designed to engage rather than to educate "bad lads". These schools offered them constructive avenues for the expression of their masculinities as well as physically exhausting them.

The question that arises is: What happens to these men when they return to their neighbourhoods in which the resources are inadequate for the purposes of expressing their gendered identities through "constructive" activities? Boarding schools (with their alternative curriculum, time away from loved ones, the opportunity to reside with peers who are experiencing similar difficulties, the experiences of fighting and challenging the institution's authority) of this kind do not prepare their pupils for Oxbridge entry as elite boarding schools do but rather, as I show later, to serve time.

Indeed, Lee and Harry—as quoted above—had their boarding experiences interrupted when they reached the age of 15 and had to serve their first prison sentences. All of the others who attended boarding school followed soon after—before they had turned 18. Alternative education provision, failing schools, time on the streets, the care system and the peer groups that are formed in these spaces all contribute to the matrix in the construction of protest masculinities that saw nearly all of the informants imprisoned before they reached the end of their teens.

5.5   Criminal Trajectories

5.5.1   "Buzz" Crime

As observed by other scholars researching working-class men, the respondents in this study were keen to prove their manhood from an early age. Legitimate and conventional routes to configuring respectable masculinity via employment proved to be challenging to find and difficult to sustain in this period of profound economic change. More accessible avenues could be found by emulating the behaviours and choices of older peers who were already deeply invested in criminality. The participants looked up to those who, as Billy put it, "were always having a laugh, and buzzing, and who knew how to 'graft'". Notably, the vast majority of the respondents' early acts of criminality were not motivated by the prospect of monetary gain. Rather, the participants sought the "buzz". Their early offences were typically linked to their obsessions with motor vehicles and, as Lee admits, "just wanting to drive all the time". Almost all of the respondents had long histories of vehicle-related offending. It is important to emphasise, here, that—from their place at the margins, in neighbourhoods that had been decimated by deindustrialisation and political neglect—skilful stealing and the deft handling of cars and motorcycles offered an easily accessible and highly valued currency by which they could achieve a "hard"-masculine status and gain respect (see Campbell 1993; Corbett 2003; Cunneen 1995; O'Connor and Kelly 2006). It is noteworthy that the respondents' masculine protest through car crime, often involved stealing the middle-class symbol of success—the luxury or performance car—and the use of it in acts of provocation and resistance against state authority:

> the police wouldn't come around our estate at one time, I mean, we used to do absolutely crazy things like get a can of spray paint and write on the car "chase us", "coppers are bastards" and things like that. And [we would] just drive through town until the police [would] come and try and get us, and we'd just take off...we had a £67,000 Mercedes, once, and we was [*sic*] just driving around town like it was ours, all the windows down and smoking weed and just taking the absolute piss... (Isaac)

Billy, too, describes the status that comes with taking a performance car from an affluent part of the area and making something that he is never likely to legally own his—at least for a very short period:

> *Billy*: I remember we did this big house back in the village and drove back to the estate in the Porsche...that felt good, I mean, joyriding a Porsche, pulling up outside my mates' houses and bibbing the horn, and them saying "where the fuck did you get that from?"
> *DM*: Did you take them for a drive in it?
> *Billy*: I was a bit funny [about] who I let in it, I did not want loads of people diving in and out; I treated it as [if] it was [*sic*] my own car. I took it for [a] car wash and kept it for a few weeks.

Brian was insightful about the role that car crime plays in creating status and confirming masculine identity in his neighbourhood.

> *Brian*: everybody loved the police chase...it was just about the buzz and the thrill...everybody knows about it, and they are all talking about it around where I live: "did you see that police chase last night, it was buzzing blah blah blah?" And, yes, it gives you a bit of an adrenaline rush, you know, and I did enjoy it.
> *DM*: What was it like if you got caught?
> *Brian*: That weren't a problem either. That was a buzz as well, you know, getting locked up. You know, at the time, I was young, and nothing much was really happening to me. I was just getting a slap on the wrist,

so it wasn't a problem...if you got away then everybody would talk about it more and then I would go around saying "the police can't do this and do that". I was seen as, like, maybe a hero back then. On the estate, people liked watching stuff like that. They like watching it all because they are not involved in it. They are just looking at it from a distance. They are not the ones who are going to end up in the police cells at the end of the night.

Brian claims that the spectacle of instigating a police pursuit enabled him to accrue masculine capital as well as respect from many of the individuals in his neighbourhood. However, joyriders, as Campbell (1993) found, were not "heroes" but the major cause of distress for many of the residents who live on poor estates. Those who complained were often targeted and intimidated by the minority of car criminals. Vehicle-related crimes and underage forms of thrill driving were costly, too, for those who were involved in them. A number of the respondents named friends or associates whom they had lost due to reckless driving and police chases. Sadly, for some of them, this was also part of the attraction of doing it, as Lee describes:

...you would get a bit nervous when other people were driving. That was another excitement factor – if he crashes that, he crashes in it, let's see how bad it turns out. It was another excitement factor and a lot of us enjoyed that...(Lee)

The men's accounts of their early experiences of offending provide insights into how this behaviour constituted the outcome of weaving identity and masculinity both into and from an estate culture that valued high-risk, high-speed and anti-authority activities. Two performances were going on, here, each of which for the benefit of a different audience: one for those who were deemed to be in positions of authority and one for peers. Anti-authority, highly skilled displays—often in unattainable vehicles that seemed to have been reserved for ownership among the successful middle classes—are clearly forms of protest. Being adept at taking cars—the higher the performance, the better—skilfully driving them and evading capture is seen as being a valuable source of masculine currency among one's peers.

A notable finding that links to the subject of vehicle crime and driving prowess is the role it plays in transitions to more profitable and prolonged criminality. A number of the respondents reported that being a skilled car thief and proficient driver—and having a proven track record of not talking to the authorities—attracted the attention of older criminals who would recruit their juniors into profitable and more serious forms of offending:

> I got into the wrong crowd, then. Because I was good at driving, I used to go with the older ones and they would use me to drive the cars to get away...(Isaac)

> ...[they] quickly realised that I was an alright driver and so it was not long before they started asking me to pick big parcels of drugs up from Doncaster services and Sheffield services and that...(Marcus)

Other respondents talked of having some kind of epiphany and suddenly realising the immaturity and futility of spending their time in and out of prison, simply for the sake of "the buzz" and to entertain the estate. Some calculated that, if they were going to keep going to prison, then they might as well earn money out of it. Billy perfectly sums up this transitional process:

> ...when I first started offending, it was like petty theft, really – stealing cars and ram-raiding shops. It was not really about the money; it was more about the buzz of it and the respect I would get from my peers. Like, if you did a job and you got loads of money out of it – and people thought it was a bit difficult to do and that you pulled it off – you would get more respect for it. When I was younger, it was more of an ego trip. As I got older, I thought "well, I'm doing all that, nicking cars, what was the point in nicking cars? It's silly, going to prison for silly things, you might as well do something – if you're going to go to prison, it might as well be worth earning some money out of it" ...(Billy)

Billy encapsulates the experiences of many of the other respondents. Their early adrenaline- or "buzz"-based primary form of offending eventually shifted into a secondary or "grown-up" phase in which their motivation to commit crimes was, then, to earn an income.

5.5.2   *Material Crime*

As many of the respondents got older, their high adrenaline, thirst for risk-taking, spirit of anti-authority and protest masculinity found expression through a range of other more materialistic agendas. From their early teenage years on the streets, they explored the highs of street drugs and understood the currency that they carried both in terms of monetary value and status. After "growing out" of "buzz-related" offending—and as a means of "grafting" or "earning a wage"—most of the respondents believed that they ought to progress to more mature criminal ventures like drug dealing and associated crimes such as robbery and targeted car crime.

In neighbourhoods that experience extreme levels of structural poverty—such as those from which these men had come—the prospect of selling drugs offers an attractive means to accrue street capital (Sandberg 2008) or etch out respectable masculinities (Bourgois 2003; Gunter 2010; Ellis 2016) as Aidan and Aaron explain:

> …easy money, fast cars, drugs. I got sick of running around like an idiot, giving all my money to somebody for drugs, I wanted to have some dignity, a family, a home, a life, kids. Fuck it – I'm going to be the one involved in this, I'll be the one selling the drugs; heroin and cocaine, back then on the streets of ≫>, was non-existent,

> …I went on to more serious things…drug deal[s] or [you] do things for people, you do robberies and get into more serious kinds of crime and even that, even though you are doing it for the money, it was about getting the respect of the lads who you hung out with…(Aaron)

The interplay between the material benefits, power and status that results from dealing means that drugs played a significant role in the formation of a number of the respondents' identities and criminal trajectories. However, for several of them, using drugs became a way of life and—as Jack recounts below—a main driving force behind their offending behaviours:

> … I'd get the keys from the house, go at night time and break into get the keys, push the car off the driveway…You'd get a grand per car, so a couple of cars a week is a couple of grand, but I've been a drug addict for a long time as well – and so, when you are a drug addict, you can spend that kind of money easily…(Jack)

Less than a third of the men reported that their criminality had been driven by drug use. All of them explained that they had long criminal histories and had experienced imprisonment before their out-of-control drug misuse took over. While acknowledging that drugs and substance abuse played a role in some of the respondents' materially driven criminal activities, it is important in this study to avoid using it as a catch-all explanation for the prolonged criminal activities and incarceration of the respondents (for an interesting discussion about how drug careers play a central role in shaping exclusionary transitions, see MacDonald and Marsh 2002; Mayock 2005; McCrystal et al. 2007; Parker and Egginton 2002; Webster et al. 2004).

In many cases, the informants' offending was controlled, planned and was often about a desire for status and respect, as Charlie and Geoff explain below:

> Out there, I was earning £700 a day, you know, selling heroin. But I was selling on a big scale. I was getting parcels vacuum-packed every week with...I bought motorbikes, quads, everything – a bigger house – I was on about 40 grand a week. People knew I was doing well for myself; some respected that and other were jealous...(Charlie)

> ...it's always been about money...it's always big money, it's money that is going to keep you going and having a lifestyle of nice houses and nice cars, women. With money comes power and respect; when you've got money, it comes with a lot of envy...(Geoff)

It is well established in criminology literature that many criminals share the operational and commercial acumen that those who work in legitimate entrepreneurial/business enterprises also exhibit (Sandberg 2009). This was also shown to be the case with regard to some of the respondents in this study. Even those who were at the lower end of the criminal spectrum—at which Geoff and Charlie had operated—talked of their crimes in the same way that a self-employed tradesman might—calculating the potential benefits but also the sanctions that they might incur should they be caught:

> ... oh, I always know what the consequences are. I don't just, you know what I mean, do it. If I'm out there – like, since that IPP come out – it's like a life sentence in it, errm, robberies, I won't touch robberies. A mate

might ring me and say I've got a robbery on. Fuck that – do you know what I mean? – I'll do other things, just not things that you know are going to get you lifed off. What, just for a few quid?...(Gibson)

5.5.3   Violent Crime

In this discussion of the respondents' criminal trajectories, the propensity for violence that was at the core of their protest or street masculinities has been absent. Whether stemming from criminality or masculine honour (Ellis 2016; Polk 1994; Tomsen and Gadd 2018), violence played a central part in the lives of all of the informants. In "this game", as Gibson acknowledged, there are many things that you cannot control; events always have the potential to quickly turn violent:

..... you might do something and things will just go wrong, man. You might be doing a shop or something and someone will run downstairs and grab you. Obviously, you'll try and fight them off. Your first thought is always to get away...(Gibson)

This instinct to get away at all costs can go tragically wrong, as we can see from Mark's extract below:

I did a burglary one night. There was an elderly person...he grabbed hold of me...got him in a headlock and he died, and fucking hell I went to prison at 24 and stayed in until I was 37. (Mark)

This is an extreme case and in the world that most respondents inhabit, as will be explored in more detail later in chapter, there exists an unwritten criminal or inmate code. Although in and out for other crimes since his release at 37, Mark's past offence against the elderly was a breach that positioned him near the bottom of the masculine status hierarchies that exist in prison.

Some of the most extreme cases of violence that the men talked of being involved in were against other criminals and had occurred during the act of "taxing" or taking the proceeds of crime from one another:

...the kid who I was with said this is a good graft, a drug dealer, [he's] got loads of money...We've just gone in, opened his backdoor, he was stood there so I just whacked him, put him out cold, put him to sleep...it just got a bit stupid really. ...papers said ... it's something you only see in horror movies...(Lee)

In Geoff's case, his actions in trying to rob another criminal led to him being charged and later convicted of murder.

> ... the drug game, I believe that, to be the best you have to take out the competition... so that's what I did and I've messed with the wrong people...I am in for murder...a gun has gone off and that was it. ... (Geof)

A number of informants undoubtedly felt that drug dealers were "fair game". Perhaps, as Hobbs (1997) found in his research on organised crime, the notion of a code of honour existing among criminals is often overstated and, mostly, mythical.

The propensity to resort to severe violence was common among all of these respondents. It is what Polk (1994) has described as "masculine honour" violence. James, a fully qualified and well-paid electrician who came from a better part of the neighbourhood, was given his first sentence for launching a prolonged, violent attack on another man who had verbally abused his partner in a driving incident. This was not James' first violent encounter. He had established his "hard masculinity" through acts of football violence—but had never been caught or convicted.

The respondent who had the most convictions—and, conversely, was also the smallest in stature among the group of participants—was Paul. Having come from a notoriously violent family, fighting and violence had been a major part of Paul's identity from a young age. Both of his parents had been to prison for violence and, at the age of just 15, he followed in their path. His many offences and multitude of prison terms had all resulted from his acts of violence against another person. Below, he describes how his family's legacy had influenced the ways in which other people saw him and how this, in turn, contributed to his decision to live up to that reputation:

> ...people was giving me a bad name because of my family name. It got to a stage where I had enough...I may as well live up to it. That is when I started fighting...Then, when I was nineteen, I went up for the training for the army...then somebody beat me up with a weight bar...gave me 49 stitches in my head and nearly killed me and, then, because I had a head injury, they told me I wasn't allowed in the army for another two years and so I went off the rails again...(Paul)

The cycle and everyday currency of violence that has been described by Paul and the other participants corresponds with Polk's (1994) assertion that "masculine scenarios" that lead to serious violence or homicide often stem from minor disputes that relate to perceived incidences of disrespect and challenges to honour. Similarly, as Messerschmidt (1993) claims, men like Geoff and Lee who are structurally limited will behave violently in an attempt to live up to the powerful representations with which hegemonic masculinity is associated.

Once violent criminal masculinities have been established, however, they must continually be backed up (Ellis 2016). To lose face is to be seen as weak and to become a potential target. Indeed, the experiences of these informants confirm what is constantly being signalled by most of the UK's statistical representations of intra-male violence. Working-class men are not only the main perpetrators of violence—but they are the most likely group to become victims of violence.

5.6   Conclusion

The respondents' negotiation of impoverished neighbourhoods—and the key institutional spaces within them—significantly contributed to their construction and reproduction of marginalised masculinities. From an extraordinarily young age, most of them had spent a great deal of time on the streets in all-male peer groups, usually avoiding adult supervision and surveillance. Under these conditions, their primary performances of protest masculinity were influenced and informed by an existing and pervasive sub-estate culture in which there was little regard for formal authority while great value was placed on acts of violence. "Care" institutions and educational establishments—especially alternative boarding schools ("for bad boys"),—were often the places in which the respondents refined and learned behaviours and attitudes that reinforced and contributed to their early configurations of protest masculinities. From these key sites, gendered criminal trajectories followed processes of transitions. By late adolescence, most of the respondents had progressed from "buzz" to more material—and—violence-based forms of offending. Their early investment in protest and criminal-based gendered performance proved to be costly and set them on the pathways that contributed to their exclusion, marginalisation and inevitably to incarceration. Before exploring the men's accounts of entering and surviving the prison space, I firstly want to chart their experiences of navigating the local labour market and it is this subject that I turn to in the following next chapter.

References

Adler, A. (1978). Masculine protest and a critique of Freud. In H. Ansbacher & R. Ansbacher (Eds.), *Cooperation between the sexes*. New York: Anchor.

Bourdieu, P. (1984). *Distinction: A social critique of the judgement of taste*. Cambridge, MA: Harvard University Press.

Bourgois, P. (2003). *In search of respect: Selling crack in El Barrio*. Cambridge: Cambridge University Press.

Broude, G. J. (1990). Protest masculinity: A further look at the causes and the concept. *Ethos, 18*(1), 103–122. https://doi.org/10.1525/eth.1990.18.1.02a00040.

Campbell, B. (1993). *Goliath: Britain's dangerous places / Beatrix Campbell*. London: Methuen.

Charlesworth, S. J. (2000). *A phenomenology of working-class experience*. Cambridge: Cambridge University Press.

Connell, R. (1995). *Masculinities*. Cambridge: Polity.

Connolly, P., & Healy, J. (2004). Symbolic violence, locality and social class: The educational and career aspirations of 10-11-year-old boys in Belfast. *Pedagogy, Culture & Society, 12*(1), 15–33. https://doi.org/10.1080/14681360400200187.

Corbett, C. (2003). *Car crime*. Crime and Society Series. Cullompton: Willan.

Cunneen, C. (1995). *Juvenile justice: An Australian perspective*. Melbourne and Oxford: Oxford University Press.

Ellis, A. J. (2016). *Men, masculinities and violence: An ethnographic study*. London: Routledge.

Evans, G. (2006). *Educational failure and working class white children in Britain*. Basingstoke: Palgrave Macmillan.

Fitzpatrick, C. (2016, October 26). Why have so many people in prison spent time in care as children? *The Conversation*. Available online https://theconversation.com/why-have-so-many-people-in-prison-spent-time-in-care-as-children-66941. Accessed 1 June 2018.

Gunter, A. (2010). *Growing up bad? Black youth, "road" culture and badness in an East London neighbourhood*. London: The Tufnell Press.

Hobbs, D. (1997). Professional crime: Change, continuity and the enduring myth of the underworld. *Sociology, 31*(1), 57–72. https://doi.org/10.1177/0038038597031001005.

Laming, L. (2016). *In care, out of trouble*. London, England: Prison Reform Trust.

Mac an Ghaill, M. (1994). *The making of men: Masculinities, sexualities and schooling*. Buckingham: Open University Press.

MacDonald, R., & Marsh, J. (2002). Crossing the Rubicon: Youth transitions, poverty, drugs and social exclusion. *International Journal of Drug Policy, 13*(1), 27–38. https://doi.org/10.1016/S0955-3959(02)00004-X.

Maguire, D. (2019). Vulnerable prisoner masculinities in an English prison. *Men and Masculinities*. https://doi.org/10.1177/1097184X19888966.

Mayock, P. (2005). "Scripting" risk: Young people and the construction of drug journeys. *Drugs: Education, Prevention and Policy, 12*(5), 349–368.

McCrystal, P., Percy, A., & Higgins, K. (2007). Exclusion and marginalisation in adolescence: The experience of school exclusion on drug use and antisocial behaviour. *Journal of Youth Studies, 10*(1), 35–54. https://doi.org/10.1080/13676260701196103.

McDowell, L. (2003). *Redundant masculinities? Employment change and white working class youth*. Oxford: Blackwell.

Messerschmidt, J. W. (1993). *Masculinities and crime: Critique and reconceptualization of theory*. Lanham, Md.: Rowman & Littlefield.

Messerschmidt, J. W. (1997). *Crime as structured action: Gender, race, class and crime in the making*. Thousand Oaks, CA and London: Sage.

O'Connor, C., & Kelly, K. (2006). Auto theft and youth culture: A nexus of masculinities, femininities and car culture. *Journal of Youth Studies, 9*(3), 247–267.

Parker, H., & Egginton, R. (2002). Adolescent recreational alcohol and drugs careers gone wrong: Developing a strategy for reducing risks and harms. *International Journal of Drug Policy, 13*(5), 419–432. https://doi.org/10.1016/S0955-3959(02)00154-8.

Parsons, T. (1964). *Essays in sociological theory* (2nd ed.). London: Collier Macmillan.

Polk, K. (1994). *When men kill: Scenarios of masculine violence*. Cambridge: Cambridge University Press.

Sandberg, S. (2008). Black drug dealers in a white welfare state: Cannabis dealing and street capital in Norway. *British Journal of Criminology, 48*(5), 604–619. https://doi.org/10.1093/bjc/azn041.

Sandberg, S. (2009). *Street capital: Black cannabis dealers in a white welfare state*. Bristol: Policy Press.

Skelton, C. (2001). *Schooling the boys: Masculinities and primary education*. Buckingham: Open University Press.

Tomsen, S., & Gadd, D. (2018). Beyond honour and achieved hegemony: Violence and the everyday masculinities of young men. *International Journal for Crime, Justice and Social Democracy, 8*(1), 17–30. https://doi.org/10.5204/ijcjsd.v8i2.1117.

Webster, C., Simpson, D., & MacDonald, R. (2004). *Poor transitions: Social exclusion and young adults*. Bristol: Policy Press.

Willis, P. (1977). *Learning to labor: How working class kids get working class jobs*. Farnborough, England: Saxon House.

CHAPTER 6

(Non)Working Lives

6.1 Introduction

In the previous chapter, I showed how the respondents had developed their early gendered identities both within and against the backdrop of their street cultures, homes, local authority "care" institutions and mainstream or alternative schooling. In this chapter, I explore how investments in masculinity that were made under these adverse conditions of their childhood and adolescent environments not only seriously disrupted their entries into a recession-ravaged and changing deindustrialised local labour market but also compromised their ability to sustain long-term employment.

Charting the men's disrupted school-to-work transitions, I highlight that—in spite of encountering significant barriers—many of the respondents had managed to gain some experience of legitimate employment, albeit of types of work that were mainly low-paid and unskilled. For the vast majority, their "fast track" or quick routes from school to the workplace were not too dissimilar from what has been found in other research into the transitions of disadvantaged young adults. However, with many of their working lives having been punctuated by criminal activity and periods of imprisonment, I show how these respondents were at the severe end of the demographic of undereducated men found to have been the most adversely affected by widespread economic restructuring.

© The Author(s) 2021
D. Maguire, *Male, Failed, Jailed*,
Palgrave Studies in Prisons and Penology,
https://doi.org/10.1007/978-3-030-61059-3_6

I then show how respondents added to their own marginalisation by attempting to reconcile protest masculine ideals with workplace transitions and how this often led to the loss or abandonment of employment. The difficulty turning away from the monetary rewards and visceral pleasure linked to criminal lifestyles and how this furthered their exclusion is discussed. Prolonged criminal careers and the years that they had already lost to incarceration left most respondents with a desire to be "normal" and with aspirations of "growing up and getting a job".

Notwithstanding the respondents' stated enthusiasm, I show how their unchanging masculine ideals undermined their best intentions of gaining employment. I conclude the chapter by analysing the role that the prison played in supporting the men in their efforts to overcome some of the post-prison challenges that they would face. I argue that the prison education and training provision—mainly based around traditional masculine trades—were woefully inadequate in preparing these men for changing workplaces on their release.

6.2   School-to-Work Transitions

There are more than 20 years in age difference between the youngest and the oldest participant in this study. For a quarter of a century, from 1984 up until 2008—under a Conservative and, then, New Labour government—these men were, or should have been, negotiating school-to-work transitions. Despite the significant passage of time between the informants' transitions, there is little to separate their early labour market experiences. As I highlighted in the previous chapter, the vast majority of the respondents were either excluded from school or completed their schooling as soon as they could, leaving with poor (if any) qualifications. There was a slight difference in the "fast" transitions of the older and younger participants, though. Four out of the five eldest (aged between 41 and 45) managed to secure—albeit in a short-lived capacity, as I explain later—apprenticeships ranging from butchering to factory-based engineering.

Out of the eight younger participants (aged from 21 to 30), three reported getting to their mid-twenties without having ever worked. A further two respondents claimed to have only ever done cash-in-hand work around the estate. Evidently, for the older respondents, there were still some options available to them in terms of following traditional working-class routes to adulthood, as documented by Willis (1977) and others (Young and Willmott 2007). However, as I show in the subsequent section, a couple of the respondents who entered the workplace some years later were able to find what might be described as "traditional" work.

On the whole, the post-schooling routes to adulthood for the vast majority of these men depressingly resonate with some of the young people in MacDonald's and Marsh's (2002) study of socially excluded young adults in the North East of England as well as those in Nayak's (2003, 2006) study of "Charvers" in the same region. Like the individuals in these studies, the respondents' school-to-workplace transitions were disrupted and fragmented as many of them had been imprisoned during their mid- to late-teens. Entrenched criminal careers, coupled with limited post-schooling options, compounded the existing disadvantages that they encountered in finding legitimate work in their regions.

Despite facing barriers, though, most of them—at some stage, mainly in the first five years after they had completed or left their formal schooling—engaged with legitimate forms of waged work. Usually, these were low-paid, low-skilled, unstable factory positions. Several worked in a local factory building caravans for a well-known local employer who mainly provided temporary seasonal jobs. A small minority, primarily the younger respondents, talked of "getting on" a building, mechanic or plumbing course, largely with local tradesmen or through family contacts—or at the local college.

Geoff and a couple of the other younger respondents explained that they had tried—usually under pressure from youth or criminal justice workers—to study for vocational courses at local colleges. With the exception of two notable cases, a consistent factor that ran through the respondents' training or work experiences was that they had not been on their courses for long enough to be able to generate valuable experiences or qualifications. The limited or short-lived nature of these transitions could not, however, be attributed to the idea that the respondents were not willing to put in "a day's work". Many of them had managed to sustain "cash-in-hand" work around the estate for local builders or businesses. "Cash-in-hand" options minimised the likelihood of experiencing rejection, formal scrutiny and the low pay of limited legitimate "cards-in" work options. The respondents rightly understood that they would be at the wrong end of a long list of more attractive candidates when applying for legitimate "cards-in" work—especially in the context of one of the UK's worst cities in which to find employment. Several of the participants indicated that they felt that they had no chance of "passing the interview" (Rob) or "getting a foot in the door" (Harry) or that—alternatively—they would not "stick them jobs; they pay shit money" (Dwayne).

6.3   Protest Masculinities: Workplace Exclusion

The small minority who fared better with their transitions under challenging local economic circumstances were respondents who came from families that had some social capital and, albeit limited, economic resources. The experiences that I reported earlier of the youngest participant, James, for instance, differ from those of the others in several ways. Both of James' parents were in long-term forms of stable employment, were relatively financially secure and were supportive of his learning, sporting and working options. Unlike many of the other respondents, James' early masculine resources were generated not through criminal activities but by means of his rugby prowess, drinking and (under the police's radar) football violence. Having been excluded from mainstream education for fighting, James still gained credible GCSE results in an alternative "learning centre" that facilitated his entry into the armed forces.

Unfortunately, James reported that, after only a short period of time, he was discharged from the army on health grounds. From the family home, he—to a much greater extent than the other respondents—demonstrated resourcefulness and (from his rugby playing days) social capital that helped him to find a legitimate "trade" or "respectable" route to manhood:

> ...I got somebody to do me a CV and sent the CV...I literally got the Yellow Pages and opened it and chose hundreds of people out of the Yellow Pages. I then seen an apprenticeship in the paper, went and had an interview, had a second interview and I got the job...work eventually dropped off...I did it again, I sent a CV out to tons and tons of companies, I know someone who works for [the local paper] and he put me in the paper as an electrician looking for work. An executive from BAE rang me up and offered me an interview...they gave me the job...(James)

James' "hard" rugby masculinity and early protest masculine resources, stemming from a readiness for violence, stayed with him—and eventually culminated in a long prison sentence, a loss of professional reputation and a loss of employment.[1]

In structurally impoverished regions that have few opportunities, hard-won job prospects are often undermined or, as with James, sabotaged as a result of the residual effects of earlier gender trajectories or the continuation of protest masculine posturing. Charlie's experiences encapsulate how past gender performances that contributed to his exclusion and childhood incarcerations in the first instance served as a catalyst for his family to draw on their contacts and limited resources to invest in trying to save his future:

> My first time in prison was at 15...I got out of Wetherby just before my 16th birthday and my mum and dad said to me, "look you're going to have to do something with your life", my dad said he would pay for my sea survival because my dad was a fisherman, so we paid for my sea survival £500 and I went away to sea...it was only a short trip about six weeks, but I come home with about £1000...[then] I was allowed to go away on the ships for three months at a time...(Charlie)

Sadly, as with so many of the others, Charlie struggled to sustain his position as a trawlerman. Fighting prowess, the ability to hold one's drink and drug taking are the core components of a particular form of protest masculinity. Such conduct—dating from their early years on the estate and sustained throughout their schooling—contributed to the exclusion of many of the respondents. This continued into young adulthood, compounding their marginalisation and "ruining"—as in Charlie's case below—rare opportunities to secure stable and well-paid forms of traditional employment:

> ...[I] would come home from sea and have lots of money... would go in the clubs and sniff cocaine and take ecstasy tablets...I ended up having a fight with a bouncer and that's when I come to prison, so I got sacked from the firm I was working for, because I come to prison and when I got arrested, I got found with a bunch of cocaine on me and stuff...(Charlie)

---

[1] James noted that his attack was widely reported on local television news and in the press. He felt that he had been represented as a "monster". Shortly afterwards, his employer wrote to him to inform him that the company wished to terminate his work with them, cutting ties.

During his time away, Charlie became more heavily involved in taking an increasing number of drugs. Having served a number of years in prison by this point, he found it difficult to get back into this kind of work. He felt that it had become a more closed industry by then—although he managed to secure a couple of final trips out to sea as a result of a favour from an old boss. Ultimately, though, "it just did not work out".

In many respects, Charlie's experiences ran in parallel to the decimation of Hull's fishing industry and, with it, the decline of one of few local pathways to attaining respectable forms of masculinity (Gillett and MacMahon 1989). Although several of the respondents' fathers, uncles and grandfathers had worked at sea, Charlie was the only one among the other 29 participants who had any significant trawler experience. His clubbing, drinking and partying with the "good money" that he had earned was similar to the sort of masculine behaviour that is common among trawlermen, as described by Ulyatt (1985). Unfortunately, Charlie took his hedonism and protest masculinity too far and "ruined" his work chances to the extent that he could no longer compete for or "hack" this work:

> ...I ruined myself and I just couldn't hack it and I ended up jumping the ship in Norway and it took me five days to hitchhike home. Within 10 minutes of being home, I was in a nightclub in Hull taking ecstasy...(Charlie)

A further and important factor in exclusion from the workplace—especially for those whose early working experiences were in less-skilled and lower-paid jobs—was (in the same way as it was on their streets and throughout their schooling) their inability to respect the authority of the shop floor management, as Billy explains:

> I did not take well to being told what to do...if you had left me alone to do the job and not been nagging on at me I'd be fine, but as soon as I started to feel a bit of authority, trying to talk down to me, I would just walk out and not think twice, I did not think "I need this job, I have to stick at it, I need the money, I've got all these responsibilities", it did not matter...(Billy)

Like Billy, the vast majority of the respondents had, from a young age, learned to resist most forms of authority. They had minimal or no experience of managing their lives around timetables or schedules—except with regard to the ones that had been forced upon them during the time that they had spent in various institutions. Moreover, as most of them had spent time in prison before they reached the age of 20, they were not averse to transgressing rules, regulations and laws. Taking a risk, pulling off a good "earner", having a "buzz" and "taking no shit" were the core components of their masculinities. Trying to contain or harness these behaviours in any workplace was a monumental challenge—not only for the employer but also for the employee himself.

For the participants of this study, a further important factor to consider with regard to their exclusion from the contemporary workplace was their refusal to "take shit" for "shit pay" and "shit work". These jobs demanded long hours for relatively low pay; the respondents were well aware that just one night and the "right graft" or crime could cover a week's—or, even, a month's—wages:

> I tried jobs, different jobs…they did not last because I was more interested in…well, I thought "what was the point of earning 250 quid when I could go robbing and earn it just like that?" [clicked fingers]…(Billy)

The perceived material rewards of crime impacted the men's early attitudes and their levels of motivation to undertake legitimate forms of work. Later, while experiencing prison, though, many recognised the true cost of the years that they had lost to imprisonment. With some having accrued up to 20 prison sentences, the idea of an ordinary working life had become highly desirable to them:

> I could earn more going out grafting, selling drugs. I could earn more than two and half hundred pound a week for a 40-hour week, which is like minimum wage, that's not asking for owt special, do you know what I mean? I could earn a thousand pound a week more, selling drugs but now I would rather work…(Marvin)

This desire to secure legitimate minimum-wage work might seem appealing during yet another period of imprisonment—but the prospect of completely giving up "grafting" and living on a low weekly wage proved to be much more challenging when on the outside.

6.4   "Grafting" and Work

In criminology, there is a growing body of scholarship that explores the later stages of criminal careers and desistance from crime (Gadd and Farrall 2004; Laub and Sampson 2001; Maruna 2001). The consensus across much of this work is that desistance grows out of a complex matrix of psychological and sociological variables including age or maturity (mid-30s to 40), subjective shifts in attitude, stable employment and the formation of a family (Gadd and Farrall 2004; Laub and Sampson 2001; Maruna 2001; McNeill 2006). Almost half of these respondents were in their mid-30s or over 40, with many of this group still very much stuck in this revolving-door cycle of criminality and imprisonment.

Employment, as previously discussed, did not prevent many of these respondents from offending. Nor did, as I show later in Chapter 8, the experiences of being in a relationship or being a father keep the men out of prison. Several of them tried to sustain relationships, fulfil their paternal responsibilities and hold down legitimate jobs alongside their criminal careers. Marcus, for instance, worked extremely hard after receiving a prison sentence to achieve the credentials required to secure a relatively well-paid, stable and senior position within the railway engineering sector. It was, he claims, the economic pressures of everyday living and—ironically—the cost of being "road legal", paying overly expensive car insurance, that kept him hooked on crime[2]:

> I got the car, I got all insured and everything was brilliant for a while...I was working to pay for my insurance...working on the railway...then, last year, I got involved with some armed robbers...I was basically paying for them to stay in hiding while they were going out doing jobs for me. They done a job the night before and hid the money, I went to pick the money up with two of them in the car and the police tried pulling us...I thought to myself, "of all the police chases I've had over the years, I can get away from these", I got away from them and a vehicle pulled out on me and I crashed into it about 100 miles an hour...it all come crashing down...(Marcus)

[2] People who have unspent convictions face difficulties in securing house and motor insurance; they are often charged much more by "specialised" brokers.

Cooper, like Marcus—after serving a previous prison sentence—managed to find a job in the building and construction sector and worked his way up into a supervisory position:

> I had a job in 2010...I lasted a full year...I got up to a supervisor and ended up having a beer and taking some tablets and thinking that it was all right and ended up trying to brain somebody and ended up back in jail...(Cooper)

Both Marcus and Cooper proved to be resourceful in finding relatively good forms of employment that reinforced "respectable", hardworking masculine performances. However, their early criminal careers and the contacts that they had generated from these lifestyles continued to exert powerful influences over them. Instead of a good job effectively pulling many men away from crime, as has often been shown in desistance literature, criminality instead served to disrupt good adult working opportunities for the respondents on several occasions. It was clear that, for many—even after having had numerous spells in prison—they were not able to commit themselves fully to adhering to law-abiding lifestyles.

Gibson's words capture many of the significant obstacles that men face when they try to completely turn away from the criminal careers that, in many instances, they have relied upon since childhood—both in terms of constructing their gendered identities and for material resources. He admitted to enjoying the challenges that sometimes come with crime and explained how everyday activities can turn quickly into an opportunity for "graft":

> ...even if I'd just go out to the shop, right, I start thinking if they've got real high security on it, they've got some real good shutters on it and blah blah blah, I like to think that I'm going to have to do this or I'm going to have to do that to get in or I'm going to have use this or that to get that...(Gibson)

Substantial masculine capital and visceral pleasure can be gained through the processes of beating commercial security systems and flaunting the subsequent rewards of having done so (Copes and Hochstetler 2003; Katz 1988). Crime or "grafting", despite efforts to "go straight", will be a fall-back option for many because it seems to offer a way out from mundane and economically marginalised forms of existence:

...I won't stop committing crime, even if I got a real good job, I think I
would still do little bits and bobs on the side, I don't know, it's just, it's
brilliant, I think it's brilliant...(Gibson)

Gibson's struggle to commit to "going straight" because crime is "just
brilliant", Marcus' armed robbery enterprise and the experiences of many
of the other respondents suggest that the emotional pay-off of criminality
plays a key role in their prolonged and persistent habits of offending (see
Katz 1988). Visceral pleasure-seeking is a heavily masculinised activity
(Courtenay 2000) and, as Winlow (2004) and others (MacDonald and
Shildrick 2007) have suggested, the types of pleasure or leisure that
individuals enjoy are influenced by their specific social and economic
backgrounds.

The criminal careers of many of the respondents—from early forms
of "buzz-based" offending to transitions into materially motivated
crime—are loaded with examples of "thrilling and intrinsically enjoyable"
(Winlow 2004, p. 18) experiences. "The adrenaline rush, the nervous
energy, the gratification" (ibid., p. 18) that can be derived from violent
encounters stand out among many of the respondents' narratives.

In the context of their deprived neighbourhood, "doing crime" was,
in many cases, a more emotionally exhilarating route to a locally valorised
version of performing masculinity than the employment options that were
open to many of them. These masculinities that were configured through
acts of crime and violence, however, led to the prolonged loss of liberty—
at a cost that was far greater than any perceived instant pay-off.

6.4.1   Work-Willing

Notwithstanding the devastation that many had left "on the out" in the
wake of their offending, an obvious cost of their criminal careers took
the form of multiple prison sentences and the years that they had lost,
locked behind a cell door. Nearly all of the respondents said that they had
"had enough" or just wanted to "be normal". In their current periods of
confinement, this desire for an ordinary existence seemed to accompany
suggestions, by some, that they were much more willing to undertake
legitimate forms of work than they had been in previous years. This senti-
ment can be seen in the accounts of Dwayne's and Paul's experiences
below, both of whom claimed to have never undertaken any form of
legitimate employment:

Dwayne: They've set up a new [scheme]...my probation officer is seeing if she can get me on it, it's like six weeks unpaid work and I'd do that, you get £25 toward your shopping and like a fiver on your gas, a fiver on your electric, which is only 35 quid and you get your dole...[It'd] be really good because I'd be getting experience and, at the end of it, it leads to a proper job.

DM: Could you do a "yes, sir, no, sir" type of job?

Dwayne: Yeah, I'd do anything—any job—because I'm really good, like my mam says, I can work in jail so why can't I work outside?...but I can work out there if I'm given a chance.

Paul, like Dwayne, was aware that he needed to acquire some skills in order to find a way into the world of work; the only job he had ever had was working in a newsagent's as a lad:

Paul: I worked in a paper shop as a kid, but I am doing [a] maintenance course now, it's painting and decorating, roofing, bricklaying, plastering, tiling and get my certificates from that, I've got a better chance of getting a job when I get out there.

DM: Have you tried to get a job?

Paul: Yeah, I've tried, I'm no good at like group work, I always end up arguing—because of my anger problems—even if someone sits there and gives me a funny look and I'll be fine for a bit and then I'll just snap.

Paul recognised that a key challenge in finding and maintaining his first real job would be to improve his poor coping skills with groups; he needed to be able to manage his unpredictable temperament and his tendency to quickly turn to violence.

Despite facing significant barriers, Paul and several other respondents said that they were desperate to find an alternative way of life. Having had a great deal of time to think, they talked of trying to map out their crime-free futures. For some of the respondents—most of whom had extremely limited experience of the labour market—the post-prison working lives that they envisaged were modest and, in some cases, had an air of desperation about them:

Billy: You could think...would you wanna be a road sweeper? And now you kind of think, the way things are now, you'd be lucky to get that—like, if you got a job, you're lucky to have one. There are people who really want jobs and are struggling to find jobs. It doesn't matter if you['re] cleaning toilets to being a stockbroker; if you have a job, you have some respect and independence.

DM: So what do you think changed—to the point that you are at, now, that you would take any job?

Billy: Maybe I'm just a bit more mature and growing up.

DM: Do you see any jobs as being "women's work"?

Billy: Maybe working in a perfume shop—retail, maybe, you know, clothes shops...Ann Summers, that's probably one job I wouldn't do, yeah, those type of jobs.

Billy's "mature" outlook on working life is very different from what he described as being his ethos in his early teens. After having served many sentences, and in the cold reality of the prison cell, road sweeping, cleaning toilets or pretty much anything else was better than spending more years being trapped in a revolving-door lifestyle of imprisonment. As with many of the other informants, Billy recognised that—if he were to secure employment—it was likely to be low-status service-sector employment, albeit under conditions that were not too feminised such as selling perfume or lingerie.

Isaac, like most of the others, expressed his desperation to secure legitimate work—and the "respect" and independence that comes with it. However, influenced by his upbringing, he was more prescriptive about what he was looking for:

DM: What would keep you out of jail, would you do any job?

Isaac: Yeah, just about.

DM: Would you stand in McDonald's?

Isaac: No, I couldn't do that...I'd end up fucking spannering someone, cheeky little bastards...Building sites or manual jobs, you know labouring, jobs, that you use your hands with...I couldn't work in an office or shop, I don't think; too enclosed.

Isaac proudly noted that he was from a travelling community and that he had been taught to have a strong work ethic. He had far more employment experience than Billy, mainly as a result of having done "fiddly" cash-in-hand work tarmacking or collecting scrap metal. Billy's short and sporadic employment history included a period of a few months in a safety-clothing factory and just over a year landscaping.

Even with their lack of labour market engagement, many of the men were aware of some of the major local economic challenges and changes—but had little overall idea of the extent of this shift. They demonstrated some awareness of the fact that "tough jobs" in "all-male environments" had become scarce and highly sought after. Most of the respondents were less knowledgeable, however, about the global and national economic shifts that were underway, as well as about how they would impact their future work prospects. What they were fully aware of, though, is of how hard the 2008 crash had hit their local region—and of the immediate employment situation that awaited them outside the gates of the prison. It is quite probable that, despite all of their enthusiasm to get to work, Billy, Isaac and most of the others would struggle on their release to compete amidst and adjust to the challenges of a demanding and shifting local labour market.

From the deprivations of prison, it is easy to understand how the respondents' hopes for a "normal" life had become pinned on low-end, low-paid work. The reality of life "on the out", as I discussed earlier in the chapter, is much more complex and difficult than the respondents acknowledged in their work-willing narratives. The masculine strategies from childhood and prison that have contributed to their work-place exclusion or the struggle to sustain now-rare forms of "traditional employment" will continue to be a major barrier for them upon their release. This will especially be the case in labour markets where limited work opportunities are increasingly short-term and one must accept "doing deference" in return for a minimum wage (McDowell 2014). In these conditions, it will be especially difficult for the respondents to resist being tempted to return to their past criminal activities—the more accessible resources of crime and violence—in order to "do" adult masculinity.

6.4.2   Ex-Con

Without following the men out of prison, it is difficult to predict with any certainty how the vast majority of them will meet the challenges that are involved in turning away from crime and securing waged work. The process of having explored their previous post-prison experiences, though, has highlighted the struggles that led many of them back to prison. One of the major barriers for those who have previously been entrenched in criminality—as many of these respondents have—in desisting from criminal and violent activities—is the way in which their criminal histories continue to disrupt their attempts to construct crime-free futures. Even in the face of these structural difficulties, many continued to hold firmly to their belief that finding work would offer them "a way out". As Brian illustrates, some of them were very persistent and proved to be quite resilient in their efforts to find a job:

> I was just sick to death of this life…agencies always have work. Wages [are] not too good but earning 200 pound[s] a week is better than earning 7 pounds a week in prison…I've actually applied for a job at McDonald's before, I never got the job but I applied for the job…I'm honest and I tell them I've got a record…you don't have to specifically go into what you've been in trouble for, you've just got to tell them you've been in prison…but I think, if Jo Bloggs turns up and he hasn't got a criminal record, and I turn up and I have got a criminal record, they're obviously going to go with him over me…(Brian)

"Going straight", for men like Brian, is much more of a process than an event (Maruna 2001). On this occasion, Brian, aged 32, managed to spend a record continuous year out of prison. It is important to note that Brian's criminal history had excluded him from even fast-food service work that most of his peers believed to be too humiliating to consider doing.

Other respondents, several of whom had much more serious offending histories than Brian, were acutely aware of the potential exclusion from contemporary labour markets that awaited them upon their release:

> [when released]…I'll be on licence again, basically, it's back to Jobseeker's [Allowance] because you cannot really get a job when you're on license, it's hard enough getting a job nowadays, when you've got no criminal record or nothing it's hard, I think Hull has just been voted the worst place ever to get a job, it's even harder when you've got a criminal record, because you have to disclose it. As soon as you disclose it: "oh, what were you in prison for?" "Attempted murder!" "Oh, we'll call you." So it's not easy, a lot of people will fall back on criminal stuff just to make money…(Lance)

> …it's hard for me to get a job because of my record, because I've got arson, violence, theft. I've even got weapons and firearms on my record. I've got domestic violence…I've been in the paper that many times, everybody knows me, as soon as I fill a form in or write my name and they notice who I am, they refuse straightaway because of what they've heard about me…(Paul)

Potential employers do not necessarily need to have access to official records that document long histories of dishonesty, violence, drug and alcohol for the men to find themselves excluded from the few local employment opportunities. Research that has been conducted by Hardgrove et al. (2015) in the UK, for instance, has shown that many of their young adult male research subjects felt excluded from employment opportunities because of their bodily presentation—if they had visible tattoos or piercings for example—or because they seemed to exhibit the wrong attitudes. A further hurdle to being able to secure work in a service-dominated labour market for many of these respondents, then, stems from their bodies that carry the marks, decay, scars and/or symbols of resistance and protest resulting from their long criminal careers, violence and years in institutions. Even after they have managed to surmount such hurdles to secure a position, these men often embody performances that they have honed on the streets or in institutions. This reveals far too much to employers and, as Andy's extract perfectly captures, it can result in rejection:

> Last year, I was required to go on a back-to-work scheme. I said, "is this really viable for me?" "Yes, yes you've got to do it." I know it's a complete waste of time, introduce my record into the equation, who I am, boom, boom, nobody on this planet is going to employ me…I'm required to go to the [well know charity] for an interview, for voluntary work, this was unpaid, this was through Social Security benefits, and I've gone through…I mean, I spent years not even claiming just to stay out of the system, and I've gone through, gone for this interview.

> It's all good, then they said "how would you feel standing outside the shop with the bucket asking people for donations?" and it just rolled off the tip of my tongue and I said: "don't you think I'd be better at the bank across the road with a shotgun?" Being funny, there was nothing, no seriousness to that at all: funny, amusing. It was funny to me, anyway. I saw the look on their face, and I thought "you are fucking joking". I knew, at that point, that it was finished…I walked out and got a phone call about an hour and a half later: "sorry but the position that we had given you is no longer available". I thought "fuck you, if I can't work for nothing what chance have I got of getting a paid job?" That's the reality that I'm faced with…(Andy)

Andy's sense of personhood, as with most other informants, had been built on the estate and in prison—when living among other men like him. In this "back to work" scenario, he was having to go it alone in a female-dominated space and, evidently, found it difficult to know how to behave or what conduct was expected of him. This was a humiliating experience and a significant blow for Andy to have his labour—offered for free as part of a government-backed initiative—refused. It is important to acknowledge that this was Andy's individual experience, though, and that there are many successful examples of instances where men—as part of their resettlement programmes—can leave prison on a daily basis to volunteer in charity sector shops and other business.

Mark's experience—almost 15 years earlier and for a paid role in the more traditional shop floor manufacturing sector—provides an example of how one's personal history could, in some instances, be of little concern in industrial work contexts where "toil" and fit bodies are highly valued attributes:

> ...I was really upfront in the interview, I said, "listen, I've been a bit of a bad lad, I just hope you give me a chance"...he was willing to give me a chance and said "I'm not interested about your past", he said "I'll give you a chance", great, and I was there for quite a while...(Mark)

Mark later stole the petty cash from the office of the employer who had given him a chance and never went back to work. Marvin, who had more recent experience of seeking work, believed that—although his history of offending will no doubt exclude him from many opportunities—there are still some jobs "if you look hard enough" that value strength, hard work and common sense over historical transgressions:

> *Marvin*: I'd do any work, anywhere that would pay me a decent wage...it's just getting the work once you got a criminal record, that's the thing—once you['ve] got a criminal record, it's hard to get the work.
>
> *Interviewer*: Have you gone for jobs where people have asked you about your criminal record?
>
> *Marvin*: Yeah, normally, in the building trade, you're normally alright, if you know how to fucking graft hard and you are not totally stupid, you will get took on, but not in any shops or nowt like that, forget it...

Marvin's and Mark's experiences suggest that more traditional workplaces that rely on strong bodies rather than emotional labour are less likely to be interested in the life histories of their employees and are more open to the idea of offering employment to people who have convictions or who have been in prison.

6.5   Prison Learning

A key part of the answer to ending the revolving cycle of crime and imprisonment is to consider how time in prison could be used to better equip these men so that they are able to undertake forms of training, education or employment upon their release. One important aspect of this is how prisons and other services can harness the men's attempts to change their attitudes, behaviours and perceptions of self as just criminals. The majority of the respondents disclosed that it was, in fact, while they were in prison that they had first learned to read and write properly. Brian explained that, in some ways, the experience of being in prison had had a positive impact on him:

> ...prison can be a good thing in certain ways, I never went to school, I never got any qualifications and, now, I've done all the education I can do in here...I can write perfect, I can spell perfect—and I'm quite bright...[when I] first started coming to prison, you had nothing, you worked on a sewing machine and now you can do bricklaying courses and you can get qualifications...(Brian)

Brian was not the only one who felt that he had enjoyed a positive learning experience during his time away. A high proportion of the men indicated that they had improved their basic literacy in prison, noting that it was when they were locked behind the cell door that they had truly come to value the importance of having the ability to read and write fluently.

Lance—who came up through the care system and who had previously experienced little encouragement or motivation in respect of his formal schooling—explained that, when he first came to prison, he undertook all of the possible learning on a course that prepared him for a career in the armed forces:

...I did a lot of my education stuff here. For young offenders, obviously, education, education is a big thing. I took part in this new scheme that they was doing, this APTC training scheme, army preparation training course...it's basic training like you do in the army but obviously to a lesser skill. You learn the phonetic alphabet, you learn all the code words, first aid, field craft, camouflage, covering and conceal, they had a place in the gardens at the back where you would take your trenches. They learnt you like military knowledge and military intelligence, military history, weapons training theory and stuff like that...we all got proper uniforms, we got proper boots and polish and we had to polish boots, every Sunday. We have to sort ourselves out, fold everything away, all creases and every-thing...50 of us started that second course and only two of us passed out, me and this other kid from Doncaster, and basically what that sets you up for is when you got released from young offenders you would go straight to Army Careers.

DM: Did you go to Army Careers?
Lance: I did, yeah, I went one time and then didn't go back, I did want to go in the army, it was something I wanted to do, but I chose the criminal world instead.

Military masculinities are built on hegemonic ideals that have many parallels with the tough masculine performances that most of these respondents sought to enact and live up to (see Atherton 2009). For Lance, the shift from the care home to the prison and, then, the armed forces would probably not have been too big a leap in terms of his sense of self and the behaviours that are valued in each institution. In the absence of a supportive family, he "chose" what he already knew: the "easy route" into the criminal world. This choice had resulted in him serving a number of sentences. During his time in prison, however, Lance had made the most of the system to "better himself"; like Brian, he had reached the pinnacle of what the prison had to offer in terms of improving one's education and skills.

Several of the men explained that they had, long ago, achieved the maximum Level Two in the "Key and Basic Skills" programmes that prison educational provision typically offers (see Coates 2016). Paul, following the advice of his ex-prisoner dad, was still enthusiastic; with some way to go, he proudly noted that he was trying to "do every-thing...[he] could whilst [he was] away rather than doing fuck all, all day".

Others were not as positive about some of the official learning opportunities and workshops that were available to them. Jack pointed out that his previous experiences of prison learning and training had no impact in terms of preventing his return to jail. He proposed that only he could make the decision to end his current lifestyle: a decision that depended on him growing up and taking responsibility for his own actions. He explained:

> ...they go on about education – and this and they can do that and they can do this – but there is nothing in jail that is going to help you on the out. If you want to stay out of prison, only you can do that; nothing you do in here is going to help you, everybody reaches a point in the[ir] life where they have had enough and they say that it is usually when you hit 30, 35, if you're going to stop you'll stop at that age. I am now nearly 32 and nothing I've done in jail is going to help me along the way. I've got a business plan for mobile car valeting, I got my provisional license when I was out for that seven days, but that was through my own perseverance – nothing to do with the prison service, they've never help[ed] me in any way, I had to get my own college application, I wrote my own business plan, had no help with that, maybe these do find it helpful the education thing but I don't...(Jack)

Like Jack, Gibson—when asked if there was anything that his time in prison had done to prepare him for living on the outside—simply replied: "no".

Larry had an interesting take on how prison time had better prepared him for his efforts to secure employment on the outside. Although he was happy to engage in education and training as part of the regime inside, he argued that he gained nothing from it in the formal sense. The most valuable learning experiences, he explained, came instead from the informal aspects of having to navigate the prison space and "surviving being around the other inmates". This learning, he suggested, would be beneficial to him when running his "security business":

> ...my experience with prison and this life in general helps me in supplying doormen and defusing situations if you like...because of the reputation of who I am and how I can talk in a tranquil manner.

Learning in the prison space enhanced Larry's credentials to run a business that is highly masculinised and where enterprising men who have an appetite for violence and intimidation are able to sell their physicality as part of their labour. For Larry and several other respondents, the official learning programmes that were offered by the prison service had little to offer them by way of their prospects upon their release.

However, learning—in some cases—was born out of a necessity to communicate with partners and one's family outside. It was a much better option, in most instances, than simply sitting in a cell for up to 23 hours, as was the case in their earlier days of prison. Regardless of the motivation, the respondents' levels of engagement with the limited provision for education and training inside can only be positive. Evidently, though, this is itself will not be enough to end the revolving cycle of incarceration for many of these men.

In labour markets that demand more and more credentials, it is questionable as to how much currency "up to Level Two" qualifications in English and Maths will carry. Furthermore, with clusters of short-term sentences, the transitory nature of being moved from one prison to the next at a moment's notice, the physical confines of the prison space and its timetable have caused several of the respondents to complain that the provision to teach skills and training—especially in the trades—could not often be completed. Additionally, they could only be taken to a very basic level.

It is noteworthy, too, that—in this prison, as with most local prisons—many of the vocational training schemes centre on traditional masculine trades or on bodybuilding and fitness. In the competitive climate for mainly service-based local work opportunities or specialised roles in Hull's emerging energy sector, it is doubtful that these respondents will see much transferable value in their gym instruction credentials or in partly completed "City and Guilds" certificates in bricklaying and joinery.

The failings of prison education and training that have been highlighted by the respondents' experiences feed into wider political and academic debates about prison education (see Coates 2016; Creese 2016; Czerniawski 2015 for a helpful overview of these debates). Since 2010, there have been several different Conservative Justice Secretaries; as part of their strong pledges regarding the punishment and rehabilitation of offenders, each of them has successively aimed to overhaul forms of prison training and education.

In the ministerial foreword in the report on the government's 2011 review, *Making Prison Work*, the government admitted that the current system "is not performing well, as repeatedly confirmed in many reports from Independent Monitoring Boards and the Prison Inspectorate. Recent reports from Ofsted confirm this" (Department for Business Innovation and Skills 2011, p. 3). In 2016, the Coates Review into prison education set out proposals to completely overhaul delivery to make more use of ICT and to devise more personalised learning plans. This recognition, though, comes rather late for many of the respondents. Further research will be needed to see how effective the Conservatives' "rehabilitation revolution" has been in delivering employability skills to prisoners and what purchase they will have in the changing workplace.

6.6   Conclusion

In this chapter, I have explored the respondents' post-compulsory schooling transitions, exposing the major difficulties that they encountered in finding and following lawful routes to acceptable and legitimate versions of manhood. In opposition to the so-called "choice biographies" (Beck 1992; Woodman 2009) and theories of individualism (Giddens 1991) that have been posited by some scholars, it is clear that the respondents' avenues to manhood were severely restricted by structures of poverty and inequality.

The challenges that were encountered by the participants parallel those that are faced by the majority of undereducated working-class men. As national and regional economic restructuring processes took hold, so did their experiences of disadvantage in local labour markets. For many of these informants, their criminal careers and inevitable entrenchment in the criminal justice system meant that, by the time that they reached working age, they carried the burden of more substantial disadvantages into the job market than other men of their age and social class.

Compounding their exclusion and marginalisation, the respondents' protest masculinities—configured in response to the earlier structures of inequality—were carried into the workplace. Often, this resulted in the termination of their employment and/or incarceration. Several respondents had tried to run criminal activities alongside legitimate forms of employment: jobs that, in some cases, were stable and relatively well-paid. This involvement in criminal activity while in employment was more than simple monetary gain, it was also linked to a particular masculine approach to visceral pleasure-seeking, emotional satisfaction and status gained by involvement in crime.

These men were not beyond redemption in terms of their future prospects. Their long criminal careers and the years lost to incarceration led many to claim that they had "had enough" and want to change "on the out". The prison's provisions for learning offered little—if anything—in terms of preparing the respondents for understanding and minimising the barriers to employment that they will face upon their release. Indeed, as I go on to show in the next chapter, the inadequate vocational training and forms of education that are provided in prison constitute just one way—of many—in which the prison contributed to trapping many of the respondents in prolonged cycles of marginalisation and incarceration.

References

Atherton, S. (2009). Domesticating military masculinities: Home, performance and the negotiation of identity. *Social & Cultural Geography, 10*(8), 821–836. https://doi.org/10.1080/14649360903305791.
Beck, U. (1992). *Risk society: Towards a new modernity*. London: Sage.
Coates, S. (2016). *Unlocking potential: A review of education in prison*. London: Ministry of Justice.
Copes, H., & Hochstetler, A. (2003). Situational construction of masculinity among male street thieves. *Journal of Contemporary Ethnography, 32*(3), 279–304. https://doi.org/10.1177/0891241603032003002.
Courtenay, W. H. (2000). Constructions of masculinity and their influence on men's well-being: A theory of gender and health. *Social Science & Medicine, 50*(10), 1385–1401. https://doi.org/10.1016/S0277-9536(99)00390-1.
Creese, B. (2016). An assessment of the English and maths skills levels of prisoners in England. *London Review of Education, 14*(3), 13–30. https://doi.org/10.18546/LRE.14.3.02.
Czerniawski, G. (2015). A race to the bottom—Prison education and the English and Welsh policy context. *Journal of Education Policy, 31*(2), 1–15. https://doi.org/10.1080/02680939.2015.1062146.
Department for Business Innovation and Skills (BIS). (2011). *Making prisons work: Skills for rehabilitation: Review of offender learning*. Available at https://www.gov.uk/government/consultations/call-for-evidence-review-of-offender-learning. Accessed 12 February 2016.
Gadd, D., & Farrall, S. (2004). Criminal careers, desistance and subjectivity interpreting men's narratives of change. *Theoretical Criminology, 8*(2), 123–156. https://doi.org/10.1177/1362480604042241.
Giddens, A. (1991). *Modernity and self-identity: Self and society in the late modern age*. Cambridge: Polity.

Gillett, E., & MacMahon, K. A. (1989). *A history of Hull* (2nd and extended ed.). Hull: Hull University Press.

Hardgrove, A., McDowell, L., & Rootham, E. (2015). Precarious lives, precarious labour: Family support and young men's transitions to work in the UK. *Journal of Youth Studies, 18*(8), 1–20. https://doi.org/10.1080/13676261.2015.1020933.

Laub, J. H., & Sampson, R. J. (2001). Understanding desistance from crime. *Crime and Justice, 28*, 1–69. https://doi.org/10.1086/652208.

Katz, J. (1988). *Seductions of crime: Moral and sensual attractions in doing evil.* New York: Basic Books.

MacDonald, R., & Marsh, J. (2002). Crossing the Rubicon: Youth transitions, poverty, drugs and social exclusion. *International Journal of Drug Policy, 13*(1), 27–38. https://doi.org/10.1016/S0955-3959(02)00004-X.

MacDonald, R., & Shildrick, T. (2007). Street corner society: Leisure careers, youth (sub)culture and social exclusion. *Leisure Studies, 26*(3), 339–355. https://doi.org/10.1080/02614360600834826.

Maruna, S. (2001). *Making good: How ex-convicts reform and rebuild their lives.* Washington, DC: American Psychological Association.

McDowell, L. (2014). The sexual contract: Youth, masculinity and the uncertain promise of waged work in Austerity Britain. *Australian Feminist Studies, 29*(79), 31–49. https://doi.org/10.1080/08164649.2014.901281.

McNeill, F. (2006). A desistance paradigm for offender management. *Criminology and Criminal Justice, 6*(1), 39–62. https://doi.org/10.1177/1748895806060666.

Nayak, A. (2003). Last of the 'Real Geordies'? White masculinities and the subcultural response to deindustrialisation. *Environment and Planning D: Society and Space, 21*(1), 7–26. https://doi.org/10.1068/d44j.

Nayak, A. (2006). Displaced masculinities: Chavs, youth and class in the post-industrial city. *Sociology, 40*(5), 813–831. https://doi.org/10.1177/0038038506067508.

Ulyatt, M. E. (1985). *Trawlermen of Hull: The rise and decline of the world's greatest fishing port.* Dalesman: Lancaster.

Willis, P. (1977). *Learning to labor: How working class kids get working class jobs.* Farnborough, England: Saxon House.

Winlow, S. (2004). Masculinities and crime. *Criminal Justice Matters, 55*(1), 18–19. https://doi.org/10.1080/09627250408553590.

Woodman, D. (2009). The mysterious case of the pervasive choice biography: Ulrich Beck, structure/agency, and the middling state of theory in the sociology of youth. *Journal of Youth Studies, 12*(3), 243–256. https://doi.org/10.1080/13676260902807227.

Young, M. D., & Willmott, P. (2007). *Family and kinship in East London.* London: Penguin.

CHAPTER 7

Boys to "Cons": Adolescent-to-Adult Transitions in the Local Prison

7.1   Introduction

In this chapter, I chart the respondents' youth-to-adult transitions in penal spaces. I have divided the discussion into two main parts. In the opening subsections, I explore the informants' first and early encounters with imprisonment; in the second section, I focus on their adolescent-to-adult transitions in local penal establishments. I start the chapter by showing how the respondents' first-time prison narratives reveal the various dimensions of their gendered constructions of self and the idea that they formed about "appropriate" masculinities in prison. All of the respondents were able to recall their prison terms in graphic detail. Almost unanimously, they admitted to a profound fear of prison prior to the actual experience. I then focus on how and why many of the respondents—after only days or, even, in some cases, just hours of imprisonment—experienced a significant shift from a feeling of terror to finding prison to be like a "home from home".

Having outlined the respondents' first and early prison encounters, in the second part of this chapter, I then track their youth-to-adult transitions in carceral spaces, showing how adulthood was institutionally imposed on them through uncompromising age-based markers. On turning 18 and becoming young adult prisoners, the respondents had to navigate some of the most impoverished and violent regimes of the prison estate.

© The Author(s) 2021
D. Maguire, *Male, Failed, Jailed*,
Palgrave Studies in Prisons and Penology,
https://doi.org/10.1007/978-3-030-61059-3_7

I argue that these carceral spaces were not resourced or equipped to challenge the street-based forms of protest masculinity that characterised the respondents on their entry to prison. Furthermore, I contend that these sites failed to encourage or open up alternative avenues to manhood. In the closing section of this chapter, I consider how the pressure to live up to the hypermasculine identities of prison during their most formative years contributed to the respondents' final institutional transitions from "young adult prisoner" to full "con" status. The transition to adult "con" status brought about a significant shift in terms of what constituted respected prison masculinities—and, consequently, was met with some relief by the men.

7.2   First Time "Inside"

The first prison sentence that each respondent received constituted one of their most memorable and significant life-changing experiences. Almost half were aged just 15 when they got their "first jail", two-thirds by 18 and all, except three, had experienced prison by the time they had turned 21. The generational differences between the respondents meant that the types of carceral spaces that they first encountered were varied: some were housed in a Young Offender Institution (YOI) while several of the respondents were initially placed on a segregated wing for young prisoners (YP) at Hull prison.[1] Every one of the men, some going as far back as three decades, was able to describe—in graphic detail—what it was like to receive their first custodial terms and arrive at the prison. From the youngest to the oldest respondents, their subjective and emotional responses to first having entered prison were virtually unanimous. All of them admitted to having been consumed with fear from the instant that they were sentenced; as they approached the prison, they described how their feelings of fear grew more and more intense:

---

[1] Up until the creation of the Youth Justice Board in 1998 and the establishment of their role and responsibility in commissioning *Custodial Places 2000*, it was common for local prisons to have a young prisoner wing that housed young people who were aged between 15 and 21. Local prisons still house some young adults, between the ages of 18 to 20.

...it don't really hit you when you're in the court room, it's like, later on when you['re] downstairs in the cell and you know you're going soon, you finally realise, you know, nine months in prison and you think of all the things that you've heard from the street, what prisoners are you going to be with and just worrying in the showers, stuff like that...(Lance)

...your head just goes, you're not really thinking, it's when you're actually on the bus, on the way to the jail, that's when you start, your mind starts to go "am I gonna be all right? Am I gonna get hurt?" The stuff you see on telly about prisons...[The] first time I come in, as soon as they put me behind my door, I sat on my bed and started crying...(Paul)

Paul's and Lance's responses were virtually typical of all of the respondents. Their fears mostly stemmed from their concerns about whether or not they would be able to "hold their own" as "one of the lads". They were terrified of being exposed as "weak" and, as a consequence, being sexually assaulted and emasculated by bigger and stronger prisoners.

A further—but related—fear concerned whether or not they would be able to stand up to the subtle daily challenges and tests to their masculinity that would be levelled at them by other prisoners. As with the vast majority of prisoners, these men were from the most deprived neighbourhoods in the UK in which valorised masculine identities are configured and dependent on a heavily managed front (Ellis 2016)—or "face work" (Connell 1995)—and on the preservation of male "honour" (Polk 1994). Having navigated childhood masculinities on deprived streets and other sites of extreme exclusion, these men were acutely aware of the costs of failing to live up to the accepted masculine ideals of all-male spaces. For most of the respondents, their concern was that being in prison would require more "keeping face" than they would be able to live up to.

...I was petrified...I was quite comfortable in the kids' homes and foster care homes, being one of the lads, you like, lead the pack...To be going somewhere where you don't know nobody or what they are capable of...it's a scary thing, to be honest. Yeah: I was scared...(Marcus)

Not all of the respondents' anxieties about prison life were about the prospect of being raped in the showers or not being "hard" enough. Isaac recognised, as did several others, that he was not used to being constrained or adhering to any forms of authority in any way; he worried about how he would adjust to and cope with being in prison:

DM: What do you think your fears were before actually experiencing prison?

Isaac: Not being able to do what I wanted to do, that was the only thing, I mean, I knew prison was alright, I mean, I wasn't expecting to get gang-raped or anything like that, you know, I don't mean, not them type of fears, fear of, I don't know, not being able to do what I wanted, you know, being told what to do, I've always had a problem with authority...

For a small number of the men whose first time away could have—and, indeed, did, in a couple of cases—result in lengthy prison sentences, their dread of what might happen on the inside was coupled with the fears about what they had left behind, or lost, on the outside. Larry—whose first time in prison was as a result of having been remanded in custody, awaiting trial for a serious kidnapping and other violent offences—spoke openly about his first days inside:

DM: Talk me through the minute the judge remanded you.

Larry: ...being locked up, I just had this insecure feeling that I would lose everything whilst I was inside...the main problem wasn't actually being in jail...it was more of a mental thing and that's the main reason I couldn't cope, the main reason I couldn't cope because one day for me away from family – it's like two weeks for other blokes being away from their family.

Geoff—who claimed to have been a major drug dealer and robber of other dealers from a young age—managed to avoid prison for a relatively long time when compared with most of the other respondents. However, at the age of 21, he finally found himself on remand, accused of having committed a serious offence. The quotation from him reflects one of a number of moments during the interview when he allowed glimpses of himself—past his hard "gangster" masculine identity—and exposed his fears of what it meant to him to lose his liberty and everything he had on the outside:

...I think I'm good at hiding how I feel...I've never been so scared in my life...rather than do 30 years of my life, I would rather they brought the death sentence back and put me to sleep, I've got too much out there, I am not like a lowlife who hasn't got nowt to look forward to – or I could get on with it – but I have...(Geoff)

Larry's and Geoff's first experiences of prison were shaped by the fact that they were looking at extremely long sentences. Consequently, their fears—as other studies into the experiences of long-term prisoners have also shown (Wright et al. 2016; Drake 2012)—centred on the prospect of losing their masculine reputation and honour outside the walls of the prison. Often, this linked to a respondents' worries about the loss of their partners, or their loyalty, and an unbearably prolonged loss of liberty. The predominant fear of incarceration that united most of the respondents—whether they were old or young, whether they were serving long or short sentences—was that of the perceived threats to their manhood identities.

7.2.1 Representations of Imprisonment

Most imprisoned men will have spent a large part of their lives perfecting their "tough" or hypermasculine exteriors. As such, it was extraordinary to hear so many members of this group openly talking about their fears and tears during their early days of imprisonment. It raised the question of where—having had no previous personal experience of prison—they had acquired their knowledge or ideas about prison life. Criminologists have established that most people's understandings of crime, criminals and prisons are informed vicariously through forms of media or texts such as films, television (news/documentaries), books and newspapers (Mason 2006). Even though they had been involved in the criminal justice system from a young age, the respondents' knowledge of life on the "inside" had, for the most part, also been gained vicariously. Popular films and television programmes about prison life—like the 1979 films *Scum* (a violent depiction of life, including male rape, in a British Borstal) and *Sense of Freedom* (the life story of a Glasgow gangster and hard man who, sentenced to life, resists the violent prison system)—were commonly cited.

Several of the respondents also spoke of having heard real-life stories of individuals' experiences of incarceration from people "on the estate". Some of these cases involved respondents' siblings and parents who had tales to tell of "doing bird". Post-prison narratives of surviving the brutal and violent conditions that are often depicted on television—or of doing "easy time"—were, as evident in Brian's interview extract below, often a potent form of currency in the construction of gender identities among some of the older peers on the estate:

DM: Where did you get your information about what prison was like before you actually got here?

Brian: Just from the guys that I knocked about with on the estate...they spoke about jail, they never really spoke about [it] in a scary way, they talked of it as a brilliant place. I don't know, people see you as [being an] even...bigger man...Well, if you've been to prison, you've got out alright, it ain't bothered you, it ain't affected you, but I was absolutely terrified. I wasn't going to put it on like they was, I know a lot of them was scared when they first come to prison, I know for a fact they was, but they try to put on this front, make out as though they are bigger than they are...(Brian).

The men's narratives about the origins of their early insights into imprisonment resonated with Kearon's (2012) assertion that popular cultural representations of imprisonment are fragmented and contradictory. He found significant distinctions between the representations of imprisonment that were presented in popular British news media and fictional representations in film. Cinematic or dramatic representations mostly portray prisons as being dangerous and brutal sites at which there are rampant instances of violence that are perpetrated both by and against both prisoners and staff. Populist journalistic and news outlets, meanwhile, peddle oversimplified stories of prisons as being like "holiday camps" at which prisoners have too many privileges: in-cell televisions, games consoles and weekends out shopping. On top of all these kinds of privileges, prisons are often reported as being awash with contraband; they are presented as being places at which prisoners can enjoy using mobile phones and throwing drug- and alcohol-fuelled parties. Recently, however, a number of factual programmes have been screened that seek to portray the harsh realities of austerity-hit prisons across England and Wales. With "fly on the wall" documentaries[2] exposing the reality of prison life, a wider audience is becoming aware of the brutal and atomised experience that those in prison endure.

These media representations are not passively consumed, interpretation or readings will vary depending on what individuals bring to the text in terms of class, gender, group/individual interests and lived experiences and so on (Ferrell et al. 2008). Brian and a small number of others, for

---

[2] See, for example, Paddy Wivell's "'Prison', on what prison life is really like". And ITV's "Welcome to HMP Belmarsh" with Ross Kemp.

instance, claimed that they had not fully subscribed to the widespread "easy prison" narrative that was often espoused by their friends and older peers. They recognised the fact that, on their estates, talk of "doing your jail" easily was, for some, just another way of "doing masculinity". As the chapter unfolds, I show how many of the respondents continually conflated and harnessed these contradictory narratives of "doing easy jail" against the backdrop of brutal prison regimes. In doing so, the respondents sought to implement a strategy through which they could project revered forms of street and prison masculinity.

7.2.2 "Hitting the Wing": "Home from Home"

As I highlighted in Chapter 1, most of the respondents had long histories of having been bounced around institutions and having their life trajectories interrogated by professionals. Even their experiences of the first few hours of imprisonment, as Lance captures below, echoed the mortification process that has been described by Goffman (1968) in his classic study, *Asylums*:

> ...it's just a lot of questions, a hell of a lot of questions...your age, your name, next of kin, your home address and your offence that you're in for, any medical conditions, any worries... and they tell you a little bit about how things work, they take all your clothes off you and you get strip-searched, you see a nurse and you see an officer and then they take you to the wing, so like, in the space of a couple of hours, you go through quite a lot...(Victor)

Most of the respondents were children when they first had to come to terms with this loss of liberty, identity and dignity—or, what Goffman terms, "civil death" (1968, p. 25).

After having had what many of the respondents described as their "outside identities" stripped away, they were escorted to their living spaces on the residential "wing" and allocated a cell or a "pad". The wing is the part of the prison in which prisoners eat, sleep, shower and interact with others. It is at this point when the men talked about "hitting" the wing that, remarkably—and almost consistently across all of the respondents—the mood and tone changed completely. The ways in which the respondents described entering this space for the very first time says a great deal about not only where they had come from but also about why they have ended up returning to prison, time and time again.

> ...when I come from Reception to D Wing, as I walked past the wing, my mates were shouting [to] me out of the window...it sounds daft, but I felt a bit at home...(Doug)

> ...I walked onto the wing, expecting there to be some big, hairy-arsed cons, and – honestly – it was like being back on my own estate...I walked on the wing and I knew everybody and that was the worst thing for me because, then, I started enjoying prison...(Brian)

These extracts sum up the experiences of nearly every respondent. Fear, loss of identity, the unknown or mortification was almost immediately replaced with relief and a confidence that comes with familiarity.

In his research into the experiences of young prisoners at Feltham YOI, Harvey (2006) found that they had struggled to a much greater extent to adapt to the early days of imprisonment. Harvey (2006), like others (Tomczak 2018), found that prisoners are at their most vulnerable at the time of entry; it is at this point that self-harm and suicide are more likely. Harvey has talked of the "liminal phase" during which the young men who were participating in his study were coming to terms with the transition from the outside to the prison world. In these early days, the boys were preoccupied with their personal safety, their loss of liberty and their separation from their outside attachments (*ibid.*). In this "liminal phase" of adaption, prisoners were hesitant to leave their cells and reluctant to engage with staff, other inmates and structured activities (*ibid.*).

A small number of the respondents in my study—as I detail later in the chapter—acknowledged some of their difficulties in adapting to the penal space during their first few days inside. For the most part, however, they did not report the same liminal phase struggles that were described by the boys in Harvey's study. These differences may be partially explained by the fact that Harvey interviewed his boys only days after they had arrived to serve their first sentence in an institution that has a long and troubling history (see Crook 2018): a prison that the Howard League for Penal Reform reports as being one of the most violent in England and Wales (*ibid.*).

The retrospective first-time prison narratives of the respondents in this study, however—with some reflecting back on their experiences over a decade later—may have softened their accounts of their initial experiences in a range of penal institutions. The respondents' versions of street-based protest masculinity and the ease which many claimed to have transferred these identities into the prison space differed from Harvey's (2006) findings—but shared interesting parallels with what the geographer Shabazz (2009) has described as "post-industrial carceral masculinity". Shabazz found that many young black men constructed this version of masculinity as a way of adapting to the structural poverty and spatial organisation of one of Chicago's biggest and most disadvantaged housing projects. Trapped in housing projects that were built in the 1970s—in accordance with the "carceral logic" of restrictive architecture, surveillance and containment—poorly educated men, faced with high rates of unemployment in a context of rapid deindustrialisation, turned to the underground economy. A daily "hustle"— that often-involved drug dealing and inevitable outbreaks of serious violence—led to high rates of incarceration among young men who came from the same projects. Shabazz found that gender performances already "prisonised" adapted relatively effortlessly to a carceral space not much different to the housing project from which they came.

Although Shabazz's study reflects America's heavily racialised penal system, while most of the men who participated in this study were white working-class males who came from post-industrial estates in England, there are some obvious similarities between the two groups. Shabazz's description of a "circular system" of black bodies "vacillating between prison" (p. 286) and their poor neighbourhoods parallels the way in which estate masculinities both reflect and affect prison masculinities and vice versa.

This strong connection between the respondents' neighbourhoods and local penal establishments makes it easier, as Billy highlights, to import already well-established "hard masculinities" from the "estate" into the prison space:

DM: What was D Wing like?
Billy: It was alright, there was lots of fighting with the older lads because it was like 15 to 21. I knew them all, especially the hard cases on the wing. I mean, I were mates with them on the out[side] so I was all right, it didn't bother me, [not] one little bit.

Not all of the respondents reported having experienced such easy transitions from the streets to the wing. Paul, like Billy, was just 15 when he was first sentenced. He did not have the same confidence, stature or masculine capital as Billy, though—and, crucially, he was not from the nearby estates. Despite his appetite for violence, he struggled through the liminal phase, finding it difficult to adapt to life on the wing:

> ...really nervous, I didn't come out of my pad. When you do start coming out of your pad and start chatting to people, you find people from my area – other lads from Grimsby – and stick with them, because that is the way it is in jail: everyone looks after their own...so, like, if I'm fighting with someone else and the Grimsby lads see it, they will join in, because we are all from the same town...[even] when I know there are some lads in there I knew, I was kind of still nervous...but was careful because of all the stabbings that went on...(Paul)

It would be difficult to overstate the importance of locality and local identity in shaping the men's early experiences of incarceration. The small minority of respondents who came from neighbourhoods that were far away from the penal establishment were the ones who admitted to struggling the most in the early days of their first sentence. Prisoners' local areas, towns or cities contribute significantly to the organisation of prison masculinities (Phillips 2012). The longer the distance that the prisoner is from home, the more important that their regional identity becomes in their efforts to find a sense of belonging and to try to fit into the existing masculine hierarchies.

The vast majority of the respondents, however, reached the wing to find "lads" who they had been in "care" with, "lads" they went to school with, "lads" from their street corners, "lads" with whom they had committed crime, and cousins, uncles and older siblings. It is easy to understand, then, why Doug "felt a bit at home" and Brian likened his experience of being in prison to being back on his "own estate". They were, clearly, on very familiar territory, with lads and men who they had been around for most of their lives: those who, like them, had accessed the same resources, in the same spaces, in pursuit of the same masculine ideals.

For many of the respondents, their initial experiences of prison did not conform to their expectations that had, themselves, been built on the back of the brutal representations they had seen on the "telly" or some of the myths that they had heard on the estate. Instead, the "worst thing", Brian admits, was the realisation that it was from this point onwards that he started "enjoying prison"; Jack, too, felt that—rather than deterring further sentences—his first time instead signalled the "start of something". Andy, in his careful, reflective statement below, captures the significance of experiencing and surviving the first prison sentence and how in some ways doing so was like passing a test that then permitted greater criminal freedom.

> ...from my experience, prison is a bigger deterrent before you actually go...the thought of prison was horrendous, going to prison was emotional – but a relief – and it removed a lot of inhibition like, yeah, I've done that, I've survived that, it wasn't that bad and I forgot about it a couple months after I got out...(Andy)

The surprising ease with which Andy adjusted to prison life and his accompanying relief at having done so, as described above, was common to nearly all of the respondents. For them, the reality of prison was "easier" than the myths, threats and anticipation that surrounded the idea of it.

7.2.3   "Easy Jail"?

It is important to unpack the reasons as to why the respondents talked of their first prison experiences as being "a relief" and not as hard as they had originally imagined them to be. For these men, their projection of the illusion that prison was "easy" says more about their pre-prison social environments and the ideas of masculinity that were circulated in them rather than legitimising any claims that prisons are not "punishing-enough" places. As I indicated earlier, the biggest and most consistently reported pre-prison fear among the respondents related to their anxiety about being potential victims of sexual violence. In reality, the necessity of fighting off predatory forms of male sexual violence was not—as represented in the movies or according to estate legend—a daily occurrence. Indeed, in this local prison (or YOI) in which sentences were highly transient—with most serving relatively short sentences of four years or less—anyone who was found to be involved in, or even suspected of, predatory sexual behaviour would be at risk of sustaining grave harm.

The other main terror with which the idea of being sent to prison was linked was the fear of being locked in a carceral space with harder, more violent and dangerous men. There was some substance to these anxieties. Research has shown prisons to be brutal institutions in which masculinities are constructed and positioned in accordance with individuals' fighting prowess and levels of willingness, if necessary, to engage in serious acts of violence (Jewkes 2005; Ricciardelli 2015). For Sykes (2007) and other penal scholars (Crewe et al. 2020; Gooch 2017; Tynan 2019), one of the most severe forms of deprivation with which imprisonment is associated is that of security, where the biggest—and constant—dangers to personal safety (security) were posed by other prisoners. Prisoners often respond or adapt to threats to their personal security—whether real or imagined—through hypermasculine displays that centre on individual or collective acts of violence (Gooch 2017; Ricciardelli et al. 2015). Pre-prison lives and intervening periods 'on the out' for many of these respondents, however, involved having to navigate and construct masculinities in similar—mostly all-male peer spaces—and in comparable conditions:

> It was like the detached exclusion centre that I went to, they was all near enough my age and, yeah, there were some bad lads and some people doing like five and six or seven years – but to talk to, they were alright lads…(Richard)

> …to me, it was just like boarding school, just a stricter regime than the school I was at, so it didn't really bother me, but I remember being scared, yeah. I remember being very scared, but at the same time, I knew I didn't need to be scared – nowt was going to happen, nowt worse than what I've already been through with boarding school…(Lee)

The ease with which the men talked of adapting to their first prison sentences is not, by any means, because imprisonment was easy. The experiences of being frightened and suffering the other "pains" of imprisonment—or structural deprivations such as missing families, girlfriends, children and the loss of their liberty—were widely reported as being difficult. With many of the respondents having being imprisoned at such young ages—in many cases, as children—they did not realise the extent of these "pains", as I explore later in the chapter, until they were older and had fallen much further into the "revolving-door cycle". The important point to emphasise here—and as shown in Richard's and Lee's extracts above—is that most of these respondents had been learning to serve time long before they had first "hit the wing". What is presented as being "easy" jail is, in reality, just familiar.

The respondents' claims of initially being able to adapt easily to the familiar carceral space are not to challenge the research that has shown prison environments to be brutally violent, psychologically harmful and deprivational in nature. Rather, it is to suggest that they were able to quickly adapt to the deprivation or pains of imprisonment because these experiences—to a large extent—paralleled their earlier lives. As the evidence that I have highlighted in Chapters 3 and 4 indicates, the respondents—like most of the men in UK prisons—have spent their lives configuring and negotiating a particular version of working-class masculinity in the context of extraordinary levels of deprivation. The localities from which they came, as I discuss in more depth in the following chapter, have some of the highest rates of mortality in relation to poverty and significantly higher-than-average rates of death—linked to drug overdoses and alcohol abuse—as well as high rates of violent crimes. Many of the men in prison—including those with whom I spoke—had been victims and/or perpetrators of violence.

This is not to suggest—as posited by some proponents of the classic importation thesis (Irwin and Cressey 1962)—that imprisonment is just another aspect of these men's lives, par for the course, and that the criminal identities that they have constructed on the outside simply import into the prison space. As Connell and Messerschmidt (2005) have shown, masculinities are situationally accomplished and have to be continuously worked and reworked. In the prison space—with nowhere to which to retreat from—the constant scrutiny of gendered performances and the pervasive threat of violence, masculine hierarchies that are based on power structures of domination and subjugation—although influenced by the outside world—will be much more pronounced. The "hard men" who enter prison spaces may well find that they have to "up their game" in order to maintain the same levels of respect that they commanded on the outside. Those who lack adequate physical masculine capital find that they have to rely on other performances or forms of masculine capital—like being "funny", the "jail lawyer", "artist" or wheeler-dealer.

The particular type of prison, as Sim (1994) has noted—whether it has long-term (high security), local or open conditions (low security)— also determines the different types of masculine hierarchies and performances. On many occasions, for instance, the respondents made statements that suggested that they understood that there were certain modes and behaviours in the local prison that would not be enacted in long-term establishments. Jack, for instance—in reference to a wing bully—noted that "he wouldn't last a day...in a proper jail like Frankland; they'd put a jug of boiling water and sugar over his fucking face".[3] Early criminal identities combine with the varying levels of deprivation that are found in different (prison) spaces to create dominant, subjugated and other forms of prison masculinities. For these respondents—many of whom had long-term investments in sustaining their forms of protest masculinity—the experience of hitting the residential wing, filled with others from their neighbourhoods, meant that most of them were well-equipped to adapt to and negotiate the masculine hierarchies of the local prison.

7.2.4   *Initiation Test*

As the respondents' narratives unfolded, it became increasingly evident just how much their previous cultural conditioning had enabled them to navigate the countless pitfalls, challenges and tests of early imprisonment. Any mishandling of their masculine performances in the first days and months of their imprisonment could have a damaging impact on all of their future prison experiences. From the very first night, new prisoners are scrutinised and tested in what are often attempts to try to gauge the attitudes and reactions of the latest arrival to the wing:

> ...the first night with the lads not seeing you on the wing, I remember some kids shouting out their windows, trying to make me sing a song for them – Baa Baa Black Sheep song – out of the window. I just went to the window and shouted "listen, if you want me to sing a song, come down in the morning and make me sing a song"...(Lee)

A number of the other respondents, like Lee, talked of the window test. They reported how initially innocuous conversations can often quickly shift to demands or threats in attempts to try to persuade the new prisoner to do something that might expose him as being naive and weak, including the recitation of nursery rhymes (see also Gooch 2017).

The trainer test is another common means by which prisoners assess a new man "in the jail". On the surface—and to the uninitiated—it seems like a simple compliment about trainers and an enquiry as to the size of a

---

[3] A high-security prison that houses some of the most violent and longest-serving prisoners in the UK.

man's feet. Those who are used to all-male, hostile environments under-stand that this is not a friendly enquiry; instead, it is a test to explore just how easy he is to intimidate and have his trainers (property) taken from him. Researchers have commented on the significance of "trainers" or designer sporting clothing as a medium through which men express their masculine identities in prison (Wilson 2003). Wearing trainers is a highly visible way in which one may convey masculine ideals that suggest that the individual in question is an "earner" and is still able to main-tain aspects of his outside identity. Many prisoners literally wear "their masculine credentials on their feet" (Jewkes 2002, p. 57). The respon-dents referred to the importance of being able to wear their own trainers; most of them understood the implication that lay behind the trainer test. This was a clear strategy, as Dillon explains, that would be used by one prisoner to try to assert his masculine dominance over another:

> ...when I first started coming to jail, it was hard to wear your own trainers or anything like that because there was a lot of taxing going on, people coming in and saying all that: "oh, they are nice what size are them"? A size 8, "I'm a size 8", and the next thing you know, he's getting done in and getting the trainers took off him...(Dillon)

To lose footwear to another prisoner is an emasculating experience that leaves the individual vulnerable to further and continued forms of exploitation. The time that they had already spent in typically all-male street spaces and all-male peer groups meant that most of the respon-dents would have faced or been involved with similar challenges in the past. As such, most of them would have been aware that their standing in the prison rested, as Doug outlines, on providing appropriate responses to such scenarios—namely, ones that communicated a willingness to use violence:

> I'd have to be cold to have my trainers took off my feet. I've been asked what size my trainers are – and they are: "about the size of your mouth" ...or "my size"; that's how it's got to be...(Doug)

For young prisoners, there were many other things of which they had to be alert to when presenting and sustaining respectable masculine iden-tities to and among the other prisoners. Gibson highlights the extent to

which masculinities are monitored for weaknesses—as well as the importance of recognising and quickly dealing with all types of (often subtle)
challenges:

> ...when you first come to jail, you can't just overlook little things...my
> mate might say "what are you looking at, you dickhead?"...you just
> wouldn't even bother outside, but when you come to jail...you have to
> fucking fight it out, because otherwise someone else will hear and, number
> one, he knows that he can talk to you like that so he's going to keep doing
> it and, number two, other people are going to hear him talking to you like
> that and think "he's a muppet". Fuck it! You've just got to jump on it
> straight away...(Gibson)

The challenges are not always as clear-cut as they would seem from
Gibson's example above, as he himself elaborates:

> ...let's say I'm not hungry...they're [servery workers] meant to give
> everyone the same, obviously, if your mate comes through, he gets a
> bit more than everyone else...so, like, when you come walking through,
> it's like – I might not even be hungry but I want as much food on my
> plate as I can get so I don't look like a dickhead when I walk through,
> because otherwise my mates...he will be like, haha, you've been stitched
> up...(Gibson)

As Gibson's accounts—and those of the other respondents—demonstrate,
their knowledge of how to present and sustain their versions of respectable
masculinity was critical to their first prison experiences. If a prisoner can
successfully project or establish early on that he is willing to fight and
"stand up to" all confrontations, "win or lose", then it is likely that things
will be much easier for him inside in the medium to longer term. It is
notable that the men whom I have just quoted had come through alternative learning/boarding school routes and/or the care system en-route
to prison; they consequently understood how to jostle for position in
masculine hierarchies.

However, this boarding school and "care" system experiences failed to
prepare a fifteen-year-old Dillon for sharing a cell with an older prisoner
who suffered from what he describes as "bad mental health problems":

...I woke up in the middle of the night with him bull whipping me...he'd rolled towels up, the nutter, and he'd wet the end of it...I was only just coming on 16 and he was nearly 21. I was like "what do you want, what do you want?" ...he was just laughing like a lunatic and I thought "fucking hell!" I couldn't sleep all night and I came out in the morning with bruises all over me and I pulled the screws up, like, told them what was going on and they moved me out the cell and put me in a cell on my own and he ended up getting put on governor's [report]...(Dillon)

Following his instinct to protect himself, Dillon reported the encounter with his "lunatic" cellmate and, by doing so, went against the inmate or convict code. Prison masculinities, as I explore in detail in the following chapter, are situationally constructed and sustained largely through one's adherence to, and enforcement of, the inmate code (Clemmer 1958; Kupers 2001; Maguire 2019). Dillon noted that, after the incident, he was seen as being "weak" and labelled a "grass" (informer). As I have discussed elsewhere, managing this type of highly stigmatised masculinity in prison is difficult and dangerous (Maguire 2019). After a short time, feeling that he could no longer live with the risk of reprisals, Dillon requested "protection" from the prison officers. Consequently, he was categorised as being a "vulnerable prisoner" (VP) and was segregated from the main prison population for his own safety.

This categorisation, that of being "vulnerable", is given to those who are thought to be at serious risk of harm from other prisoners. It often proves to be, as shown in more depth in the following chapter, a permanent marker of subordinate status. No matter where they serve time, these men will always be situated near the bottom of the masculine hierarchy; they are seen as being "shithouses and tossers who can't be trusted" (Isaac). In his insightful comments, as presented in the extract below, Isaac captures the importance of constructing respectable masculinities in the early days of one's imprisonment:

...if you do something wrong in YPs, it sticks with you for the rest of your prison sentences...I mean, I know lads in here, now, who might have done something wrong in YPs and went on protection – and every time they come back in, they have to go on protection, not because they have done anything wrong this time, it is just because someone would say: "you was on protections last time", not knowing what they were on protections for, and so its back on protection. So, whatever you do that first day you land in jail –whether it's 10 months or 10 years down the line – it stays with you...(Isaac)

Isaac's remarks confirm both the fragility and the tentative nature of normative gendered prison identities while at the same time pointing to the durability and legacy of undesirable forms of masculinity.

The prison was not easy for the respondents. However, brutality and cruelty were not so much inflicted by the regime or by the officers—as commonly reported in other penal accounts—so much as by other prisoners. The targeting of those who failed to meet the particular standards for masculinity in prison, however, could reportedly be just as brutally unpleasant in old schooling environments, residential "care" homes and the streets of the respondents' estates. Many of these men had, long ago, refined their masculine identities and learned to enact acceptable or desirable gender performances in these spaces, resulting in easier adaptation to the culture of masculinity encountered in prison. Dillon's experience reveals that, when confined in a prison space, one's performance of masculinity is under much more intense and constant scrutiny and just one breach of the dominant codes can have harsh and lasting consequences.

7.3   TIME SERVED: COMING-OF-AGE TRANSITIONS

The ongoing criminal careers that most of these men found too difficult to avoid saw well over two-thirds of the respondents being returned to prison, time and time again, after they had served their first sentences. A consequence of the prison journeys that had started early in their teens meant that the key formative years—that profoundly shape people's identities and during which they lay the foundations for their adult existence—were spent behind walls in their local prison. Only three of the respondents were serving their first prison sentence at the time at which I undertook my fieldwork; the remaining 27 were serving anywhere from a second to a twentieth custodial term. Most of them were well into double figures in relation to the number of prison sentences that they had received from the courts. Time served was often measured through birthday milestones or age-based transitions:

> ...I had my 18th, my 21st, and my 22nd and 23rd inside...I've had about ten birthdays out since the age of 16...(Jerry)

...all my 20 s in jail – and just about, nearly, every Christmas since then...yeah, 18th and my 21st, all the milestones, 30th, I just had a birthday last week, is just like any other day now to me...(Nigel)

As others "on the out" might have been marking their 16th birthdays by concluding their formal education and entering college or training—or reaching 18 years and celebrating having been accepted onto a training programme or apprenticeship—many of these participants were marking their transitions into young adulthood through institutional-based markers within the criminal justice system.

In the criminal justice system in England and Wales, turning 18, for example, means that young men like these are no longer deemed to be juveniles who have to be accompanied by an adult when attending special youth courts.[4] Instead, they are processed in accordance with the guidelines of the adult criminal justice system.

Other institutional markers at 18 meant that the respondents advanced from being "juvenile prisoners" to "young adult prisoners" (YPs), leading to a notable change to their regime in terms of their rights and privileges. For many on the outside, this important birthday milestone may have involved the commemorative—but legal—pub-crawl or alcohol-fuelled party, and/or perhaps triumph at a coming-of-age income increase. One may even just simply enjoy their newly acquired right to vote. For these respondents, however—as many fondly remember—turning 18 in prison meant that they were entitled to buy and smoke tobacco and that they were permitted to wear more of their own clothes and, as a result, had to wear fewer items of prison uniform.

7.3.1   Abrupt Transitions: Young Adult Offenders

Although the men welcomed this significant coming-of-age shift, many scholars, policy experts and campaign groups have expressed concerns about this "dramatic transition". Lösel et al. (2013) have highlighted the serious failings for this group once they have moved from juvenile prisoners into young adult prisoners. As I have already outlined in Chapter 2, economic change and its impact on labour market relations have contributed to the creation of extended transitions to adulthood.

---

[4] Serious offences like murder and rape would still be passed from the Youth Court for sentencing or trial at the Crown Court.

"On the out"-delayed routes to adulthood have been met with a legislative push for the extended provision of education and training as well as—although they have been in decline under the coalition and current government—a multitude of youth support services that extend to those who are 25 or younger. In the criminal justice system, however, institutionally determined transitions are fixed. This age-based, uncompromising approach only serves to perpetuate—as has been the case for most of these respondents—patterns of long-term, revolving-door incarceration. A major concern is that prisoners, on their 18th birthdays, face the statutory transition from the youth justice system—centred on rehabilitation—to the adult criminal justice system, that focuses more on punishment. (Barrow Cadbury Trust 2005; Lösel et al. 2013)

Widespread concerns about this group of young adult offenders led the charity Barrow Cadbury Trust to establish an independent Commission on Young Adults and the Criminal Justice System in 2004. The Commission's report, *Lost in Transition*—that followed in 2005—was one of the most important reports to have been written on young adult offenders in England and Wales since the early 1970s (Lösel et al. 2013). The report highlighted the failure of the criminal justice system to factor in the varying levels of maturity when dealing with young adult offenders. The Commission found that the police and judiciary's universal approach when dealing with offenders as adults from the age of 18 ignores the vast body of scientific evidence that shows that there is a broad spectrum of ages at which boys emotionally, mentally and physically mature into men. A later study (Prior et al. 2011), that was also instigated by the Barrow Cadbury Trust, set out to review advances in neuroscience research regarding levels of maturity.[5] It was found that, although one could reach intellectual maturity by the age of 18, the higher functions of the brain that involve planning, memory and impulse do not fully develop until the age of 25 (*ibid.*).

A recent review by Lord Harris into deaths that occur in custody among the young adult population acknowledged these findings concerning maturity. In his 2015 report, *Changing Prison, Saving Lives,*

---

[5] Leading on from their 2005 Commission on Young Adults and the Criminal Justice System, the Barrow Trust conveys and funds the Transition to Adulthood Alliance (T2A Alliance). The T2A alliance is a broad coalition of organisations that promote the need to adopt a distinct approach to young adults (18–25 throughout the criminal justice system). More information is available at: www.t2a.org.uk/t2a-alliance/.

he noted: "...given [the] current understanding of maturity...we feel it no longer makes sense to expect that young adults...should be sentenced as an adult solely on the basis of their age" (Harris Review 2015, p. 81). A decade earlier, the Barrow Cadbury Trust's report, *Lost in Transition*, had recommended the introduction of specialists who would be able to assess offenders' levels of maturity and present their findings to courts before sentencing took place. The report further recommended: "As most young offenders stop offending at 23[,] it would make more sense to require sentencers to refrain from imposing custody in all but the most serious cases until after then" (Barrow Cadbury Trust 2005, p. 62).

As a key argument of this book is that interconnected spaces of exclusion amplify and reproduce marginalised or protest gender trajectories, it is worth emphasising once again that 23 out of the 30 respondents received a custodial sentence before they had reached their twentieth birthdays. Well over half of these 23 informants were initially imprisoned for low-end acquisitive offences—mainly, "buzz-related" vehicle crime that many claimed to have been "a phase" that they outgrew and out of which they eventually matured.

7.3.2   Carceral Purgatory

For many of these respondents, turning 18 and spending their final teenage years as young adult prisoners meant that, at some point, they had been or were part of a population that has been variously described as the "lost generation" (Prison Reform Trust 2012), the "abandoned generation" (Howard League for Penal Reform 2010b) or the "forgotten group" (Allen 2013, p. 7). Young adult prisoners have been found to have been in receipt of the poorest levels of statutory support and protection (Lösel et al. 2013). In recent years, as Allen (2013) has noted, there has been much more extensive policy-related interest in how best to deal with under 18 at the expense and neglect of 18- to 20-year-olds. Although coming too late for some respondents, the overhaul of the youth justice system that was started under New Labour saw the creation of the Youth Justice Board, Youth Offending Teams (YOT) and improved custodial regimes for under 18. Over recent years, there has been a significant reduction in the number of under 18 who are being charged with criminal offences, being brought to court and sentenced to custody. Young adult prisoners, in contrast, have been languishing in a political and policy vacuum for a number of decades.

During their time in young adult custodial settings, the respondents' forms of masculinity were continuously being tested. Masculine hierarchies were maintained through acts of fighting and violence, confirming the precarious state of the constantly reported areas of concern across the youth estate. In his 2017 annual report, the Chief Inspector of Prisons, Peter Clark, concluded that: "there was not a single establishment that we inspected in England and Wales in which it was safe to hold children and young people" (HM Chief Inspector of Prisons 2017, p. 9). He added that the "Assault rates were [staggering]...18.9 per 100 children. Our own surveys showed that 46% of boys had felt unsafe. The number of those reporting being victimised by other boys had risen significantly" (*ibid.*, p. 9).

With this prolonged lack of policy and political strategy for young adult carceral spaces—the institutions that have previously housed most of these respondents there has not, for some time, been an effective means by which to challenge and address the issue of street-based protest masculinities. Indeed, as I have argued in the previous sections, many of the respondents adapted and adopted more intensified versions of violent masculine performances in order to survive these volatile young adult penal establishments. In the absence of any real or meaningful institutional interventions, many respondents completed the all-too-predictable transition from being young adult prisoners to adult convicts.

7.3.3   *"Con" Status*

—Given some of the challenges that have been reported in the previous section, it is hardly surprising that most of the respondents celebrated—albeit with some fear—the institutional transition that came at the age of 21 when they were no longer deemed to be "young adult prisoners" and so moved to "con" status: that of adult prisoners. Anxieties about transitioning to "con" status, for some, centred on the prospect of having to endure "mixing" with older men who had been convicted of serious violent offences and had "nothing to lose", as Lee explains below:

> ...in YP, you don't really think [about] it being full of murderers and rapists...But a cons jail, like Hull, say, for instance, or a prime example is, like, Wakefield...it's one of them where you think, my God, rapists and murderers – and you just think "I don't want to be mixed in with that"...(Lee)

In reality, however, the adult prison space—as Billy highlights below—allows men to enact less aggressive forms of masculine performance:

> ...there was a lot more pressure on you to be seen to be able to handle yourself and to survive in prison as a young person. As you get older, it is not so much the case – but, definitely from 15 to [your] early 20 s, you have to be seen as...like, if someone talks down to you a little bit, you'd have to go and fill them in...now, as you're older, you would maybe say to them: "look, don't talk to me like that or else we will fall out"...it would probably not come to blows. But as a young kid, it would always come to blows...(Billy)

For most of the men, reaching 21 marked a clear transition from youth to manhood and, with it, a substantial shift in what constituted respectable prison masculinities. Despite their initial fears and reservations, many noted that they were happy to get away from the young adult prisoner environment in which masculinities were contested daily through overt acts of violence. They felt that, among "cons", they were able to "grow up".

The men did not claim to have woken up on their twenty-first birthdays as "mature" "cons". From the interviews, it is clear that there were some tensions, contradictions and uncertainties about these identity transformations. Many of the newly adult prisoners whom I interviewed, for instance, talked of the sheer relief once they had been moved out of the highly physical "young prisoner" environments—but noted, too, their distrust of the older cons. The older respondents denigrated their juniors, suggesting that they were unable to "handle their jail" and that their immaturity and resistance just made serving time harder for everyone. Strangely in parallel with elderly individuals' perceptions of young people in the outside world, the more senior respondents were fearful—or, at the very least—cautious of the younger generation of prisoners. Indeed, they often suggested that they were the ones who were responsible for most of the violence and disruption that occurred on the wings:

> ...they're mixing YOs with adults now...one minute, it can be all adults and be all quiet and then, all of a sudden, fights break out and somebody gets their ear bitten off or somebody gets slashed – and it's always YOs that are doing it...(Rob)

Years ago, I'd be down playing snooker every night, arguing over the snooker games and all that – and I just can't be bothered with it any more...I'm 35, I'm too old, it's a young man's game, I just want to finish this sentence...I've grown out of all that but a lot of these young ones...it's all bravado..."I've knocked so and so out, I can punch this hard"; I'm past that, I'm 35...(Nigel)

A great deal of the conduct that was once seen as being an acceptable— or, even, a celebrated—behaviour among young prisoners was denigrated by many cons as being "childish" or "immature" and lacking any purpose or sense. The unprovoked forms of violence and bullying that had been so core to the construction of the young prisoners' forms of masculinity were, by "con" standards, too overt, unpredictable, unnecessary—and too hard a way of doing time.

Normative or revered "con" masculinities are configured more through the use of measured, calculated and—often strategic—acts of violence (see also Ricciardelli et al. 2017). Those who turn to indiscriminate and uncontrollable forms of intimidation and violence too quickly generate little genuine respect and are often avoided by other prisoners (Kupers 2005; Evans and Wallace 2008). Most of the interviewees' carceral trajectories from boyhood to manhood have reflected these distinctions in age and space-appropriate masculine performances. They acknowledged that, during their time as young prisoners, fighting was the only way to ensure that they were not being exploited. Although this can be the case as a "con" too, random occurrences of violence and fighting are less common. Most of the respondents welcomed the shift to "con" versions of masculine performances that, on the whole, meant "doing your own jail like a man" in the easiest way possible and "getting out when you're supposed to"—at the earliest opportunity (Lance).

7.4   Conclusion

In charting the respondents' carceral transitions from boys to men in this chapter, I have shown how street-based masculinities—once imported into local prisons—can easily be adapted to the existing "extreme" culture of masculinity. Sim's (1994) observation that prisons are linked to wider "society by the umbilical cord of masculinity" (p. 116) neatly captures the essence of why "being inside" was not too difficult an adaptation for most of the respondents. It explains their "easy prison" narratives while, at the same time, disrupting the notion that prisons are not punishing-enough sites.

Indeed, nearly all of the respondents were sent, by the courts, to impoverished and violent prison regimes before they had been afforded the time or opportunities to see if they would "grow out of crime" and "mature" into responsible adults. At crucial and formative stages of their lives, many of the respondents found themselves in penal spaces that—after decades of political and policy-based neglect—offered no real strategic or rehabilitative measures to help the men to address the protest masculine performances that led them there in the first instance.

Under intense scrutiny—and having endured testing at the hands of the other young adult prisoners—, hyperaggressive and violent masculine performances were adopted by some as a strategy for survival in these highly volatile carceral spaces. Extreme masculinities—that the respondents had configured so as to navigate the impoverished young adult penal regimes—contributed to their transitions from being young adult prisoners to attaining their current status as adult "cons". These youth-to-adult transitions—and the subsequent long journeys across penal spaces that have resulted from them—have come at a great cost for many. In the following, and final, empirical chapter, I explore some of the long-term consequences of the respondents' early investments in performing specific forms of masculinity.

REFERENCES

Allen, R. (2013). *Young adults in custody: The way forward*. T2A Alliance Barrow Cadbury Trust.

Barrow Cadbury Trust. (2005). *Lost in transition: A report of the Barrow Cadbury Commission on young adults and the criminal justice system*. London: Barrow Cadbury Trust.

Clemmer, D. (1958). *The prison community*. New York: Holt, Rinehart & Winston.

Connell, R. (1995). *Masculinities*. Cambridge: Polity.

Connell, R., & Messerschmidt, J. W. (2005). Hegemonic masculinity rethinking the concept. *Gender & Society, 19*(6), 829–859. https://doi.org/10.1177/0891243205278639.

Crewe, B., Hulley, S., & Wright, S. (2020). *Life imprisonment from young adulthood*. London: Palgrave Macmillan UK.

Crook, F. (2018). *Reinventing different ways of locking up children— A cautionary tale*. Howard League for Penal Reform. Available

162   D. MAGUIRE

at https://howardleague.org/blog/reinventing-different-ways-of-locking-up-children-a-cautionary-tale/. Accessed August 2018.

Drake, D. (2012). *Prisons, punishment and the pursuit of security*. Critical Criminological Perspectives. Basingstoke: Palgrave Macmillan.

Ellis, A. J. (2016). *Men, masculinities and violence: An ethnographic study*. London: Routledge.

Evans, T., & Wallace, P. (2008). A prison within a prison? The masculinity narratives of male prisoners. *Men and Masculinities, 10,* 484–507. https://doi.org/10.1177/1097184X06291903.

Ferrell, J., Hayward, K., & Young, J. (2008). *Cultural criminology: An invitation*. London: Sage.

Goffman, E. (1968). *Asylums: Essays on the social situation of mental patients and other inmates*. Harmondsworth: Penguin.

Gooch, K. (2017). 'Kidulthood': Ethnography, juvenile prison violence and the transition from 'boys' to 'men.' *Criminology & Criminal Justice, 19*(1), 80–97. https://doi.org/10.1177/1748895817741519.

Harris Review. (2015). *Changing prisons, saving lives: Report of the independent review into self-inflicted deaths in custody of 18–24 year olds*. London: The Crown.

Harvey, J. (2006). *Young men in prison*. Cullompton and Portland, OR: Willan Publishing.

HM Inspectorates of Prisons and Probation (HMIPP). (2017). *HM Chief Inspector of Prisons for England and Wales: Annual report 2016–17*. London: HMIP. Available at https://assets.publishing.service.gov.uk/government/uploads/system/uploads/attachment_data/file/629719/hmip-annual-report-2016-17.pdf. Accessed 22 October 2017.

Howard League for Penal Reform. (2010b). *Access to justice denied: Young adults in prison*. London: Howard League for Penal Reform.

Irwin, J., & Cressey. D. R. (1962). Thieves, convicts and the inmate culture. *Social Problems, 10,* 142–155. https://doi.org/10.2307/799047, https://www.jstor.org/stable/799047.

Jewkes, Y. (2002). *Captive audience: Media, masculinity, and power in prisons*. Cullompton: Willan.

Jewkes, Y. (2005). *Men behind bars: Men and masculinities, 8,* 44–63. https://doi.org/10.1177/1097184X03257452.

Kearon, T. (2012). Alternative representations of the prison and imprisonment: Comparing dominant narratives in the news media and in popular fictional texts. *Prison Service Journal, 199*(January), 4–9.

Kupers, T. A. (2005). Toxic masculinity as a barrier to mental health treatment in prison. *Journal of Clinical Psychology, 61*(6), 713–724. https://doi.org/10.1002/jclp.20105.

Kuppers, T. A. (2001). Rape and the prison code. In D. Sabo, T. Kupers, & W. London (Eds.), *Prison masculinities*. Philadelphia, PA: Temple University Press.

Maguire, D. (2019). Vulnerable prisoner masculinities in an English prison. *Men and Masculinities*. https://doi.org/10.1177/1097184X19888966.

Mason, P. (Ed.). (2006). *Captured by the media: Prison discourse in popular culture*. Cullompton: Willan.

Phillips, C. (2012). *The multicultural prison: Ethnicity, masculinity, and social relations among prisoners*. Oxford: Oxford University Press.

Polk, K. (1994). *When men kill: Scenarios of masculine violence*. Cambridge: Cambridge University Press.

Prior, D., Farrow, K., Hughes, N., Kelly, G., Manders, G., White, S., & Wilkinson, B. (2011). *Maturity, young adults and criminal justice: A literature review*. Birmingham: University of Birmingham.

Prison Reform Trust. (2012). *Old enough to know better?* London: Prison Reform Trust.

Ricciardelli, R. (2015). Establishing and asserting masculinity in Canadian penitentiaries. *Journal of Gender Studies, 24*(2), 170–191. https://doi.org/10.1080/09589236.2013.812513.

Ricciardelli, R., Maier, K., & Hannah-Moffat, K. (2015). Strategic masculinities: Vulnerabilities, risk and the production of prison masculinities. *Theoretical Criminology, 19*(4), 491–513. https://doi.org/10.1177/1362480614565849.

Roberts, M., Stanley, C., & Cavadino, P. (2002). *Young adult offenders*. London: National Association for the Care & Resettlement of Offenders.

Shabazz, R. (2009). "So high you can't get over it, so low you can't get under it": Carceral spatiality and black masculinities in the United States and South Africa. *Souls, 11*(3), 276–294. https://doi.org/10.1080/10999940903088309.

Sim, J. (1994). Tougher than the rest? Men in prison. In T. Newburn & E. A. Stanko (Eds.), *Just boys doing business? Men, masculinities and crime*. London: Routledge.

Sykes, G. (2007). *The society of captives: A study of a maximum security prison*. Princeton, NJ: Princeton University Press.

Tomczak, P. (2018). *Prison suicide: What happens afterwards?* Bristol: Bristol University Press.

Tynan, R. R. (2019). *Young men's experiences of long term imprisonment: Living life*. London: Routledge.

Wilson, A. (2003). Nike trainers—My one true love, without you I am nothing. In J. Androutopolous & A. Georgakopoulo (Eds.), *Discourse constructions of youth identity*. Amsterdam: John Benjamins Publishing Company.

Wright, S., Crewe, B., & Hulley, S. (2016). Suppression, denial, sublimation: Defending against the initial pains of very long life sentences. *Theoretical Criminology*, *21*(2), 225–246. https://doi.org/10.1177/136248061664 3581.

CHAPTER 8

Vulnerable Masculinities: Absent Men and Imagined Futures

8.1   Introduction

In the earlier chapters, I have shown that the gender identities of the men who participated in this study were heavily constructed through aggressive and violent displays. Closer scrutiny of their narrated experiences, however, reveals that this image alone is too superficial; the identities of these men were more complex and contradictory than the common portrayals of prisoners would suggest. In this chapter, I seek to disrupt dominant media, political and, indeed, some academic representations of forms of working-class masculinity, especially those of prisoners. In doing so, my focus will be on the less understood and underacknowledged—yet widespread—gendered vulnerabilities of the men who fill our prisons.

Vulnerability is not often associated with the "hard" and violent (hyper)masculinity that we typically attribute to the figure of the prisoner. Much of the existing scholarship on prison masculinities has tended to focus on the revered, hyper, dominant or hegemonic forms of masculinity, affording scant attention to the men who struggle to navigate their identities at the bottom of prison hierarchies. A third of the men in this study, for instance, were unable to live up to or sustain these widely reported, revered forms of prison masculinity. At various stages in their prison journeys, they were officially categorised as being "vulnerable prisoners". In this chapter, I will firstly explore how this cohort configured their masculinities in the context of the "vulnerable category" and in

© The Author(s) 2021
D. Maguire, *Male, Failed, Jailed,*
Palgrave Studies in Prisons and Penology,
https://doi.org/10.1007/978-3-030-61059-3_8

a segregated penal space. I will show how these men—influenced by their previous prison experiences, statuses and criminal histories—adopted different, more costly and high-risk situationally adaptive strategies in order to negotiate their masculinities at the bottom of prison hierarchies. By exploring their subordinated prison identities, I reveal the dynamic, relational, fragile and spatial elements of prison masculinities.

Following this I will then discuss another important dimension of the gendered vulnerabilities of the participants: their absences as men. I will show how being trapped in "revolving-door" imprisonment led to the men's absence from significant life events. As a result, the respondents experienced subsequent feelings of shame and failure at having been unable to live up to their own—and wider culturally valued—masculine obligations of being both a "protector" and a "provider".

In the final section, I will highlight the extent to which the men mostly longed "to be normal": a "normal" that meant looking to the traditional masculinities of their fathers and past generations to guide them in their crime- and prison-free futures. I will show how these men's imagined futures, post-prison, relied heavily on an outdated breadwinner model that had been unattainable or unsustainable for most of these men in the past.

8.2   VULNERABLE PRISONERS

In the previous chapter, I highlighted how the men's experience of being on the streets, in "care" and alternative education sites provided a solid gender foundation upon which they were able to construct prison masculinities. The men described how they had survived and navigated hypermasculine young adult carceral spaces and the fact that they had, unanimously, welcomed their transition to "con" status. With this shift, they felt that they had reached what constitutes a form of adult prison masculinity. However, from childhood through to adulthood, across these interconnecting sites of extreme exclusion, the pressures of navigating and sustaining normative masculinities—with all of their intrinsic contradictions, fragilities and challenges—would prove to be too much for a third (10) of the respondents. Prison, as Hans Toch (1992) has identified, traps men in hypermasculine performances, long after they can meet the criteria for this identity.

At various stages in their prison journeys, with their alleged shortcomings in meeting masculine ideals having been exposed, these 10 men were compelled to follow the emasculating process of being formally categorised as "vulnerable prisoners" (VPs). Prisons are duty-bound to segregate those who are thought to be at risk of attack and reprisal from mainstream prisoners.[1] This, in many cases, means—as with this prison—having to share the vulnerable prisoners' unit (VPU) with other at-risk (mainly those convicted of sexual offences) prisoners and, in doing so, having one's position near the bottom of the prisoner hierarchy confirmed.

8.2.1 Situationally Stratified VPU Masculinities

The reasons as to why these men went from being mainstream prisoners to sharing the VPU with those convicted of sexual offences varied. All of the respondents were deemed, however, to have gone against—or to have been in breach of—the inmate code (see Clemmer 1958; Copes et al. 2013). None of them identified as being—or were labelled by the other VPs as being—"sex offenders". Mostly, they were believed to have informed on or "grassed" up other criminals. Two of the respondents were suspected of having committed crimes against "their own"—which is to say, bigger and better-connected criminals—and, therefore, faced serious risks in the form of retribution.

Among all lower-status prisoners, a great deal of hierarchical movement still takes place as multiple masculinities are, similarly, configured through the power dynamics of domination and subordination that can be found among the main population. In their paper, in which they explore the situational construction of prisoner identities among sex offenders, Levines and Crewe (2015) have reported subdivisions in prisons whereby those convicted of rape against women have been hierarchically positioned above those convicted of sexually assaulting children. Similar stratifications, as I will shortly discuss in more detail, could be identified among

---

[1] There are rules, regulations and guidelines regarding the running of prisons. Under rule 45, prisoners might be segregated from the main location for two main reasons: (1) as a means of punishment and for the smooth running of the penal establishment, a disruptive prisoner might be segregated and placed in isolation under "good order and discipline" (GOD); (2) the segregation of vulnerable prisoners for their own interest. Unlike segregation for GOD, this is not a form of punishment that limits privileges; it reflects a duty to keep vulnerable prisoners safe.

these respondents as they attempted to salvage some sense of their previously respectable forms of masculinity and prisoner status. The existence of intra-group masculine power struggles did not detract from the collective and individual strategies that were adopted to try to resist their continual "lumping together"—by officers and main location inmates—with what they described as the "beasts" and the "nonces" with whom they shared the Unit.

Alert to their inferior status among main location prisoners, most of the respondents expended a great deal of effort in configuring their masculine identities through opposition to, denigration of and separation from the sex offender "other" who held a still-lower status in the prison hierarchies. This strategy of separation and stratification at the lower end of the prison hierarchies generated a form of solidarity among this VP cohort, as one of them, Scott, comments:

> ...paedophiles seem to know who the other[s]...are...the others they call them "debt heads[2]" you've got them and...the non-sex offenders like me, who stick together...(Scott)

On the whole, this group—in a manner that was entirely consistent with the main population's values—felt that they were in a position of moral superiority over the other inhabitants on the Unit. This othering and dominance over the sex offenders—or "beasts" and "nonces"—proved, as I go on to show, a valuable resource that allowed a number of the participants to salvage some sense of their previous masculine status.

8.2.2   VPU Adaptation Strategies

Sim (1994) has emphasised that the nature of the specific type of penal space contributes to the forms of masculine identities that are configured therein. Hierarchies, Sim has argued, are built on complex horizontal and vertical dimensions of power. The dominant or revered forms of masculinity that are performed by both prisoners and male staff, for instance, will be different in a low-security open prison to those that will be enacted in a high-security prison or a mainstream location, especially when compared with those of denigrated carceral spaces like the VPU.

---

[2] Those who have run up debts with other prisoners that they cannot pay.

In all penal sites, however, masculinities have to be continuously "achieved", are constantly contested and, as such, are fluid or always shifting (Ricciardelli et al. 2015). What was especially interesting about this VP cohort is the fact that, influenced by their previous prison statuses and criminal histories, they adopted a variety of situationally adaptive strategies for "doing masculinity" in a segregated carceral space for low-status prisoners. As I have discussed elsewhere, three distinct—but with some inevitable overlap between them—categories of adaptation stood out: "protest adaptation"; "subversive adaptation" and "pragmatic adaptation" (see Maguire 2019).

8.2.3   Protest as Adaptation

Geoff and Jack, as can be seen from the extracts below, were the main figures among this cohort. Both of them claimed to have well-established pre-VPU reputations and solid criminal credentials:

> ...I've been to two category A [high-security] prisons, I've done about five category B prisons, all long-term...I went on the roof in one jail, dirty protests. I've been caught with mobile phones and drugs, I've been shipped out for assaulting a member of staff in another prison, so a lot of people knew me...(Jack)

> ...I've got bounties on my head...people are trying to do me in...it's exciting for me with someone trying to do me in. I'd love to see them try...(Geoff)

These "solid" prisoner and gangster masculine narratives—proudly shared while being under the prison's protection in the VPU—are fraught with contradictions and tensions that will not be immediately obvious to those who are outside of prison and criminal cultures. To live among "beasts" and "child rapists" and to take official protection from the prison—regardless of the circumstances, and despite one's past criminal exploits and previous hierarchical positioning—erodes any previously revered masculine status. In the eyes of those who inhabit this world and appear to live by the inmate/criminal code, both of these respondents have shown extraordinary weakness that is consistent with subordinated masculinities.

In the relatively small pond that is the VPU space, Geoff and Jack played up to the idea of—and generated significant masculine capital from being—the "big fish". However, their ability to sustain this kind of gender identity was, largely, reliant on importing or salvaging aspects of their previous masculine statuses. For the most part, they tried to do so by performing and enacting these identities through their overt protesting at being on the unit in the first place—as well as denigrating the "other" with whom they were "forced" to live.

Jack reported that he was regularly warned about his treatment and intimidation of sex offenders. His uncontrolled hatred for them had, on occasion, resulted in him being moved to the punishment block for "cooling-off" periods. Similarly, Geoff's resistance to being housed with sex offenders was palpable through his expressions of disgust and shame: "I believe there should be a death sentence for pedophiles because pedophiles can't change…disgusted…I am embarrassed, so embarrassed".

Both Jack and Geoff reported that they had no agency or choice when it came to the decision to move them to the new surroundings of the VPU. They asserted that their current formal statuses as vulnerable prisoners were due to protocol or out of their control. The two men's experiences demonstrate just how easily those with higher-status masculine identities can fall downwards to the lower end of the prison power structures. Once one is at or near the bottom, the likelihood of being able to return to any previous status is extremely low.

8.2.4   Acceptance as Adaptation

Dilan's and Brian's shared adaptive strategy directly contrasts with that of Jack and Geoff. Both Brian and Dilan described having had difficulties and having struggled among the main population for some time before accepting protection from the prison. Brian's troubles started back in 2000 after a "pad" was searched for drugs and he was implicated in having allegedly tipped off the officers about the contraband. Meanwhile, Dilan's difficulties began after he reported his cellmate for the wet towel "bullwhipping" incident that I discussed slightly earlier in the book.

The officers were not so subtle with regard to Dilan's predicament. From that point forward, as he explains, he was shrouded in suspicion—accused of being an informer—and lived in constant fear of being "called out":

I've always worried that somebody's going to say something to me, and I start going bright red – and it will be for fight or flight, which in most cases is fight – and, when you get older, you can't be arsed with all that, that's why I'm on here now…(Dilan)

After six more years of being in and out of prison, Dilan was the victim of a brutal incident involving drugs. Word had got out that Dilan had returned from a domestic visit with a large parcel of cannabis secreted in his anal passage. A large mob, he recounts, barged into his cell, held him down and threatened to forcibly remove the parcel with a spoon—known in prison argot as "spooning". He explained how he feared that "they would come and try it again" and "I got sick of it so I thought 'fuck it'"—and, with this, he sought formal protection status.

Dilan and Brian had served a considerable portion of their prison time as vulnerable prisoners who were segregated on the VPU. Unlike the other respondents, in what can arguably be interpreted as an act of subversion, both of them openly rejected the main location prison culture and its masculine hierarchies that positioned them as being subordinate. They went as far as to suggest that "it takes balls to do prison this way":

…it like undermines me, it's like "you're weak, you've gone on there because you're weak and you can't hack it out on the mains", which, in a way, it is a way out. I put my hands up, I couldn't…I'm on here because I've had a hard time, I've been turned over and all the rest of it, people jumped on me. I'm on here for an easy life, at the end of the day. I think most of them, given the choice out there – if they had the balls – would be on here as well…(Brian)

Brian and Dilan accepted that they had struggled to live up to mainstream prison masculinities and admitted that they found it a relief to be away from the main location. Brian went as far as to reject the futile jostling for position in the main part of the prison and saw his acceptance of his vulnerability as an act of courage and resistance against the dominant prison identities.

For Brian and Dilan, their strategy of adaptation was one way of subverting the vulnerable category to, instead, suggest that they had courage and were not afraid to show a spirit of resistance. They reasoned that serving time among the sex offender population—who are not as invested in prison hypermasculine culture and, as others have shown, are usually much older, middle class and less likely to be embroiled in illicit drug use/dealing and the disputes that follow (Levines and Crewe 2015)—would make for an easier and "chilled jail time". It is worth cautioning, here, that we must not overestimate the extent of Brian's and Dilan's agency in opting out of these mainstream power struggles to move to the relatively drug- and hypermasculine-free VPU. Both claimed that they had been forced to embrace their new VP status as a result of acts of staff incompetence or betrayal. It is more accurate, though, to suggest that their strategies for adapting to their vulnerable status were linked more closely to the fact that their pre-prison/criminal masculine identities were far less established than those of prisoners like Jack and Geoff.

8.2.5   Pragmatic Adaptation

The other men in this VP cohort were pragmatic in terms of how they adapted to the unit and configured their masculinity, having been placed in the formal category of being "vulnerable". A key strategy was to avoid acknowledging the predatory crimes of the "others" as well as sources like newspapers and other forms of media that might expose them to the truth about the whom they were living with. For Malcolm, "it is not too bad…don't get me wrong, I don't want to know what they've done regarding children and stuff like that…put it into the back of your mind, what's the point, just forget it". He goes on to say that if he, the lads and the staff "thought about it too much it would drive them mad". Likewise, Lance comments that it is "that mentality that, if you don't know what they're in for, you can turn a blind eye; when you know what they're in for, it's a different ball game". His difficult times in the Unit, he observes, are when the crimes that have been committed by the "others" are exposed as being so awful that it is impossible to deny the type of predatory men among whom they are forced to live and, accordingly, by whom they, too, are "tarred":

> When you find out what they're in for – read it in the paper and then you know – and you see them on the landing, you just want to crack them, you want to leather them up and down, but then you're just causing more trouble for yourself…you've got to learn to live with them, when it's people that you shouldn't be living with, you shouldn't have to be nowhere near them, but unfortunately you are…(Lance)

Among this pragmatic category of respondents, they justified the suppressing of their perceived masculine obligation or compulsion to act against those labelled as predatory "others". Deeply ingrained masculine notions as being protectors of the weak, women and children have been well-documented (Segal 2007). So, too, has the expectation in criminal and prison cultures to practice—or to be seen to advocate—retribution (and, by doing so enhancing/reinforcing revered masculinity) against those who commit predatory offences against the vulnerable, innocent and defenseless. For these prisoners, though, it was not worth the risk of facing sanctions or of compromising their protective space. The majority of this VP cohort lived daily with the contradictory pressures of trying to prove that they did not meet the core criteria of the unit while, at the same time, living with the fear and insecurity of losing their place in it. Wayne—a respondent who was intuitive to the function of the "other" or of the role of the subordinated in gender configurations—comments:

> ...sexual offenders, people who tell tales and people in debt who go to protection wings, VP wings, are looked upon as scum. I mean, there is always the argument that we all need somebody to look down on...(Wayne)

As much as they try to deny their surroundings, the respondents have to face the daily and emasculating reality of what it means to be vulnerable prisoners. The whole prison regime—and all movements—centre upon the priority of protecting them from the main population. The relief or joy of being visited by a loved one—events that are usually scheduled at different times from those of (and segregated from) the main population—is marred by the constant abuse that the respondents face when being escorted to and from the visitor centre, as Scott explains below:

> ...we all get called, we get threatened, when we are moved around the prison there's those that throw things out of the window at you: "who'd visit you, you fucking beast" and all that – "nonce"...I just cover myself and look the other way, it sickens me. I'm a grandad and I've got a daughter...(Scott)

All of the movements of the prisoners—going to and from forms of work and education—are managed in such a way as to allow the VPs to be moved first and to be safely back on the wing before the mainstream men are free to return to their wings. Gym visits, healthcare appointments and so on are often secondary, timetabled to fit around segregation arrangements to keep the VPs from the mainstream prisoners. Even when on the unit, and despite their pragmatism at dealing with neighbours, they are reminded of their inferior prison identity:

> I don't like the term "vulnerable" …you feel ashamed, I guess…unless an officer knows you and knows what you're in for, they just treat you the same…(Ken)

8.2.6   Liminal Prison Masculinity

The focus, up to this point, has been on those who have been officially categorised as being vulnerable prisoners and are segregated in the VPU. A core part of the argument that I have presented throughout this book is that, in penal spaces—indeed, in all of their sites of exclusion—men are forced to negotiate a dynamic, precarious and liminal existence between subordinated and normalised (prison) masculinities. In prison, manhood is a tenuous condition that is always subject to the possibility of being lost (Kupers 2001). As I show with the following two case studies, lower-status prisoners on the main location are at the sharp end of this prison reality. They must utilise a whole spectrum of high-risk and extraordinarily dangerous adaptive strategies so as to avoid being culturally and institutionally emasculated. In prison argot, they have adopted the strategies that are known as "blending it" and "blocking off" to stave off the highly denigrated and subordinate vulnerable status.

"Blending it" is a term that describes how some men try to continue to "blend" into, or perform, mainstream prison identities—even when their behaviour or offence, if exposed, would be deemed to have transgressed the conditions of the criminal/inmate code and, as such, fallen short of the expected forms of masculine conduct. In their attempts to embody normalised versions of prison masculinity, male prisoners conceal or deny their code breaches; instead, they amplify their criminal and prisoner credentials in order to present a more acceptable frontstage performance (Goffman 1969; Jewkes 2005).

Paul—who was not in the VP cohort but was part of the wider study—revealed during his interview that he had informed on, or given a witness statement against, an individual who had brutally assaulted him. This had culminated in the perpetrator being sentenced to years in prison.

Paul accepted that this decision to report the incident has marked him as being a "grass" or an "informer". However, rather than taking up VP status and living with "nonces" under the protection of the prison, he adopted the potentially deadly strategy of "blending" in with the general population.

As Paul continued with the interview, he casually stated that—during a previous prison term—the individual against whom he had given evidence had been in the same jail as him. To avoid bumping into him and fighting every day, Paul took the decision to go "on protection" and "keep a low profile" until his attacker had moved on. Other individuals who were in the VP cohort were clear that, once it is "out there" that you have taken "protection" from the prison, a return to the main location—even under a new prison term—is both incredibly dangerous and unlikely to last. Unlike Geoff, Jack and some of the other respondents, Paul's relatively low criminal/prisoner status is perhaps why—at least up until the time of being interviewed—he had been able to successfully "blend" it. Carrying the emotional stress and daily fear that he might be found out at some point was, for him, preferable to dealing with the emasculation, shame and humiliation that comes with living in the VPU. As he explains:

> We can see the VPs out the window and so all it takes is for me to be on VP and someone spot me from my area and that's it. It gets spread around the town that I was on the VP and everyone will start, because VPs are rapists and sex offenders, that's what I'll get associated with. I'd rather risk it on here…(Paul)

Another high-risk and costly strategy for preserving one's main location masculine status and for dealing with the threat of serious violence is "blocking off": intentionally going against prison authority/discipline to instigate being "dragged" off and put in the punishment "block" or "segregation unit" and, consequently, out of harm's way. Isaac explained how, while in prison—a long way from his own local one—he found himself in a position in which he felt that "blocking off" was his only option. He spoke of how he had been confronted on the wing by a mob who accused him of having robbed the elderly relative of another prisoner:

> …he said "you robbed my uncle" ra ra ra…it genuinely wasn't me…I don't rob old people. He said "I am getting you stabbed up"…I thought "fuck this, I don't know where this knife is going to come from"…shut

my door, packed all my stuff up and then got opened up for dinner – and then a lad come in and stabbed me. It was only in the leg, but I thought "fuck this, it's not going to end here", and so I smashed my pad up and a screw came up...I kicked the door in his face and said "take me down the block"...then they shipped me out...(Isaac)

Having spent much of his life in and out of prison, Isaac was only too aware of the danger of being associated with crimes against the elderly; he knew that asking for protection from the prison would only add credibility to the allegation, thereby serving to further emasculate him and profoundly compromise his safety and status in the prison. "Blocking off" proved to be effective; the punishment block, housing unruly and high-risk/security prisoners, is a very different penal space to the VPU. Prisoners are usually kept in solitary confinement, with the added loss of most of their privileges and remission. These, though, are sacrifices that, for Isaac, were preferable to the prospect of being formally labelled as being "vulnerable" and a "wrong un". In this way, he not only preserved but, actually, probably enhanced his prisoner masculine status.

8.3   Life Behind the Door: Absent Men

Another form of vulnerability—one that is not so explicitly defined but one that nevertheless ran through all of the respondents' gendered and classed trajectories—related to their absence or perceived failure as men. Regardless of their prison categorisations—segregated or mainstream, subordinated or revered—a common thread that united most of these men was the fact that they had spent more time in prison than "on the out". On the whole, the extent of the respondents' time away was not the result of having served single long-term prison sentences. It was, rather, as one respondent put it, "life in prison on a multiple instalment plan". Mark was the only "lifer"; two others were serving terms of over a decade. The respondents were mostly classed as being "persistent" offenders or "career" criminals; over the course of their long criminal histories, they had served numerous prison sentences. Sometimes, their sentences were just a matter of months for "something petty"; on other occasions, they had served sentences that had run into years. Most of the respondents talked of being out for only short periods of time before finding themselves back inside, locked away from the significant life events that help to shape and sustain meaningful masculine identities.

Their absence as (grand)sons, brothers, fathers and intimate partners seemed to be felt much more profoundly when they were coping with extremely difficult life situations. Coming from neighbourhoods that have high rates of crime and violence, several of the men had to deal with life events while they were in prison that most people would never have to face. Isaac, for instance—having spent much of his life trapped in revolving-door cycles of imprisonment—lost his father to a violent murder that took place during one of his short spells of freedom. Just weeks later, Isaac found himself back inside. During this time, he lost both his younger brother—to an accidental drug overdose—and, then, his mother, following a short illness:

> I mean, when my dad got killed in 2007, I kind of blamed myself a bit for that really......if I was with him, it would never have happened, no one would have dared hit my dad if I was with him...I should have been there...then my brother died on the last sentence...if I'd not come to prison for him, he'd still be here. My mam died two weeks after that...(Isaac)

Another respondent, Cooper, spoke of his mother's "suspected" murder just days before he was given his previous sentence. Jerry noted that the toughest jail term that he had ever served was when his partner was raped while he was in prison. He then explained how, during another term, he had lost his sister to suicide after she was sent to prison for the first time. Then, there was Dwayne; just minutes into his interview, it became apparent that he was in the process of trying to come to terms with the loss of his newborn son just days earlier.

The moving extract from the interview, as presented below—following Dwayne's refusal to abandon the interview and his insistence on continuing—captures his grief and reflects the difficulty that he experienced at not only being locked away as a grieving father but also at the fact that he was not able to fulfil his responsibilities in terms of being present for his partner:

> I pleaded with the judge to not send me to prison, but he gave me four weeks, which means only doing two – and, with me doing big sentences, I thought "two weeks is nothing", but I was going to miss...my baby's birth...But, like, I've come to jail, missed it and then found out that he was born with brain damage and then died. He lived a week; he lived a

week...I need to be out there to look after her. I'd like to be able to go to the funeral, not in this [special escape tracksuit], I don't want to be at a funeral, my own kid's funeral, in this...(Dwayne)

What makes Dwayne's case even more tragic is the fact that, after meeting and settling down with his partner—and getting "the flat sorted"—he kept out of trouble for over two years. During this stable period, he was then arrested and charged for a historical offence. After being sentenced, a rare mistake meant that there was an opportunity for him to abscond from the courtroom: an opportunity that he seized. He explained that he only wanted to be out until after his son was born. He was subsequently picked up before this could happen, though, and deemed to be an escape risk. As a result, he was made to wear "stripes" everywhere, even to his son's funeral.[3]

Several of the other respondents talked of having experienced the death of a parent or a significant other while they were away. These losses—and the struggles/suffering of those close to them on the outside—brought their absence from the outside world sharply into focus and, with it, a sense of failure and shame for being unable to fulfil what they considered to be traditional working-class masculine obligations to protect and provide for their families. Dwayne's distress, for example, was partly caused by the fact that he was not able to "be there" and to look after his partner. Isaac, similarly, felt that, as the eldest child, he had let his recently deceased father down by not being present to prevent his brother's drug-related death and "not being there" to look after the remaining siblings. Cooper, too—as he expresses in the words below—felt the weight of not fulfilling the responsibilities of the oldest male sibling after the death of his mother:

...not having my mum, and my brothers growing up in jail, it reflects on me, I feel guilty for that, knowing that I showed him what I didn't want to show him if you know what I mean...I sit here and I think that's my fault that, knowing that I haven't had a physical part in it, but I have emotionally and mentally [been a] part of it, it does, it does my head in, because I'm like his stepdad in a way...(Cooper)

[3] Highly visible blue prison uniform and brightly striped yellow uniform for prisoners who are categorised as posing escape risks.

It is notable that Cooper felt that his absence as a "father figure" had contributed to his younger brothers following him into the prison system.

8.3.1   Locked Inside

The respondents offered snapshots of some of the highly difficult life events with which many of them had to cope as part of their "revolving-door" cycle of existence alternating between prison and their estates. With such high incidences of tragedy and violence, many of them were left to deal with incredibly tough emotions while they were in a prison cell. The respondents were not only isolated from the people who were closest to them, but also surrounded by men who, given the chance, would "ruthlessly" exploit any display of emotion/grief as a sign of weakness (see Laws 2019).

Aware of this, Isaac expressed his anxiety about the prospect of losing anybody else while he was in prison. He shared his fear of not being able to conceal his emotions sufficiently well:

> ...that's the only thing that scares me these days about coming to prison is if someone else dies, because you can't show that emotion...[When] my brother died, I never came out of my pad for three weeks, I was on a sports course and I never finished that...(Isaac)

Isaac felt safer hiding himself away in his cell rather than exposing his grief and vulnerable state to the other men on the wing. Revealing too much emotion in the prison environment brings unwanted attention (Laws 2019). As Cooper explains below, exploitation and bullying campaigns often begin to manifest themselves under the guise of sympathy during tough times:

> ...when mum died...I was "under the weather", you can call it, I was depressed, I didn't want to talk to nobody and people started trying to take liberties, "oh yeah, I've got baccy if you want it"...Then they never did anything about it when it didn't get paid back...but then I started to wise up a bit...(Cooper)

"Wising up" for Cooper meant that he did not allow himself to get too deep into debt with those who were offering him credit during his tough times. What, on the surface, looks like an act of generosity could quickly turn into a debt that could not be paid and, consequently, a highly compromising position for the debtor.

This is not to suggest that prisoners do not support each other through "hard times". There is some evidence, in penal scholarship, that documents instances of prisoners showing compassion and care to each other through various struggles (Cohen and Taylor 1981; Evans and Wallace 2008). Over recent decades, there has been a movement of prisoners supporting each other to combat the issue of substance misuse by means of self-help groups/communities (see Kopak et al. 2015). Many prisoners have been trained as "Listeners" by the Samaritans so that they can offer peer support to suicidal prisoners (see Perrin and Blagden 2014).

A number of the men noted that fellow prisoners had offered them support in various guises when they were going through tough times. However, as Dillon suggests, it is difficult to strike the right balance; unofficial gestures of help from individuals—if they are to be accepted at all—have to be accepted with caution:

> ...you see, a lad who maybe his girlfriend has left him and the lads try cheering him up, or somebody that's not got any family and they've got no money, there's a lot of guys that help other guys out. But that can also be turned on its head because people can do things for people and they can turn it on the head by saying "I've done that for you now [you] owe me this, you've got to bring drugs in for me on a visit" and stuff like that, so there is a fine balance...(Dillon)

Similarly, Mark remarked on the at-once caring and "ruthless" natures of his fellow prisoners:

> ...I mean, we all have bad stages...might have had a bereavement outside, or a bad phone call, they might have had a "dear John" letter...I've seen cons being caring and considerate sometimes...but they can also be fucking ruthless, so you've got the other end of the stick, haven't you?...(Mark)

Even at the height of his grief, Dwayne was alert to those who might try to take advantage of him at such a difficult time:

> ...when they heard about my bairn dying, all my mates kept asking if I had this or if I need that, but you do see the downside and you see bullies in here...(Dwayne)

This anxiety about the prospect of being exploited by other prisoners when trying to deal with challenging life events meant that some of the respondents, like Isaac, were very careful about how they managed their grief/emotions outside of their cells.

Building on Goffman's (1969) dramaturgical model, drawing on his work on the *Presentation of Self*, the penal scholars Crewe (2009) and Jewkes (2005) have conceptualised the ways in which prisoners manage their private emotional selves in contrast to their public presentations of identity in terms of "backstage" and "frontstage" behaviour. In the prison setting, as Jewkes (2005) has noted, backstage—or, in this case, time alone in a cell—is where the "basic ontological security system is restored" (p. 54). While they are in this isolated space, individuals can leave their "bodily, gestural and verbal codes" and their hard-masculine personas at the door.

Frontstage, meanwhile, is where the respondents—as demonstrated throughout this study—present their public, gendered performances: ones that they have refined over a "long process of socialization into male-dominated subcultures as a child, adolescent, and adult" (Jewkes 2005, p. 54). Isaac's experiences show that there are some instances in which the pressure to maintain one's frontstage masculine identity is simply too difficult. For the sake of self-preservation, he found himself having to hide away in his cell—and to retreat backstage with his emotional pain—until he felt that he was able to put on a convincing and appropriate gendered performance once more.

Many of these respondents would have established—early on in their classed and gendered trajectories—that public displays of emotional pain or struggles significantly compromise working-class hegemonic performances of masculinity (Connell 1995; Segal 2007). Such displays certainly serve to undermine dominant masculinities in carceral spaces (De Viggiani 2012; Evans and Wallace 2008; Laws 2019). Sadly, however, it is men who come from impoverished, complex and violent backgrounds who are more likely than most—as can be seen from the testimonies of these respondents—to have to come to terms with exceptionally difficult life events, often while they are in the confines of the hostile and enclosed space of the prison.

This adversity in the respondents' lives has meant that they have had to devise well-measured, brave, masculine "frontstage" performances—often in the face of extraordinary circumstances that include the alleged murder of their parents, sibling suicides, drug overdoses and the loss of a child.

Inevitably, there were also instances of other less extreme—and, arguably, more typically difficult—issues relating to the prisoners' outside lives that they had to process while being locked inside.

8.3.2   *Absent Fathers*

Having experienced feelings of failure about being unable to meet their masculine obligations as sons, siblings and partners, their cycles of revolving imprisonment meant that many of the respondents were also absent fathers. A third of the study participants reported that they were biological fathers; several of the others mentioned that they were step-fathers to the children of their partners. Walker (2010), in her study of recently released prisoners who have children, found that—as with some of the respondents—their (compromised) roles as fathers prompted them to reflect on the cost of their imprisonment more than almost any other circumstance. Some of the fathers whom I interviewed for this study calculated the cost or pains of incarceration by considering their absence from the lives of their children, partners and other family members:

> I got three kids and two grandkids. I thought it was about giving my kids everything they wanted, but it wasn't…they'd of [*sic*] rather have had me around than sat in jail, I provided for them everything that they needed but I wasn't there on an emotional level when they needed me to be there…(Andy)

Andy did not go into detail about the impact on his children but suggested that his continued imprisonment has had a significantly nega-tive effect on them. Moreover, he worries that his children are a "bit too [much]" like he was at their age. Andy's and the other fathers' experiences resonate with existing research on the subject that has high-lighted the ways in which imprisonment puts an enormous strain on family ties, amplifies the levels of deprivation that families may already be experiencing and increases the risk of intergenerational offending (Dyer 2005; Lösel et al. 2012). The fathers whom I interviewed for this study were aware of the cost and hardship that their families had to bear as a result of their incarceration. They were painfully aware, too, of their lost opportunities to be fathers:

...got released October 07, met up with my son, I felt like the floor was swallowing me because I haven't seen him since he was three, he was about 16 or something, he just done his exams and did real well and I went back to the hostel and started smoking gear, they asked for a drug test and I refused and came back...(Mark)

Mark explained that his reaction to being confronted with his lost and damaged relationship with his son, as a father, was to retreat to his hostel and to smoke "gear" (heroin). As a life-sentenced prisoner who was out on license, he was recalled back to prison, highlighting the perpetual cycle of cost and loss that some of these respondents and their families have to endure.

For other participants, their failures as fathers were marked by how many of their children's birthdays and Christmases, they had ended up having to spend in prison. These dates marked some of the respondents' "hardest days in jail" (Christian). These "absent father" experiences support Thomas Ugelvik's (2014) assertion that the deprivation of family life—especially with regard to contact with children—is one of the most painful aspects of incarceration. An important aspect of this pain, Ugelvik has found, is the male prisoner's inability to live up to the modern fatherhood ideal and to meet the shifting cultural expectations of fathers. These men's feelings of failure have intensified in the context of changing and binary definitions of contemporary fatherhood (Ugelvik 2014; Walker 2010). "Good" and responsible fathers are expected to be emotionally present and actively involved in the lives and welfare of their children. In contrast to this is the "deficit model" of the absent "bad" father who abandons his paternal responsibilities in pursuit of selfish agendas. Many of these overly simplified binary debates surrounding notions of "good" or "bad" ("feckless" or absent fathers) are part of the wider discourse on the so-called "crisis of masculinity".

The experiences of these imprisoned fathers were more nuanced than those that are suggested by the binary or false dichotomy that has been set up between "good" or "bad" fathers. My interviews with the respondents revealed that they typically had complex and difficult relationships with the mothers of their children and, in many cases, with their children themselves. Some noted that they wanted to have a more active role in their child's life but—as has been well-reported in penal scholarship—the unique conditions of incarceration are incompatible with family life.

In their attempts to avoid compromising their hard-masculine exteriors with outside emotional baggage—and, in some cases, to minimise their own levels of pain and worrying about their loved ones—a number of the participants reported that they had found it easier to end all outside contact. By severing their contact with their children, as Isaac decided to do, male prisoners feel that not only can they preserve a solid emotional masculine front but they can also, in some way, protect their child. Such decisions represent painful attempts to be good fathers:

> I would never let her bring my son to [a] place like this and see me in here. I don't want him to have anything to do with it. I don't even like talking to him on the phone because I have to lie...(Isaac)

Several of the respondents explained that there were times at which they felt that they were doing the right thing as fathers. Equally, though, others admitted that there were times at which they had encountered difficulty in putting their families first.

In his research into the experiences of imprisoned fathers, Dyer (2005) made similar claims, noting that some prisoners have "antisocial and egocentric behaviours and attitudes" (p. 202) that impede their priorities as fathers. Several of the informants believed that their chaotic criminal lifestyles, drug- and alcohol-induced hedonistic pursuits and the fact that they were continuously in and out of prison inevitably led to breakups, "betrayals" or "dear Johns" and, consequently, separation (often acrimonious) and/or decisions to distance themselves from their children.

Indeed, under such circumstances—as Lösel et al. have highlighted—the experiences of men who return from prison to relationships and families are not always positive ones—they are not always welcomed—and this can detrimentally impact the children and the man's partner. In many cases, this puts families at risk and can hinder resettlement efforts, thereby contributing to a father's speedier return to incarceration (Lösel et al. 2012).

Prison was damaging on many levels for these participants and those closest to them. The men felt that they had failed to meet basic masculine ideals and responsibilities. This sense of failure was accompanied by feelings of having to manipulate and deeply suppress their grief and/profound emotional pain in order to adapt to—and facilitate the easier navigation of—the prison space. Such adaptation strategies, though, only serve to contribute to the continued construction of problematic and dysfunctional forms of masculinity, culminating in the men being released back into their troubled environments with few solutions and, perhaps, more difficulties than before they were most recently incarcerated.

8.4   IMAGINED FUTURES

8.4.1   Role Models

As we approached the end of the interview process, I asked each respondent whether they had any role models and how they imagined their futures post-prison. Almost every single one of the men struggled to identify role models, with 23 out of the 30 claiming that they did not have any. Several of the respondents were genuinely stumped by the question and took some time to ponder their responses. Five of the men named their fathers as being the men to whom they looked up. As Christian explains below, this respect for their fathers was linked to their work ethic or how they fulfilled their "breadwinner" obligations:

> ...he's a proud man and he's done well for himself, he don't drink, he's got a beautiful home...he was like a proper man, he'd make sure we'd have food on the table all the time...(Christian)

The men looked up to their fathers because of their success as protectors and providers—success that they had achieved through legitimate hard work. Gibson, however, notes that his role model was only "possibly his dad" because of his more dodgy "little schemes" for earning money—albeit ones that were "never real high-risk things". Billy also chooses his hardworking self-employed father—but quickly adds that he has chosen other role models, too, because of their reputations as criminals or business entrepreneurs. He explains:

> ...when you are young and impressionable, you would read books on the Krays and think "I want to be like them", and you would think that you was like them when you weren't really...I like Alan Sugar, Kenneth Noye, I

respect him, I've actually met him and he's a good bloke.[4] I was in prison with him for quite a while.

Warren—like the other respondents—was taken aback by the question of role models and struggled to identify anyone. After a long thoughtful pause, though, he says:

I don't know about role models, as such, but I would love a lifestyle where I could wear a suit, a real suit, and walk the streets and click, clack, in nice Savile Row shoes...(Warren)

Further exploring their ideas around what meaningful masculinities might look like—and in an attempt to include more of the respondents—I extended the role model question by asking them what qualities, in their opinion, characterised a real man:

...a man has to...if he's married and got children, go out and work and provide for his family, looks after his family and just respects anyone that respects them...(Joe)

...what makes a man, one that works and provides for his kids, I can't stand people that have kids and don't provide for them...(Marvin)

...being able to support his family, being able to work for his family, being brave and being sensible and having polite manners...(Cooper)

These responses were typical of all of the participants, almost as though they were reading from the same script of hegemonic masculine ideals: the man has to "provide", he has to be "brave", "strong" (in character) and have "determination", "morals" and "respect". The core and pervasive masculine discourse that had significant meaning in all of their lives—and the idea that came up time and time again throughout their narratives—was the notion that a man must be a "protector", "provider" or "breadwinner". Against the powerful backdrop of political and policy-related rhetoric that suggests the existence of "intergenerational cultures of worklessness" (see also Macdonald et al. 2014), the high value that the

---

[4] Kenneth Noye is an English criminal who is said to have been involved in the famous Brinks MAT bullion robbery and later stabbed and killed a detective who was investigating the crime. He is currently serving a life sentence for a "road rage" murder that he committed in 1996.

men placed on the "breadwinner" model was, to a large extent, inspired by the respondents' role-model fathers or other men of that generation from their neighbourhoods. The cruel irony was not lost on me, or on the respondents, that the attributes for "being a man" that they held so uncompromisingly close were impossible to fulfil from a prison cell. Mark explicitly points to this failure—this inability—to live up to the masculine ideal:

> *DM*: What qualities make a man?
>
> *Mark*: Being able to cope, being able to help your spouse, being able to look after them...I'm not very masculine at the minute, I don't feel...because I can't look after my girlfriend, I'm a let-down, if anything...I don't see violence as masculinity...yeah, it's to be the provider...

Mark's words reveal a more complex picture of prisoner masculinity than that which is often portrayed. Like most of the other respondents, he felt that he had failed or was a "let-down" because he was not able to provide or to be there for the people who were closest to him outside. These words, together with the perceived failures that I have documented in previous sections, reveal how prison is—in many ways—an emasculating experience. It is notable that, despite failing to sustain their own masculine ideals for any prolonged period while "on the out", the time that the men had lost to imprisonment was often cited as being the main reason for their perceived shortcomings as men. It was deeply concerning, as I go on to show in the next section, that many of the respondents were heavily reliant on the same unattainable or unsustainable traditional working-class hegemonic ideals for their imagined crime- and prison-free futures.

8.4.2   Domesticity

When discussing their futures post-prison, an almost consistent and troubling theme that emerged was the respondents' dependence on outdated notions of masculinity and femininity and domesticity as a route to freedom or "normality":

> ...what I want to do in the future, obviously, I want to gain things, a good job, a decent bird and a good place to live, not coming back to prison and things like that...(Hough)

> ...I tried so many times to not get involved, to get away, but, like, they're actually good mates, but I've got to get away from all of that now because I want kids and want to live a normal life, work and things like that...coming home to your missus and kids and things like that. That's all I want, really: a normal life...(Dwayne)

The respondents' reliance on, or belief in, domesticity as a "way out" of offending and incarceration was, in some respects, not misplaced. It was clear that, for many of them, their most stable and sustained periods of freedom were when they were with a partner and had responsibilities. It was when they felt that they had something—a function, a role—as a man:

> ...I was very, very, very determined and I think the girlfriend that I had at the time had quite a big impact on me, her getting pregnant...I sort of had my son as a responsibility and I wanted to do the right thing...then things started breaking down with her and that is when it started going wrong, I let myself be influenced by the lads that I was with...until our relationship broke down, everything was fine...(Marcus)

Lee, too, was aware that—even from a young age—the experience of being in a relationship had a significant bearing on the type of masculine conduct that he exhibited:

> I was taking cars but, then, at that age, I took more of a liking to the lasses as well. So that kept me out of jail, you know, just being with the lasses, I was in with a new set of friends...I got with Rachel...And that was good for a good year, I stayed out of complete crime, no crime whatsoever, no thought of crime or anything. Then we started arguing, she started...I don't know...it just went bad...my mate's rung me up one night and he said "oh look, I'm driving past that estate right now, are you coming?" And as he drove past, I've jumped in the car, and I've never seen her again...(Lee)

Heterosexual relationships, waged work and taking responsibility are seen by many of these men as being the main components of "doing masculinity" right. According to desistance scholarship, these are the key values that help men to ensure that they cease offending. What stands out from Marcus's and Lee's experiences, however, is that—just as in the workplace, as I discussed in Chapter 5—when things get too difficult, many men retreat to all-male groups and to a default form of protest masculinity that has constituted the basis of their identity from an early age.

Most of the respondents' histories have shown that—whether in a job or in relationships—they have been unable to totally sever their ties with their male peers from "the estate" or "jail" and to fully distance themselves from all criminal activity. Once they had separated from their intimate partners, the trend was typically that instances of drug- and alcohol-use—and criminal and violent activities—would increase, often followed by a return to prison. In the extract below, Billy reflectively recognises the fragility of the idea of pursuing a pathway to "normality" through domesticity:

> ...I always used to think, "if I had a good girlfriend"...I had a place with her and a decent job, used to think them things would be the things to keep me out of prison, but they haven't, because I've had them all...I don't think you ever become rehabilitated fully, maybe people just stop and run out of steam, they can't take no more of prison. There is always that voice inside you, you could have it so good and have a good job, a good family life but there'd always be, to me personally, the side to me was [*sic*] somebody could offer you something and you would risk it and end up losing all that...no matter how much money I'm earning, how much I love or marry...Maybe children would calm me a little and make me sit down and think...(Billy)

Even Billy—and a minority of the other respondents who recognised the past failures of domesticity or work to "settle" them down—still held on to the belief that the right job and/or partner or children would release them from their cycle of crime and incarceration. This is understandable—as the only legitimate respectable masculinities to which many of them looked up or had ever known were those of the "breadwinners" from their fathers' generations.

Their street- and prison-based transitions meant that many of the respondents had experienced extremely limited exposure—and had gained little understanding of—some of the fundamental societal changes that now affected them, including the seismic shift from heavy industry to the service sector and nature of labour relations that have changed as a consequence. Although currently trapped in the sort of protest masculinities that have been described by Connell (1995), most of them aspire to live up to core hegemonic ideals: to legitimately provide for themselves and their families, and to be strong and present fathers, sons and partners.

Sadly, most of the respondents do not yet currently possess the necessary social, cultural and masculine capital to legitimately live up to their gender aspirations. The structural poverty that contributed to their criminal and prison journeys is still in place in their respective neighbourhoods, and the institutions that have housed them over crucial and formative years have done little to inform or equip them to meet the challenges on release. Rather, as I have shown in this chapter—together with the preceding ones—the protest masculinities that the respondents have adapted and amplified for the sake of being able to negotiate spaces of exclusion have kept them trapped in a powerful vortex of marginalisation, exclusion and incarceration.

8.5   Conclusion

In this chapter, I have highlighted some of the less-recognised aspects of prison masculinities. I have charted the men's vulnerabilities, failings, fragilities and desires to live up to the masculine respectability of past generations. In doing so, I have shown that, although most of them found it to be near impossible to break away from their destructive protest masculine trajectories that originated from their early childhoods, the process of trying to sustain these "exaggerated" masculinities in penal spaces proved to be too difficult to sustain for a third of the respondents. Officially categorised as being "vulnerable", coupled with their segregation on the VPU, these men—regardless of their prior status—have plummeted so as to be near the bottom of the prison masculine hierarchy: a position from which a return is unlikely. By making full use of Connell's hierarchal concept of "hegemonic masculinity", I have revealed how—within extreme penal spaces—these vulnerable prisoners have adjusted and adapted to their all-too-easy falls from hegemonic or dominant statuses to varying levels of subordination.

For all of the respondents—regardless of their prison status—the configuration of their criminal and prison masculinities was, by its nature, indicative of their continued absence as men "on the out[side]". This culminated in their failure to meet what are the, arguably, more culturally valued masculine obligations of the protector and the provider. Their inability to fulfil the expectations of their roles as elder sons, siblings and partners was, the respondents recognised, a high price that many regretted having had to pay. Their absence as fathers was overtly acknowledged as being the greatest cost of their imprisonment.

The respondents' sadness at their perceived failures was compounded by the necessity of having to manage extraordinarily painful life situations "backstage" in the isolation of a prison cell. Their imagined futures, free from these pains of imprisonment, rested heavily on the prospect of the "breadwinner" model that—for most of the men—has been unattainable or unsustainable in the past. Prison has not equipped these men in such a way that they will be able to readily navigate the structural challenges that they will face on their release. Rather, the experience of imprisonment has served to intensify the same masculine traits that led to their marginalisation and exclusion in the first instance, thereby trapping these men in the revolving-door cycle of imprisonment The more sentences that they serve, the more entrenched their exclusion "on the out"—and the more elusive their role as provider and protector—becomes.

REFERENCES

Clemmer, D. (1958). *The prison community*. New York: Holt, Rinehart & Winston.

Cohen, S., & Taylor, L. (1981). *Psychological survival: The experience of long-term imprisonment* (2nd ed.). Harmondsworth: Penguin.

Connell, R. (1995). *Masculinities*. Cambridge: Polity.

Copes, H., Brookman, F., & Brown, A. (2013). Accounting for violations of the convict code. *Deviant Behavior, 34*(10), 841–858. https://doi.org/10.1080/01639625.2013.781444.

Crewe, B. (2009). *The prisoner society: Power, adaptation and social life in an English prison*. Oxford: Oxford University Press.

de Viggiani, N. (2012). Trying to be something you are not: Masculine performances within a prison setting. *Men and Masculinities, 15*(3), 271–291. https://doi.org/10.1177/1097184X12448464.

Dyer, W. J. (2005). Prison, fathers, and identity: A theory of how incarceration affects men's paternal identity. *Fathering: A Journal of Theory, Research, and Practice about Men as Fathers, 3*(3), 201–219. https://doi.org/10.3149/fth.0303.201.

Evans, T., & Wallace, P. (2008). A prison within a prison? The masculinity narratives of male prisoners. *Men and Masculinities, 10,* 484–507. https://doi.org/10.1177/1097184X06291903.

Goffman, E. (1969). *The presentation of self in everyday life*. London: Allen Lane.

Jewkes, Y. (2005). *Men behind bars: Men and masculinities, 8,* 44–63. https://doi.org/10.1177/1097184X03257452.

Kopak, A. M., Dean, L. V., Proctor, S. L., Miller, L., & Hoffman, G. N. (2015). Effectiveness of the rehabilitation for addicted prisoners trust (RAPt) programme. *Journal of Substance Use, 20*(4), 254–261. https://doi.org/10.3109/14659891.2014.904938.

Kuppers, T. A. (2001). Rape and the prison code. In D. Sabo, T. Kupers, & W. London (Eds.), *Prison masculinities*. Philadelphia, PA: Temple University Press.

Laws, B. (2019). The return of the suppressed: Exploring how emotional suppression reappears as violence and pain among male and female prisoners. *Punishment & Society, 21*(5), 560–577. https://doi.org/10.1177/1462475518805071.

Levines, A., & Crewe, B. (2015). 'Nobody's better than you, nobody's worse than you': Moral community among prisoners convicted of sexual offences. *Punishment & Society, 17*(4), 482–501. https://doi.org/10.1177/1462475515603803.

Lösel, F., Pugh, G., Markson, L., et al. (2012). *Risk and protective factors in the resettlement of imprisoned fathers with their families*. Milton: Ormiston Children and Families Trust.

Macdonald, R., Shildrick, T., & Furlong, A. (2014). In search of "intergenerational cultures of worklessness": Hunting the Yeti and shooting zombies. *Critical Social Policy, 34*(2), 199–220. https://doi.org/10.1177/0261018313501825.

Maguire, D. (2019). Vulnerable prisoner masculinities in an English prison. *Men and Masculinities*. https://doi.org/10.1177/1097184X19888966.

Perrin, C., & Blagden, N. (2014). Accumulating meaning, purpose and opportunities to change "drip by drip": The impact of being a listener in prison. *Psychology, Crime & Law, 20*(9), 902–920. https://doi.org/10.1080/1068316X.2014.888429.

Ricciardelli, R., Maier, K., & Hannah-Moffat, K. (2015). Strategic masculinities: Vulnerabilities, risk and the production of prison masculinities. *Theoretical Criminology, 19*(4), 491–513. https://doi.org/10.1177/1362480614565849.

Segal, L. (2007). *Slow motion: Changing masculinities, changing men* (3rd ed.). Basingstoke: Palgrave Macmillan.

Sim, J. (1994). Tougher than the rest? Men in prison. In T. Newburn & E. A. Stanko (Eds.), *Just boys doing business? Men, masculinities and crime*. London: Routledge.

Toch, H. (1992). *Violent men: An inquiry into the psychology of violence*. Washington, DC: American Psychological Association.

Ugelvik, T. (2014). Paternal pains of imprisonment: Incarcerated fathers, ethnic minority masculinity and resistance narratives. *Punishment & Society, 16*(2), 152–168. https://doi.org/10.1177/1462474513517020.

Walker, L. (2010). "My son gave birth to me": Offending fathers—Generative, reflexive and risky? *British Journal of Social Work, 40*(5), 1402–1418. https://doi.org/10.1093/bjsw/bcp063.

CHAPTER 9

Conclusion: Marginalised from the Margins

9.1 Introduction

Largely influenced by Connell's (2000; Connell and Messerschmidt 2005) hegemonic masculinities framework and the Teesside School's scholarship on transitions—in particular, their concept of alternative careers (Johnston et al. 2000)—in this book, I have explored the classed and gendered trajectories of male prisoners. The study provides a complete picture of how the key spaces in which men transition from boyhood into (young) adulthood affect and reflect versions of protest masculinities.

I have charted the ways in which the respondents situationally constructed their masculinities on the streets of their neighbourhoods, in compulsory learning and residential "care" spaces, in workplaces—and in prison. In particular, I map how these sites interconnect and contribute to the construction and maintenance of versions of protest and excluded masculinities. On the basis of almost every respondent interview, the indisputable evidence is that these men's journeys to imprisonment started on the streets of their impoverished neighbourhoods—many years before they reached the prison gates. I contend that the institutional spaces of compulsory learning and "care" prepared these men to serve time in prison—rather than preparing them for the shop floor in the workplace. Once they were in prison, resources for more prosocial gender investments were scarce. As a result, adapting to the

© The Author(s) 2021   193
D. Maguire, *Male, Failed, Jailed*,
Palgrave Studies in Prisons and Penology,
https://doi.org/10.1007/978-3-030-61059-3_9

existing, extreme versions of prison masculinity seemed to be the most easily accessible—but costly strategy for navigating prison spaces.

In this concluding chapter, I summarise and expand upon my key findings. In doing so, I reveal how masculinities navigated over deeply impoverished spaces left these men marginalised from the margins.

9.2   Impoverished Masculine Trajectories

9.2.1   Class, Gender and Protest Masculinity

In undertaking this study, one of my key objectives was to explore how issues of class, gender and place intersect in the formation of protest masculinities. Throughout this book, I have shown how structural economic disadvantages serve to reinforce and reproduce the type of masculine trajectories that are typically experienced by young men who grow up in impoverished circumstances on local authority housing estates.

Rather depressingly, despite the rather broad age spectrum of the respondents (they were aged between 21 and 44 at the time at which I conducted the study), regional economic forces clearly played a powerful role in their experiences; their classed and gender routes to imprisonment were all too similar. In presenting this study, I have uncovered the processes by which these men's experiences of early socialisation, exclusion and marginalisation were able to contribute to the onset of their early criminal careers: ones in which most of the respondents remain trapped many years later.

The idea of "choice" biographies (Beck 1992, 2000)—or of reflexively creating individualised or portfolio identities in a knowledge-based economy (Giddens 1991)—is one that does not have much mileage in the context of these men's lived experiences. In Chapters 5–8—the empirical heart of the book—I have exposed just how limited the respondents' "choices" actually were when they were "trapped in place" and the spaces of extreme exclusion that followed. Throughout this book, I have shown that the respondents had no option but to navigate their masculinities, as best they could, in highly deprived neighbourhoods in which they were pupils at some of the country's poorest-performing schools, with several of the participants in this study finding themselves in inadequate "care" facilities in local authority children's homes. In conducting this research, I have uncovered how the men's transitions from these institutions to employment—in recession-ravaged, deindustrialised landscapes—offered them extremely limited prospects. The disadvantages that the respondents experienced were exacerbated by their involvement in crime and their confinement in impoverished young adult prison environments and regimes. These men configured versions of protest masculinities as a means of resisting and adapting to these penal spaces. In doing so, though—in performing these gendered identities—the respondents have remained stuck in a prolonged and escalating cycle of exclusion and imprisonment.

9.2.2   *Deprived Neighbourhoods, Failing Schools and Poor "Care"*

In Chapter 5, "Local Lads: Pathways to Prison", I focused on the men's early experiences of their homes, neighbourhoods and schooling. It was clear that, for most of the men, protest masculinities originated from their early childhoods; some of them had been known to the police and to the local authorities from as young as 10. Their experiences revealed the extent to which they had tried to reproduce protest masculinities. As young boys, they had eagerly wanted to emulate their "olders" who were deeply involved in neighbourhood criminal subgroups.

On their "estates", the young men who belonged to these groups constructed versions of street-based masculinities—those that were valorised among their younger (and older) peers—by stealing and driving cars, engaging in acts of violence, "hardness" and "grafting" or "earning". In response to their circumstances, growing up on one of Europe's largest and most highly deprived council estates—where choices or legitimate routes to attaining respectable masculinities were limited—these respondents, as soon as they were able to do so, followed older criminal subgroups in adopting crime and violence as accessible avenues to manhood.

A further, related important finding emerged from my focus on the respondents' childhood masculine protests. Gender and education scholarship to date has established that secondary or upper schooling is a key arena in which the construction and reproduction of marginalised or protest masculinities takes place. Schooling was certainly significant in the context of the respondents' marginalised trajectories. Crucially, though, many of the men in this group were already deeply invested in street-based masculinities before they had even set foot in secondary education sites. Most of them imported their emergent and—in many cases—well-established versions of protest masculinity into their underperforming, underfunded and poorly resourced failing schools. For example, the Local Education Authority (Hull)—that was responsible for the schooling provision of most of the respondents—has an abysmal record. Indeed, it is regularly found to be one of the worst-performing education authorities and has languished at the bottom end of performance tables since they were introduced in the early 1990s (Ofsted 1993, 2013, 2015).

Furthermore, the respondents' early street identities also contributed to several of them being placed or taken into local authority care. This happened after what the respondents described as having been "out of control" or "off the rails". The failing institutional spaces of "learning" and "care" that the men, then boys, occupied—that were ill-equipped to challenge or to undo troubling gender trajectories—created environments and resources that only served to cultivate and exacerbate these protest masculinities. Recently, there has been wider recognition that the failings of the "care" system often lead to it being an all-too-predictable stepping stone to incarceration, with care leavers being significantly over-represented in the prison system[1] (Department for Education 2018; Laming 2016). This belated recognition of institutional failings—and of the inadequacy and/or protracted nature of the political or policy-based responses to them—is of little consequence, now, changing nothing for these respondents. As I explained earlier in this study, it was jostling for position—and the pressure to live up to the dominant versions of protest masculine ideals in children's "homes", schools and in the context of street subcultures—that contributed to many of the respondents' ever-deeper submergence into ongoing criminal careers.

9.2.3   Marginalised Workplace Transitions

In Chapter 6, "(Non)Working Lives", I followed the disrupted transitions of undereducated respondents from poor-performing schools into regional labour markets that have seen some of the UK's highest rates of unemployment. One of my major objectives in undertaking this study was to explore and unpack how their street or protest masculinities have contributed to the respondents' experiences of marginalisation, incarceration and continued disadvantage. Throughout this book, I have shown that, in enacting these versions of masculinity, the men compounded their

---

[1] It is important to be clear that 94% of looked-after children in England and Wales do not get into trouble with the law (Laming 2016).

labour market exclusion in a number of ways. Their childhood forms of protest masculinities had contributed to them to rejecting their schooling and pursuing criminal careers, leading to forms of imprisonment that bolstered the existing barriers that they faced in an already-challenging economic and industrial landscape. This was especially the case for young men who were in the process of transitioning out of school and into the world of work.

The respondents' resistance to legitimate "cards in" forms of employment in favour of cash-in-hand or "fiddly" work furthered their economic marginalisation. The men, for the most part, understood that—in and around their city, that is often described as being one of the hardest places in which to find a job—their backgrounds positioned them among the least likely to be successful in finding steady work. "Cash-in-hand" work saved them from what many felt would almost certainly be rejection from workplaces that could offer a "shit job" for "shit money". The fact that these men lacked legitimate work histories added to their difficulties and further distanced them from the labour market, worsening their marginalisation.

Another process in which the respondents contributed to their own experiences of economic marginalisation and continued exclusion was in their struggle to reconcile their early street masculine protest ideals with "respectable" working lives. Despite the significant barriers that they faced, most of them secured and tried to hold down legitimate forms of employment at one point or another. The experience of having a job was, though, a short-lived one; many of these men found that they were unable to "stick" with the structure, discipline and mundane work in return for poor wages. The men's previous unstructured, adrenalin-filled and exhilarating alternative criminal careers (and networks)—that, occasionally, brought about big pay-offs—proved to retain an irresistible pull for many. This made the prospect of committing to "poor work" a significant challenge for most of the respondents.

Notably, it was not just the "shit" jobs that were lost to the respondents' protest masculine performances that they had refined on the streets and in "care" homes and alternative learning centres. Four of the respondents—either as a result of great self-resilience and/or backing from supportive families—secured well-paid and stable work in (mainly traditional) respectable masculine occupations. Among this group of respondents, two years was the longest period for which any of them held down "good" jobs before violent and drug-related forms of crime began to run alongside their attempts at "respectability". Consequently, two of the men returned to prison and the others served their first prison terms.

9.2.4   Boys to "Cons" in Impoverished Prison Regimes

A further major focus of this study has been on how gendered trajectories—across the important sites of neighbourhood, home, school, workplace and prison—interconnect in such a way as to perpetuate cycles of revolving-door imprisonment. It was striking to discover that the vast majority of the respondents had spent much more time in prison than they had in the workplace. Indeed, in many cases, these men had spent more time in prison than they had on the "outside". As I have documented throughout the book, the men's classed and gendered trajectories across these extreme sites of exclusion better prepared them to serve time in violent and hypermasculine impoverished penal spaces than to work on the shop floor. Unlike the challenges that most of them faced in trying to adjust to "legit" workplaces, their adaptation to the prison space—despite their almost unanimous, profound fear of imprisonment beforehand—proved to be far less difficult than most of them had anticipated. This is not because prison was in any way "easy" but, rather, because it was a familiar space that contained familiar groups of men—all of whom adhered to and reinforced familiar masculine values and hierarchies. Most of the respondents had been introduced to these forms of masculinity on their "estates" and/or "care" or schooling spaces for "bad lads".

Sadly, the transitions from school to prison were all-too-common experiences among these men. Twelve of them had been imprisoned before they had completed their formal schooling; a further 9 had been incarcerated before they had reached the age of 18. It is important to emphasise, here, that these respondents found themselves—as reported in research and articulated as a concern by campaign groups—negotiating penal spaces long before they had fully matured and their brains had properly developed (Prior et al. 2011; Lösel et al. 2013). With many of the respondents having been imprisoned during such formative years, it was disappointing to find little evidence that they had been offered real strategies or alternative avenues to manhood that challenged the protest street identities that had led them to imprisonment. Instead, as documented in other research, they were abandoned to long-impoverished young adult prison regimes that reproduce hypermasculine identities that rely upon violence and "hardness" (Gooch 2017; Tynan 2019).

Furthermore, official prison learning and training—one of the key aspects of penal regimes tasked with equipping prisoners with resources for alternative avenues to "respectable masculinities",—was, clearly, woefully inadequate for this purpose (see Coates 2016). This was confirmed by the respondents' testimonies that, in turn, validated external parties' long-held concerns on this subject. The fact that the respondents were introduced to and held as children and young adults in these impoverished penal conditions—before most of them had been afforded an opportunity to "grow out" of their criminal careers—played a significant role in trapping many of them in an enduring and costly cycle of revolving-door incarceration.

9.2.5   On the Margins: Outside Looking In

The men had been, in many respects, marginalised from already deeply marginalised spaces. A specific housing estate, for instance—where most of the respondents proudly proclaimed to have been "born and bred"—was regarded, a probation representative noted, as being the "worst of the worst". Even in their "worst of the worst" neighbourhoods, most of the men were part of a sub- or protest-group. They were excluded from, as Broude (1990) and Nayak (2003) have put it, the respectable working class—who, on the whole, are hardworking and law-abiding citizens. Half of the respondents had been excluded from some of the country's worst-performing schools and placed in alternative learning institutions that reinforced their statuses as "bad lads" outside the mainstream. Several of them had been taken or excluded from their family or "proper" home and placed into the "care" of the local authority. Often, the respondents had been left in residential care after other forms of "care" placements had broken down. In Hull's bleak industrial and economic landscape, the vast majority of the men felt excluded, even from "shit" jobs. Having experienced multiple periods of imprisonment, the men experienced another obvious—albeit more extreme—form of exclusion or "deprivation" from societies—that were already highly deprived.

By charting the respondents' gendered trajectories over these interconnecting sites, I have exposed just how limited their (legitimate) resources were for "doing masculinity". Moreover, I have shown just how narrow the definitions and understandings of "dominant" and "subordinated" masculinities actually were in these spaces. The respondents' options—so-called "choice"—in the vast majority of cases meant oscillating between "doing" marginalised masculinity in "failing" schools, followed by holding down "shit" jobs, or resisting the "respectable" route and instead embracing forms of street protest masculinity that inevitably led to their existence at the margins of the margins. In her review of research on working-class masculinity and schooling, Sara Delamont (2000) is critical of those whom she identifies as being mostly middle-class and male researchers who mythologise and lionise the resistance and protest of the same working-class boys from whom they hid in the school playground. There are, though, no heroes or lions in this study. Indeed, the deeper that the men invested in forms of street protest masculinity, the greater the costs to both themselves and everyone they were close to. Consequently, I have argued in Chapter 8—"Vulnerable Masculinities: Absent Men and Imagined Futures"—that the more the men added to and amplified their own experiences of exclusion, the more the cracks in this masculinity began to reveal profound vulnerabilities.

The language of vulnerability is not associated often enough with the overly portrayed aggressive masculinities of working-class men (prisoners) and this is partly Delamont's point. In this book, however, I show how the versions of protest masculinities that are sustained by men like these respondents over long periods—and in various sites of exclusion—reveal particular, but significant, vulnerabilities. Most explicitly, these vulnerabilities are evident in the space of the prison itself where a number of the participants had the status of "vulnerable prisoner". In revealing the fragility and vulnerability that lie behind masculinities constructed in sites of exclusion, like prisons, I have shown how several individuals from this "vulnerable" cohort went from being highly respected by other prisoners to embodying subordinated masculinities themselves. In these subordinate positions, the men became the victims of violence and denigration at the hands of other mainstream prisoners who used them as resources for performing dominant prisoner masculinities. I have argued how these same main location prisoners—"backstage" and alone in their cells—understood the fragility and difficulties of sustaining and living up to the expectations of prison masculinities. Moreover, I have highlighted just how easily—like the 10 men who were in the vulnerable cohort—it is to for these main location prisoners to quickly lose dominant masculine status and find themselves in the same penal spaces as the "vulnerable".

In conducting this study, I have highlighted another form of vulnerability: one that is not so explicitly defined but one that nevertheless runs through all of the respondents' gendered and classed trajectories. I found that the more the respondents sought masculine acceptance or respectability on the streets or in other sites of exclusion, the further they distanced themselves from—or failed to be—the men, they claimed they want to be. Spending more time inside than "on the out"—as the majority of the participants had—meant being excluded from, or unable to meet, the most basic cultural expectations of working-class masculinity. Regardless of whether they had a revered or subordinate street or prison masculine status, nearly all of the respondents—as I have shown in Chapters 7 and 8—felt and carried the burden of a great deal of shame for having, as they saw it, failed to fulfil their masculine obligations towards those they cared about. Decades sustaining destructive forms of masculinity had contributed to their failures as fathers, providers and protectors, disqualifying them from fulfilling the specific gendered ideals that the majority of them desired to live up to. In Chapter 8, I argued that such significant losses—and the emotional cost or consequences of their continued absence from major life events on the "outside"—revealed a particularly vulnerable side to many of the respondents.

A particularly striking aspect of the findings that highlighted the vulnerabilities of many of the respondents was their belief that they could, and would, make up for their past "failings" to be the men that they wanted and needed to be. Sadly, as demonstrated in the closing empirical chapter, many of them were looking to the "breadwinner" versions of masculinity that their fathers and previous generations had embodied in an effort to secure futures that were free from crime and prison. After having spent so long on the margins of the margins—where resources for "doing" alternative "respectable" working-class masculinities were almost non-existent—the respondents' futures rest on the precarious foundations of a masculine model that even the most so-called "respectable" working-class men are struggling to attain. More importantly, the lasting vulnerabilities of most of these men stem from their need—once they have been released from prison—to achieve a version of that traditional respectable working-class masculinity that they have failed to attain and sustain, time and time again in previous spells of freedom.

It is, as such, with concern and sadness that I argue that there is little in the narratives of most of these respondents that suggests that they are better equipped than they were before starting their sentences to attain the masculine roles of being protectors and (legitimate) providers that they so desire. One might argue that, in an increasingly austere environment—with already-limited support services and forms of welfare provision suffering from significant and growing cuts—, these men perhaps face their toughest challenge to date: the challenge of just staying on the margins.

9.3   FINAL THOUGHTS

In what has been, on the whole, a considerably bleak study, it is difficult to find uplifting words of optimism with which to conclude this book. The Teesside School's work on transitions has taken pains to point out that young people—who grow up in the same contexts of structural economic disadvantages—experience varying, albeit mainly "poor", transitions. Of course, most of those who grow up in the very same environments as the participants of this study do not end up in the local prison. It is an indisputable fact, however, that it is the men who come from deprived neighbourhoods that fill prisons like Hull. Having comprehensively charted the respondents' gender ed and classed trajectories to, in most cases, revolving-door cycles of imprisonment—and although it is difficult to see how these cycles might end for many of them—I cannot claim with any certainty, at least without conducting follow-up interviews, what their futures might hold.

My own lived and work experiences leave me reluctant to write these men off as having no way out of their current position. Had I, like these respondents, been interviewed during the course of my last prison term, I could never have imagined the future in which I find myself today. Thomson et al. (2002) and others (Shildrick and MacDonald 2008) have talked of "critical moments": events that an individual "sees as having important consequences for their lives and identities" (p. 339). These are moments that transpire when some form of interaction occurs—with, for example, a professional, a family or an associate—or an incident takes place (such as bereavement or becoming a victim of violence) that change the trajectory of one's life for better or worse. Reflecting on my own biography, a clear set of events led to my critical moment: the one that instigated change. A year into my last prison sentence, I was moved from Manchester's local prison (Strangeways) to a training prison in Thetford, Norfolk, which had a bad reputation and was a long way from home. After spending a short time in this institution, I was made aware of a specialist therapeutic unit for prisoners who wanted to address the behaviours that contributed to their decisions to commit crime. With no other agenda but to try to secure an early release, I applied to the unit and was accepted. It was while I was on this unit that I met several senior prison officers—one of whom was the Governor of Hull at the time of this study—and their team of staff, whose attitudes, actions and approaches to prisoners convinced many of us that we were more than just a number.

During my previous stints of incarceration, I had never considered undertaking forms of prison education—for many of the same reasons that the respondents identified. On this unit, though, engagement in educational activities was compulsory. I was encouraged, by the officers, to try it out. I was also remunerated at the same rate that those who undertook paid work in the main prison workshops received; this was unusual because educational programmes always paid less than prison wages. The educational programme was run by a volunteer, a retired teacher, who freely invested her time with the sole aim of introducing the rewards of learning to those who were in her class. Meeting this teacher, Maggie—who was not constrained by the core prison curriculum and who tailored learning activities to the interests and needs of the room—was a critical moment for me. Maggie's particular specialism was to convince those of us who had low self-belief—and had been through negative schooling experiences in the past—that we were teachable and that we had something of value to say. It seems fitting to reference Maggie, here, as I am sure I was neither the first nor the last prisoner to use her class-room as a gateway or an avenue to finding an alternative way of "doing masculinity".

I was paroled and left the unit, filled with more hope than I had felt when I was sentenced. In my final weeks in prison, I was supported in making the move to a new location; from this halfway house, I was encouraged to pursue higher education, where the journey to this book started.

Behind this biographical disclosure lies a tentative attempt to share a message of optimism that relates to the men who participated in this study and those like them. Most of those who surrounded me during my early years on the streets of our neighbourhood or during my periods "inside" could never have predicted that I would take this route out of crime and imprisonment. Because this study was conducted within the confines of a prison, it was only ever going to feature those men who are still stuck in their criminal and prison masculine identities. Perhaps, however, some of these respondents—who seemed so locked into prison and criminal masculinities—will encounter their own particular "critical moment" and find a way of living up to, or beyond, their aspirations for their own imagined futures.

REFERENCES

Beck, U. (1992). *Risk society: Towards a new modernity.* London: Sage.
Beck, U. (2000). *Brave new world of work.* Cambridge: Polity Press.
Broude, G. J. (1990). Protest masculinity: A further look at the causes and the concept. *Ethos, 18*(1), 103–122. https://doi.org/10.1525/eth.1990.18.1.02a00040.
Coates, S. (2016). *Unlocking Potential: A review of education in prison.* London: Ministry of Justice.
Connell, R. (2000). *The men and the boys.* Cambridge: Polity.
Connell, R., & Messerschmidt, J. W. (2005). Hegemonic masculinity rethinking the concept. *Gender & Society, 19*(6), 829–859. https://doi.org/10.1177/0891243205278639.
Delamont, S. (2000). The anomalous beasts: Hooligans and the sociology of education. *Sociology, 34*(1), 95–111. https://doi.org/10.1177/S0038038500000079.
Department for Education (DfE). (2018). *The national protocol on reducing unnecessary criminalisation of looked-after children and care leavers.* London.
Giddens, A. (1991). *Modernity and self-identity: Self and society in the late modern age.* Cambridge: Polity.
Gooch, K. (2017). 'Kidulthood': Ethnography, juvenile prison violence and the transition from 'boys' to 'men.' *Criminology & Criminal Justice, 19*(1), 80–97. https://doi.org/10.1177/1748895817741519.
Johnston, L., MacDonald, R., Mason, P., Ridley, L., & Webster, C. (2000). *Snakes and ladders: Young people, transitions and social exclusion.* Bristol: Policy Press.
Laming, L. (2016). *In care, out of trouble.* London, England: Prison Reform Trust.
Lösel, F., Bottoms, A., & Farrington, D. P. (Eds.). (2013). *Young adult offenders: Lost in transition?* Cullompton: Willan.
Nayak, A. (2003). Last of the 'Real Geordies'? White masculinities and the subcultural response to deindustrialisation. *Environment and Planning D: Society and Space, 21*(1), 7–26. https://doi.org/10.1068/d44j.
Office for Standards in Education. (1993). *Access and achievement in urban education.* London: Ofsted.
Office for Standards in Education. (2013). *Unseen children: Access and achievement 20 years on.* London.

Office for Standards in Education. (2015). *The annual report of Her Majesty's Chief Inspector of Education, Children's Services and Skills 2014/15: Education and skills*. London: Ofsted.

Prior, D., Farrow, K., Hughes, N., Kelly, G., Manders, G., White, S., & Wilkinson, B. (2011). *Maturity, young adults and criminal justice: A literature review*. Birmingham: University of Birmingham.

Shildrick, T., Blackman, S., & MacDonald, R. (2009). Young people, class and place. *Journal of Youth Studies, 12*(5), 457–465. https://doi.org/10.1080/13676260903114136.

Thomson, R., Bell, R., Holland, J., Henderson, S., McGrellis, S., & Sharp, S. (2002). Critical moments: Choice, chance and opportunity in young people's narratives of transition. *Sociology, 36*(2), 335–354. https://doi.org/10.1177/0038038502036002006.

Tynan, R. R. (2019). *Young men's experiences of long term imprisonment: Living life*. London: Routledge.

Correction to: Male, Failed, Jailed

Correction to:
D. Maguire, *Male, Failed, Jailed*, Palgrave Studies in Prisons and Penology, https://doi.org/10.1007/978-3-030-61059-3

The original version of this book was inadvertently published with some errors in the text. Those errors have now been corrected. The book has been updated with the changes.

The updated version of the book can be found at https://doi.org/10.1007/978-3-030-61059-3

© The Author(s) 2021
D. Maguire, *Male, Failed, Jailed*,
Palgrave Studies in Prisons and Penology,
https://doi.org/10.1007/978-3-030-61059-3_10

REFERENCES

Abbot, D. (2013). *Britain's crisis of masculinity: Good health, hard work and family*. A Demos Twentieth Birthday Lecture delivered by Diane Abbott MP (pp. 1–11). Demos. Magdalen House. London: Demos.

Adler, A. (1978). Masculine protest and a critique of Freud. In H. Ansbacher & R. Ansbacher (Eds.), *Cooperation between the sexes*. New York: Anchor.

Alexander, C. (2000). *The Asian gang: Ethnicity, identity, masculinity*. Oxford: Berg.

Allen, R. (2011). *Last resort? Exploring the reduction in child imprisonment 2008–11*. London: Prison Reform Trust.

Allen, R. (2013). *Young adults in custody: The way forward*. T2A Alliance Barrow Cadbury Trust.

Allen, R., Bibby, D., & Parameshwaran, M. (2015). *Missing talent: Raising the aspirations and achievement of the 7,000 highly able pupils who fall behind at secondary school*. London: Sutton Trust.

Anderson, C., & Bushman, B. J. (2002). Human aggression. *Psychology, 53*(1), 27. https://doi.org/10.1146/annurev.psych.53.100901.135231.

Anderson, E. (1999). *Code of the street: Decency, violence, and the moral life of the inner city*. New York and London: W. W. Norton & Company.

Anderson, E. (2009). *Inclusive masculinity: The changing nature of masculinities*. London: Routledge.

Archer, J. (1994). *Male violence*. London: Routledge.

© The Editor(s) (if applicable) and The Author(s), under exclusive license to Springer Nature Switzerland AG 2021
D. Maguire, *Male, Failed, Jailed*,
Palgrave Studies in Prisons and Penology,
https://doi.org/10.1007/978-3-030-61059-3

Archer, L. (2001). 'Muslim brothers, black lads, traditional Asians': British Muslim young men's constructions of race, religion and masculinity. *Feminism & Psychology, 11*(1), 79–105. https://doi.org/10.1177/095935350101 1001005.

Archer, L. (2003). *Race, masculinity and schooling: Muslim boys and education.* Maidenhead: Open University Press.

Archer, L. (2007). *Understanding minority ethnic achievement: Race, gender, class and "success".* Abingdon: Routledge.

Atherton, S. (2009). Domesticating military masculinities: Home, performance and the negotiation of identity. *Social & Cultural Geography, 10*(8), 821–836. https://doi.org/10.1080/14649360903305791.

Ball, S. J. (2003). *Class strategies and the education market: The middle classes and social advantage.* London: Routledge.

Barker, G. (2005). *Dying to be men: Youth, masculinity and social exclusion: Youth and masculinity and social exclusion.* London: Routledge.

Barrow Cadbury Trust. (2005). *Lost in transition: A report of the Barrow Cadbury Commission on young adults and the criminal justice system.* London: Barrow Cadbury Trust.

Beasley, C. (2008). Rethinking hegemonic masculinity in a globalizing world. *Men and Masculinities, 11*(1), 86–103. https://doi.org/10.1177/109718 4X08315102.

Beck, U. (1992). *Risk society: Towards a new modernity.* London: Sage.

Beck, U. (2000). *Brave new world of work.* Cambridge: Polity Press.

Beck, U., & Beck-Gernsheim, E. (2001). *Individualization: Institutionalized individualism and its social and political consequences.* London: Sage.

Bengtsson, T. T. (2015). Performing hypermasculinity experiences with confined young offenders. *Men and Masculinities, 19*(4), 410–428. https://doi.org/10.1177/1097184X15595083.

Berg, L. D. (1994). Masculinity, place and a binary discourse of "theory" and "empirical investigation" in the human geography of Aotearoa/New Zealand. *Gender, Place and Culture: A Journal of Feminist Geography, 1*(2), 245–260. https://doi.org/10.1080/09663699408721212.

Berg, L. D., & Longhurst, R. (2003). Placing masculinities and geography. *Gender, Place and Culture, 10*(4), 351–360. https://doi.org/10.1080/096 6369032000153322.

Berger, R. (2013). Now I see it, now I don't: Researcher's position and reflexivity in. *Qualitative Research, 15*(2), 219–234. https://doi.org/10.1177/146879 4112468475.

Berman, G. (2013). *Prison population statistics.* House of Commons Library. www.parliament.uk/briefing-papers/SN04334.pdf. Accessed 1 June 2017.

Beynon, J. (2002). *Masculinities and culture.* London: McGraw-Hill Education.

Bianchini, F., Bissett, V., Cavalleri, F., Grabher, B., Morpeth, N., Oanca, A., & Tommarchi, E. (2019). *Cultural transformations the impacts of Hull UK City of Culture 2017*. Culture, Place & Policy Institute, University of Hull.

Blades, R, Hart, D., Lea J., & Wilmot, N. (2011). *Care—A stepping stone to custody? The views of children in care on the links between care, offending and custody*. Prison Reform Trust.

Blokland, T., & Savage, M. (2001). Networks, class and place. *International Journal of Urban and Regional Research, 25*(2), 221–226. https://doi.org/ 10.1111/1468-2427.00308.

Boffey, D. (2015). Youth unemployment rate is worst for 20 years, compared with overall figure. *The Guardian*.

Boswell, G. (2002). *Imprisoned fathers and their children*. London: Jessica Kingsley Publishers.

Bottero, W. (2009). Class in the 21st century. In K. P. Sveinsson (Ed.), *Who cares about the white working class?* London: Runnymede Trust.

Bourdieu, P. (1984). *Distinction: A social critique of the judgement of taste*. Cambridge, MA: Harvard University Press.

Bourgois, P. (1996). In search of masculinity: Violence, respect and sexuality among Puerto Rican crack dealers in East Harlem. *British Journal of Criminology, 36*(3), 412–427. https://doi.org/10.1093/oxfordjournals.bjc. a014103.

Bourgois, P. (2003). *In search of respect: Selling crack in El Barrio*. Cambridge: Cambridge University Press.

Bracken, C. (2011). *Bars to learning: Practical challenges to the working prison*. London: CIVITAS.

Brannon, R. (1976). The male sex role: Our culture's blueprint for manhood, what it's done for us lately. In B. Robert & D. D. Sarah (Eds.), *The forty-nine percent majority: The male sex role*. Boston: Addison Wesley Publishing Company.

Brereton, S. (2015). Stolen lives and missed opportunities: The deaths of young adults and children in prison. *Probation Journal, 62*(3), 281–283. https:// doi.org/10.1177/0264550515599321.

Broude, G. J. (1990). Protest masculinity: A further look at the causes and the concept. *Ethos, 18*(1), 103–122. https://doi.org/10.1525/eth.1990.18. 1.02a00040.

Brown, P., & Scase, R. (1991). *Poor work: Disadvantage and the division of labour*. Milton Keynes: Open University Press.

Brunton-Smith, I., & Hopkins, K. (2013). *The factors associated with proven re-offending following release from prison: Findings from Waves 1 to 3 of SPCR: Results from the Surveying Prisoner Crime Reduction (SPCR) longitudinal cohort study of prisoners*. London: Ministry of Justice.

Bryman, A. (2012). *Social research methods*. Oxford: Oxford University Press.

Butler, J. (1990). *Gender trouble and the subversion of identity*. New York and London: Routledge.

Butler, M. (2008). What are you looking at? Prisoner confrontations and the search for respect. *British Journal of Criminology, 48*(6), 856–873. https://doi.org/10.1093/bjc/azn053.

Calvert, E. (2010). *Young people's housing transitions in context*. ESRC Centre for Population Change Working Article 8. Centre for Population and Change.

Campbell, B. (1993). *Goliath: Britain's dangerous places / Beatrix Campbell*. London: Methuen.

Carlsson, C. (2013). Masculinities, persistence, and desistance. *Criminology, 51*(3), 661–693. https://doi.org/10.1111/1745-9125.12016.

Centre for Cities. (2015). *Cities outlook 2015*. London: Centre for Cities.

Champion, N. (2013). *Smart rehabilitation—Learning how to get better outcomes*. London: Prisoners' Education Trust.

Charlesworth, S. J. (2000). *A phenomenology of working-class experience*. Cambridge: Cambridge University Press.

Chavez, C. (2008). Conceptualizing from the inside: Advantages, complications, and demands on insider positionality. *The Qualitative Report, 13*(3), 474–494. https://nsuworks.nova.edu/tqr/vol13/iss3/9.

Clapham, D., Mackie, P., Orford, S., Thomas, I., & Buckley, K. (2014). The housing pathways of young people in the UK. *Environment and Planning A: Economy and Space, 46*(8), 2016–2031. https://doi.org/10.1068/a46273.

Clemmer, D. (1958). *The prison community*. New York: Holt, Rinehart & Winston.

Coates, S. (2016). *Unlocking potential: A review of education in prison*. London: Ministry of Justice.

Cockburn, C., & Oaklek, A. (2013). The cost of masculine crime. *Open Democracy*. https://www.opendemocracy.net/5050/ann-oakley-cynthia-cockburn/cost-of-masculine-crime. Accessed 26 February 2015.

Cohen, P., & Ainley, P. (2000). In the country of the blind? Youth studies and cultural studies in Britain. *Journal of Youth Studies, 3*(1), 79–95. https://doi.org/10.1080/136762600113059.

Cohen, S., & Taylor, L. (1981). *Psychological survival: The experience of long-term imprisonment* (2nd ed.). Harmondsworth: Penguin.

Collier, R. (1998). *Masculinities, crime and criminology: Men, heterosexuality and the criminal(ised) other*. London: Sage.

Collier, R. (2004). Masculinities and crime: Rethinking the "man question"? In C. Sumner (Ed.), *The Blackwell companion to criminology* (pp. 285–308). Hoboken: Blackwell Publishing Ltd.

Connell, R. (1989). Cool guys, swots and wimps: The interplay of masculinity and education. *Oxford Review of Education, 15*(3). https://doi.org/10.1080/0305498890150309.

Connell, R. (1995). *Masculinities*. Cambridge: Polity.

Connell, R. (2000). *The men and the boys*. Cambridge: Polity.

Connell, R., & Messerschmidt, J. W. (2005). Hegemonic masculinity rethinking the concept. *Gender & Society, 19*(6), 829–859. https://doi.org/10.1177/0891243205278639.

Connolly, P., & Healy, J. (2004). Symbolic violence, locality and social class: The educational and career aspirations of 10-11-year-old boys in Belfast. *Pedagogy, Culture & Society, 12*(1), 15–33. https://doi.org/10.1080/1468136040200187.

Copes, H., Brookman, F., & Brown, A. (2013). Accounting for violations of the convict code. *Deviant Behavior, 34*(10), 841–858. https://doi.org/10.1080/01639625.2013.781444.

Copes, H., & Hochstetler, A. (2003). Situational construction of masculinity among male street thieves. *Journal of Contemporary Ethnography, 32*(3), 279–304. https://doi.org/10.1177/0891241603032003002.

Corbett, C. (2003). *Car crime*. Crime and Society Series. Cullompton: Willan.

Corrigan, P. (1979). *Schooling the smash street kids*. London: Palgrave Macmillan.

Courtenay, W. H. (2000). Constructions of masculinity and their influence on men's well-being: A theory of gender and health. *Social Science & Medicine, 50*(10), 1385–1401. https://doi.org/10.1016/S0277-9536(99)00390-1.

Cowburn, M. (2007). Men researching men in prison: The challenges for profeminist research. *The Howard Journal of Criminal Justice, 46*, 276–288. https://doi.org/10.1111/j.1468-2311.2007.00474.x.

Crane, M., Warnes, A. M., Barnes, J., & Coward, S. (2014). The resettlement of homeless young people: Their experiences and housing outcomes. *Social Policy and Society, 13*(02), 161–176. https://doi.org/10.1017/S1474746413000468.

Creese, B. (2016). An assessment of the English and maths skills levels of prisoners in England. *London Review of Education, 14*(3), 13–30. https://doi.org/10.18546/LRE.14.3.02.

Crewe, B. (2005). Codes and conventions: The terms and conditions of contemporary inmate values. In A. Liebling & S. Maruna (Eds.), *The effects of imprisonment* (pp. 177–208). Cambridge Criminal Justice Series. Cullompton: Willan.

Crewe, B. (2006). Prison drug dealing and the ethnographic lens. *The Howard Journal of Criminal Justice, 45*, 347–368. https://doi.org/10.1111/j.1468-2311.2006.00428.x.

Crewe, B. (2009). *The prisoner society: Power, adaptation and social life in an English prison*. Oxford: Oxford University Press.

Crewe, B. (2011). Depth, weight, tightness: Revisiting the pains of imprisonment. *Punishment & Society, 13*(5), 509–529. https://doi.org/10.1177/1462474511422172.

Crewe, B. (2014). Not looking hard enough masculinity, emotion, and prison research. *Qualitative Inquiry, 20*(4), 392–403. https://doi.org/10.1177/1077800413515829.

Crewe, B., Hulley, S., & Wright, S. (2020). *Life imprisonment from young adulthood*. London: Palgrave Macmillan UK.

Crook, F. (2018). *Reinventing different ways of locking up children—A cautionary tale*. Howard League for Penal Reform. Available at https://howardleague.org/blog/reinventing-different-ways-of-locking-up-children-a-cautionary-tale/. Accessed August 2018.

Cunneen, C. (1995). *Juvenile justice: An Australian perspective*. Melbourne and Oxford: Oxford University Press.

Czerniawski, G. (2015). A race to the bottom—Prison education and the English and Welsh policy context. *Journal of Education Policy, 31*(2), 1–15. https://doi.org/10.1080/02680939.2015.1062146.

Daly, K., & Chesney-Lind, M. (1988). Feminism and criminology. *Justice Quarterly, 5*(4), 497–538. https://doi.org/10.1080/07418828800089871.

Daly, M., & Wilson, M. (1988). *Homicide*. New York: Aldine.

Daly, M., Wilson, M., & Weghorst, S. J. (1982). Male sexual jealousy. *Ethology and Sociobiology, 3*(1), 11–27.

Davies, W. (2015). Unique position: Dual identities as prison researcher and ex-prisoner. In D. H. Drake, R. Earle, & J. Sloan (Eds.), *The Palgrave handbook of prison ethnography*. London: Palgrave Macmillan. https://doi.org/10.1057/9781137403889_25.

DeKeseredy, W. S., & Schwartz, M. D. (2005). Masculinities and interpersonal violence. In M. S. Kimmel, J. Hearn, & R. Connell (Eds.), *Handbook of studies on men and masculinities* (pp. 353–366). London: Sage.

Delamont, S. (2000). The anomalous beasts: Hooligans and the sociology of education. *Sociology, 34*(1), 95–111. https://doi.org/10.1177/S0038038500000079.

Demetriou, D. Z. (2001). Connell's concept of hegemonic masculinity: A critique. *Theory and Society, 30*(3), 337–361. https://doi.org/10.1023/A:1017596718715.

Department for Business Innovation and Skills (BIS). (2011). *Making prisons work: Skills for rehabilitation: Review of offender learning*. Available at https://www.gov.uk/government/consultations/call-for-evidence-review-of-offender-learning. Accessed 12 February 2016.

Department for Education (DfE). (2017). *York, North Yorkshire, East Riding and Hull area review final report*. London.

Department for Education (DfE). (2018). *The national protocol on reducing unnecessary criminalisation of looked-after children and care leavers*. London.

de Viggiani, N. (2012). Trying to be something you are not: Masculine performances within a prison setting. *Men and Masculinities, 15*(3), 271–291. https://doi.org/10.1177/1097184X12448464.

De Visser, R. O., & Smith, J. A. (2007). Alcohol consumption and masculine identity among young men. *Psychology & Health, 22*(5), 595–614. https://doi.org/10.1080/14768320600941772.

Dolphin, T. (2009). *The impact of the recession on northern city regions.* Newcastle-upon-Tyne: IPPR North.

Donaldson, M. (1993). What is hegemonic masculinity? *Theory and Society, 22*(5), 643–657. https://doi.org/10.1007/BF00993540.

Donaldson, S. (2001). A million jokers, punks, and queens. In D. F Sabo, T. A. Kupers, & W. J. London (Eds.), *Prison masculinities* (pp. 118–126). Philadelphia: Temple University Press.

Drake, P. (2010). Grasping at methodological understanding: A cautionary tale from insider research. *International Journal of Research & Method in Education, 33*, 85–99. https://doi.org/10.1080/17437271003597592.

Drake, D. (2011). The ""dangerous other"" in maximum-security prisons. *Criminology and Criminal Justice, 11*(4), 367–382. https://doi.org/10.1177/174 8895811408836.

Drake, D. (2012). *Prisons, punishment and the pursuit of security.* Critical Criminological Perspectives. Basingstoke: Palgrave Macmillan.

Duncan-Smith, I. (2006). *Breakdown Britain: Interim report on the state of the nation.* London: Centre for Social Justice.

Dyer, W. J. (2005). Prison, fathers, and identity: A theory of how incarceration affects men's paternal identity. *Fathering: A Journal of Theory, Research, and Practice about Men as Fathers, 3*(3), 201–219. https://doi.org/10.3149/fth.0303.201.

Earle, R. (2016). *Convict criminology—Inside and out.* Bristol: Policy Press.

Earle, R. (2018). Convict criminology in England: Developments and dilemmas. *The British Journal of Criminology, 58*(6), 1499–1516. https://doi.org/10.1093/bjc/azy016.

Earle, R., & Phillips, C. (2012). Digesting men? Ethnicity, gender and food: Perspectives from a "prison ethnography". *Theoretical Criminology, 16*(2), 141–156. https://doi.org/10.1177/1362480612441121.

Edley, N., & Wetherell, M. (1997). Jockeying for position: The construction of masculine identities. *Discourse & Society, 8*(2), 203–217. https://doi.org/10.1177/0957926597008002004.

Ellis, A. J. (2016). *Men, masculinities and violence: An ethnographic study.* London: Routledge.

Ellis, A.J. (2019). A de-civilizing reversal or system normal? Rising lethal violence in post-recession austerity United Kingdom. *The British Journal of Criminology, 59*(4), 862–878. https://doi.org/10.1093/bjc/azz001.

Ellis, A., Winlow, S., & Hall, S. (2017). 'Throughout my life I've had people walk all over me': Trauma in the lives of violent men. *The Sociological Review*, 65(4), 699–713. https://doi.org/10.1177/0038026117695486.

Enenkel, K., Quinio,V., & Swinney, P.(2020). *Cities outlook 2020. Holding our breath*. Centre for Cities.

English, C. (2014, December 9). To Hull and back: The rebirth of Britain's poorest city. *The Guardian*.

Epstein, D. (1998). *Failing boys? Issues in gender and achievement*. Buckingham: Open University Press.

Evans, G. (2006). *Educational failure and working class white children in Britain*. Basingstoke: Palgrave Macmillan.

Evans, T., & Wallace, P. (2008). A prison within a prison? The masculinity narratives of male prisoners. *Men and Masculinities, 10*, 484–507. https://doi.org/10.1177/1097184X06291903.

Farrington, D. P., Ttofi, M. M., & Coid, J. W. (2009). Development of adolescence-limited, late-onset, and persistent offenders from age 8 to age 48. *Aggressive Behavior, 35*(2), 150–163. https://doi.org/10.1002/ab.20296.

Featherstone, M. (2013). Being-in-Hull, being-on-Bransholme: Socio-economic decline, regeneration and working-class experience on a peri-urban council estate. *City, 17*(2), 179–196. https://doi.org/10.1080/13604813.2013.765648.

Fergusson, R., Pye, D., Esland, G., McLaughlin, E., & Muncie, J. (2000). Normalized dislocation and new subjectivities in post-16 markets for education and work. *Critical Social Policy, 20*(3), 283–305. https://doi.org/10.1177/026101830002000302.

Ferrell, J. (1992). Making sense of crime: A review essay on Jack Katz's Seductions of Crime. *Social Justice, 19*, 110–123.

Ferrell, J., Hayward, K., & Young, J. (2008). *Cultural criminology: An invitation*. London: Sage.

Fielding, N. (1994). Cop canteen culture. In T. Newburn & E. A. Stanko (Eds.), *Just boys doing business? Men, masculinities and crime*. London: Routledge.

Fine, M., Weis, L., Addelston, J., & Marusza, J. (1997). (In)secure times: Constructing white working-class masculinities in the late 20th century. *Gender & Society, 11*(1), 52–68. https://doi.org/10.1177/089124397011001004.

Fitzpatrick, C. (2016, October 26). Why have so many people in prison spent time in care as children? *The Conversation*. Available online https://theconversation.com/why-have-so-many-people-in-prison-spent-time-in-care-as-children-66941. Accessed 1 June 2018.

Fitzpatrick, E., McGuire, J., & Dickson, J. M. (2014). Personal goals of adolescents in a youth offending service in the United Kingdom. *Youth Justice, 15*(2), 166–181. https://doi.org/10.1177/1473225414543484.

Fletcher, D., & Batty, E. (2012). *Offender peer interventions: What do we know?* Centre for Regional Economic and Social Research, Sheffield Hallam University.

Flood, M. (2002). Between men and masculinity: An assessment of the term "masculinity" in recent scholarship. In S. Pearce & V. Muller (Eds.), *Manning the next millennium: Studies in masculinities.* Perth: Black Swan Press.

Flood, M., & Pease, B. (2009). Factors influencing attitudes to violence against women. *Trauma, Violence, & Abuse, 10*(2), 125–142. https://doi.org/10.1177/1524838009334131.

Francis, B. (1999). Lads, lasses and (new) labour: 14–16-year-old students' responses to the 'laddish behaviour and boys' underachievement' debate. *British Journal of Sociology of Education, 20*(3), 355–371. https://doi.org/10.1080/01425699995317.

Francis, B. (2006). Heroes or zeroes? The discursive positioning of "under-achieving boys" in English neo-liberal education policy. *Journal of Education Policy, 21*(2), 187–200. https://doi.org/10.1080/02680930500500278.

Francis, B. (2009). The role of The Boffin as abject other in gendered performances of school achievement. *The Sociological Review, 57*(4), 645–669. https://doi.org/10.1111/j.1467-954X.2009.01866.x.

Francis, B., & Skelton, C. (2001). *Investigating gender: Contemporary perspectives in education.* Buckingham: Open University Press.

Frosh, S., Phoenix, A., & Pattman, R. (2002). *Young masculinities: Understanding boys in contemporary society.* Basingstoke: Palgrave.

Furlong, A., Woodman, D., & Wyn, J. (2011). Changing times, changing perspectives: Reconciling "transition" and "cultural" perspectives on youth and young adulthood. *Journal of Sociology, 47*(4), 355–370. https://doi.org/10.1177/1440783311420787.

Gadd, D. (2003). Reading between the lines: Subjectivity and men's violence. *Men and Masculinities, 5*(4), 333–354. https://doi.org/10.1177/1097184X02250838.

Gadd, D., & Farrall, S. (2004). Criminal careers, desistance and subjectivity interpreting men's narratives of change. *Theoretical Criminology, 8*(2), 123–156. https://doi.org/10.1177/1362480604042241.

Gelsthorpe, L, & Morris, A. (1990). *Feminist perspectives in criminology.* New Directions in Criminology Series. Milton Keynes: Open University Press.

George, A., Metcalf, H., Hunter, G., Betram, C., Newton, B., Skrine, O., & Turnbull, P. (2014). *Evaluation of day one mandation of prison leavers to the Work Programme* (Department for Work and Pensions Research Report, No. 897). London: Department for Work and Pensions.

Gerami, S. (2003). Mullahs, martyrs, and men conceptualizing masculinity in the Islamic Republic of Iran. *Men and Masculinities, 5*(3), 257–274. https://doi.org/10.1177/1097184X02238526.

Giddens, A. (1991). *Modernity and self-identity: Self and society in the late modern age*. Cambridge: Polity.

Gilbert, R. (1998). *Masculinity goes to school*. London: Routledge.

Gill, R., Henwood, K., & McLean, C. (2005). Body projects and the regulation of normative masculinity. *Body & Society, 11*(1), 37–62. https://doi.org/10.1177/1357034X05049849.

Gillborn, D. (1997). Ethnicity and educational performance in the United Kingdom: Racism, ethnicity, and variability in achievement. *Anthropology & Education Quarterly, 28*(3), 375–393. https://doi.org/10.1525/aeq.1997.28.3.375.

Gillett, E., & MacMahon, K. A. (1989). *A history of Hull* (2nd and extended ed.). Hull: Hull University Press.

Gilmore, R. W. (2007). *Golden gulag: Prisons, surplus, crisis, and opposition in globalizing California*. Berkeley and London: University of California Press.

Goffman, E. (1968). *Asylums: Essays on the social situation of mental patients and other inmates*. Harmondsworth: Penguin.

Goffman, E. (1969). *The presentation of self in everyday life*. London: Allen Lane.

Goldson, B. (2003). *Vulnerable inside: Children in secure and penal settings*. London: The Children's Society.

Gooch, K. (2017). 'Kidulthood': Ethnography, juvenile prison violence and the transition from 'boys' to 'men.' *Criminology & Criminal Justice, 19*(1), 80–97. https://doi.org/10.1177/1748895817741519.

Gorman-Murray, A., & Hopkins, P. (2014). *Masculinities and place*. Farnham: Ashgate.

Gough, B., & Edwards, G. (1998). The beer talking: Four lads, a carry out and the reproduction of masculinities. *The Sociological Review, 46*(3), 409–455. https://doi.org/10.1111/1467-954X.00125.

Graham, B., White, C., Edwards, A., Potter, S., & Street, C. (2019). *School exclusion: A literature review on the continued disproportionate exclusion of certain children*. London: Department for Education.

Gramsci, A. (1971). *Selections from the prison notebooks of Antonio Gramsci*. New York: International.

Griffin, C. (2000). Discourses of crisis and loss: Analysing the "boys" under-achievement' debate. *Journal of Youth Studies, 3*(2). https://doi.org/10.1080/713684373.

Griffith, A. I. (1998). Insider/outsider: Epistemological privilege and moth-ering work. *Human Studies, 21*, 361–376. https://doi.org/10.1023/A:1005421211078.

Gunter, A. (2008). Growing up bad: Black youth, 'road' culture and badness in an East London neighbourhood. *Crime, Media, Culture, 4*(3), 349–366. https://doi.org/10.1177/1741659008096371.

Gunter, A. (2010). *Growing up bad? Black youth, "road" culture and badness in an East London neighbourhood.* London: The Tufnell Press.

Gunter, A., & Watt, P. (2009). Grafting, going to college and working on road: Youth transitions and cultures in an East London neighbourhood. *Journal of Youth Studies, 12*(5), 515–529. https://doi.org/10.1080/136762609030 83364.

Hall, S. (2002). Daubing the drudges of fury: Men, violence and the piety of the "hegemonic masculinity" thesis. *Theoretical Criminology, 6*(1), 35–61. https://doi.org/10.1177/136248060200600102.

Hardgrove, A., McDowell, L., & Rootham, E. (2015). Precarious lives, precarious labour: Family support and young men's transitions to work in the UK. *Journal of Youth Studies, 18*(8), 1–20. https://doi.org/10.1080/13676261. 2015.1020933.

Hardie, M., & Banks, A. (2014). *The changing shape of UK manufacturing.* Office for National Statistics.

Harkness, S., Gregg, P., & MacMillan, L. (2012). *Poverty: The role of institutions, behaviours and cultures.* York: Joseph Rowntree Foundation.

Harris Review. (2015). *Changing prisons, saving lives: Report of the independent review into self-inflicted deaths in custody of 18–24 year olds.* London: The Crown.

Harvey, J. (2006). *Young men in prison.* Cullompton and Portland, OR: Willan Publishing.

Haylett, C. (2001). Illegitimate subjects? Abject whites, neoliberal modernisation, and middle-class multiculturalism. *Environment and Planning D: Society and Space, 19*(3), 351–370. https://doi.org/10.1068/d237t.

Hearn, J. (1998). *The violences of men: How men talk about and how agencies respond to men's violence to women.* Thousand Oaks, CA: Sage.

Heath, S., & Calvert, E. (2013). Gifts, loans and intergenerational support for young adults. *Sociology, 47*(6), 1120–1135. https://doi.org/10.1177/003 8038512455736.

Hewson, A. (2013). *Bromley briefings prison factfile.* London: Prison Reform Trust.

Hicks, S. (2008). Gender role models. *Qualitative Social Work, 7*(1), 43–59. https://doi.org/10.1177/1473325007086415.

Hicks, S. (2008). Gender role models… who needs 'em?!. *Qualitative Social Work, 7*(1), 43–59. https://doi.org/10.1177/1473325007086415.

HM Government. (2005). *Reducing re-offending through skills and employment.*

HM Government. (2013). *Care leaver strategy—A cross departmental strategy for young people.*

HM Government. (2016). *Prison reform: Prime Minister's speech.* Available at https://www.gov.uk/government/speeches/prison-reform-prime-min isters-speech. Accessed 7 February 2016.

HM Inspectorates of Prisons and Probation (HMIPP). (2017). *HM Chief Inspector of Prisons for England and Wales: Annual report 2016–17.* London: HMIP. Available at https://assets.publishing.service.gov.uk/gov ernment/uploads/system/uploads/attachment_data/file/629719/hmip-ann ual-report-2016-17.pdf. Accessed 22 October 2017.

Hobbs, D. (1995). *Bad business: Professional crime in modern Britain.* Oxford: Oxford University Press.

Hobbs, D. (1997). Professional crime: Change, continuity and the enduring myth of the underworld. *Sociology, 31*(1), 57–72. https://doi.org/10.1177/0038038597031001005.

Hobbs, D., Hadfield, P., & Lister, S. (2003). *Bouncers: Violence and governance in the night-time economy.* Oxford and New York: Oxford University Press.

Holland, S., & Scourfield, J. B. (2000). Managing marginalised masculinities: Men and probation. *Journal of Gender Studies, 9*(2), 199–211. https://doi.org/10.1080/713677981.

Hood-Williams, J. (2001). Gender, masculinities and crime: From structures to psyches. *Theoretical Criminology, 5*(1), 37–60. https://doi.org/10.1177/1362480601005001003.

Hooks, B. (2003). *We real cool: Black men and masculinity.* New York: Routledge.

Hopkins, P. (2007). Young people, masculinities, religion and race: New social geographies. *Progress in Human Geography, 31*(2), 163–177. https://doi.org/10.1177/0309132507075362.

Hopkins, K. (2012). *The pre-custody employment, training and education status of newly sentenced prisoners. Results from the Surveying Prisoners Crime Reduction (SPCR) longitudinal cohort study of prisoners* (Ministry of Justice Research Series 3/12). London, UK: Ministry of Justice.

Hopkins, P., & Noble, G. (2009). Masculinities in place: Situated identities, relations and intersectionality. *Social & Cultural Geography, 10*(8), 811–819. https://doi.org/10.1080/14649360903305817.

House of Commons Committee of Public Accounts (HOC). (2013). *Work programme outcomes statistics* (33rd Report of Session 2012–13). HC936, Department for Work and Pensions.

House of Commons Educational Committee. (2014). *Underachievement in education by white working class children* (First Report of Session 2014–15). London: The Stationery Office.

Howard League for Penal Reform. (2010a). *Chaotic and violent Feltham.* Available at http://www.howardleague.org/feltham/. Accessed 2 December 2015.

Howard League for Penal Reform. (2010b). *Access to justice denied: Young adults in prison.* London: Howard League for Penal Reform.

Hull County Council. (2014). *Hull at a glance: Economic update report.*

Ingram, N. (2011). Within school and beyond the gate: The complexities of being educationally successful and working class. *Sociology, 45*(2), 287–302. https://doi.org/10.1177/0038038510394017.

Irwin, J., & Cressey. D. R. (1962). Thieves, convicts and the inmate culture. *Social Problems, 10,* 142–155. https://doi.org/10.2307/799047, https://www.jstor.org/stable/799047.

Jackson, P. (1991). The cultural politics of masculinity: Towards a social geography. *Transactions of the Institute of British Geographers, 16*(2), 199–213. https://doi.org/10.2307/622614.

Jackson, P. (1994). Black male: Advertising and the cultural politics of masculinity. *Gender, Place & Culture, 1*(1), 49–59. https://doi.org/10.1080/09663699408721200.

Jefferson, T. (2002). Subordinating hegemonic masculinity. *Theoretical Criminology, 6*(1), 63–88. https://doi.org/10.1177/1362480602006001103.

Jenkins, J. (2010). The labour market in the 1980s, 1990s and 2008/09 recessions. *Economic & Labour Market Review, 4*(8), 29–36.

Jewkes, R., Flood, M., & Lang, J. (2014). From working with men and boys to changing social norms and reducing inequities in gender relations: A paradigm shift in prevention of violence against women and girls. *The Lancet, 385,* 1580–1589. https://doi.org/10.1016/S0140-6736(14)61683-4.

Jewkes, Y. (2002). *Captive audience: Media, masculinity, and power in prisons.* Cullompton: Willan.

Jewkes, Y. (2004). *Media and crime.* London: Sage.

Jewkes, Y. (2005). *Men behind bars: Men and masculinities, 8,* 44–63. https://doi.org/10.1177/1097184X03257452.

Jewkes, Y. (2012). Autoethnography and emotion as intellectual resources doing prison research differently. *Qualitative Inquiry, 18*(1), 63–75. https://doi.org/10.1177/1077800411428942.

Johnston, L., MacDonald, R., Mason, P., Ridley, L., & Webster, C. (2000). *Snakes and ladders: Young people, transitions and social exclusion.* Bristol: Policy Press.

Jonsson, H (1982). *Friends in conflict: Anglo-Icelandic cod wars and the law of the sea.* London: Hamden, Conn: C Hurst & Co Publishers Ltd.

Katz, J. (1988). *Seductions of crime: Moral and sensual attractions in doing evil.* New York: Basic Books.

Kavanagh, L., & Borrill, J. (2013). Exploring the experiences of ex-offender mentors. *Probation Journal, 60*(4), 400–414. https://doi.org/10.1177/026 4550513502247.

Kearon, T. (2012). Alternative representations of the prison and imprisonment: Comparing dominant narratives in the news media and in popular fictional texts. *Prison Service Journal, 199*(January), 4–9.

Kennedy, E. (2013). *Children and young people in custody 2012–13*. London: HM Inspectorate of Prisons and Youth Justice Board.

Kenway, J., & Fitzclarence, L. (1997). Masculinity, violence and schooling: Challenging 'poisonous pedagogies'. *Gender and Education, 9*(1), 117–134. https://doi.org/10.1080/09540259721493.

Khattab, N., & Modood,T. (2018). Accounting for British Muslim's educational attainment: Gender differences and the impact of expectations. *British Journal of Sociology of Education, 39*(2), 242–259. https://doi.org/10.1080/01425692.2017.1304203.

Kimmel, M. (1997). Integrating men into the curriculum. *Duke Journal of Gender Law & Policy, 4*(1), 181–196.

Kimmel, M. (2004). Masculinity as homophobia: Fear, shame, and silence in the construction of gender identity. In P. S. Rothenberg (Ed.), *Race, class, and gender in the United States: An integrated study* (pp. 81–93). New York: Worth.

Kimmel, M., & Mahler, M. (2003). Adolescent masculinity, homophobia, and violence random school shootings, 1982–2001. *American Behavioral Scientist, 46*(10), 1439–1458. https://doi.org/10.1177/0002764203046010010.

Kopak, A. M., Dean, L. V., Proctor, S. L., Miller, L., & Hoffman, G. N. (2015). Effectiveness of the rehabilitation for addicted prisoners trust (RAPt) programme. *Journal of Substance Use, 20*(4), 254–261. https://doi.org/10.3109/14659891.2014.904938.

Kuppers, T. A. (2001). Rape and the prison code. In D. Sabo, T. Kupers, & W. London (Eds.), *Prison masculinities*. Philadelphia, PA: Temple University Press.

Kupers, T. A. (2005). Toxic masculinity as a barrier to mental health treatment in prison. *Journal of Clinical Psychology, 61*(6), 713–724. https://doi.org/10.1002/jclp.20105.

Lacombe, D. (2008). Consumed with sex: The treatment of sex offenders in risk society. *British Journal of Criminology, 48*(1), 55–74. https://doi.org/10.1093/bjc/azm051.

Laming, L. (2016). *In care, out of trouble*. London, England: Prison Reform Trust.

Laub, J. H., & Sampson, R. J. (2001). Understanding desistance from crime. *Crime and Justice, 28*, 1–69. https://doi.org/10.1086/652208.

Laws, B. (2019). The return of the suppressed: Exploring how emotional suppression reappears as violence and pain among male and female prisoners. *Punishment & Society*, *21*(5), 560–577. https://doi.org/10.1177/146 2474518805071.

Laws, B., & Crewe, B. (2016). Emotion regulation among male prisoners. *Theoretical Criminology*, *20*(4), 529–547. https://doi.org/10.1177/136248061 5622532.

Lee, N. (2010). *No city left behind? The geography of the recovery—And the implications for the coalition*. London: The Work Foundation.

Levines, A., & Crewe, B. (2015). 'Nobody's better than you, nobody's worse than you': Moral community among prisoners convicted of sexual offences. *Punishment & Society*, *17*(4), 482–501. https://doi.org/10.1177/146247 4515603803.

Liebling, A. (2001). Whose side are we on? Theory, practice and allegiances in prisons research. *British Journal of Criminology*, *41*, 472–484. https://doi.org/10.1093/bjc/41.3.472.

Liebling, A., & Arnold, H. (2004). *Prisons and their moral performance: A study of values, quality, and prison life*. Oxford: Oxford University Press.

Loader, I. (2006). Policing, recognition, and belonging. *The Annals of the American Academy of Political and Social Science*, *605*(1), 201–221. https://doi.org/10.1177/0002716206286723.

Loftus, B. (2009). *Police culture in a changing world*. Clarendon Studies in Criminology. Oxford: Oxford University Press.

Lösel, F., Bottoms, A., & Farrington, D. P. (Eds.). (2013). *Young adult offenders: Lost in transition?* Cullompton : Willan.

Lösel, F., Pugh, G., Markson, L., et al. (2012). *Risk and protective factors in the resettlement of imprisoned fathers with their families*. Milton: Ormiston Children and Families Trust.

Lyng, S. (1990). Edgework: A social psychological analysis of voluntary risk taking. *American Journal of Sociology*, *95*, 851–886. https://doi.org/10.1086/229379.

Mac an Ghaill, M. (1994). *The making of men: Masculinities, sexualities and schooling*. Buckingham: Open University Press.

Mac an Ghaill, M. (2019). Reconfiguring masculinities and education. Interconnecting local and global identities. In L. Gottzén, U. Mellström, & T. Shafer (Eds.), *Routledge international handbook of masculinity studies*. London: Routledge.

Mac an Ghaill, M., & Haywood, C. (2012). The queer in masculinity: Schooling, boys, and identity formation. In J. C. Landreau & N. M. Rodriguez (Eds.), *Queer masculinities* (pp. 69–84). Explorations of Educational Purpose. Netherlands: Springer.

MacDonald, R. (1994). Fiddly jobs, undeclared working and the something for nothing society. *Work, Employment & Society, 8*(4), 507–530. https://doi.org/10.1177/095001709484002.

MacDonald, R. (2011). Youth transitions, unemployment and underemployment Plus ça change, plus c'est la même chose? *Journal of Sociology, 47*(4), 427–444. https://doi.org/10.1177/1440783311420794.

MacDonald, R., & Marsh, J. (2002). Crossing the Rubicon: Youth transitions, poverty, drugs and social exclusion. *International Journal of Drug Policy, 13*(1), 27–38. https://doi.org/10.1016/S0955-3959(02)00004-X.

MacDonald, R., & Marsh, J. (2005). *Disconnected youth? Growing up in Britain's poor neighbourhoods*. Basingstoke: Palgrave Macmillan.

MacDonald, R., Mason, P., Shildrick, T., Webster, C., Johnston, L., & Ridley, L. (2001). Snakes & ladders: In defence of studies of youth transition. *Sociological Research Online, 5*(4), 1–13.

MacDonald, R., & Shildrick, T. (2007). Street corner society: Leisure careers, youth (sub)culture and social exclusion. *Leisure Studies, 26*(3), 339–355. https://doi.org/10.1080/02614360600834826.

MacDonald, R., & Shildrick, T. (2013). Youth and wellbeing: Experiencing bereavement and ill health in marginalised young people's transitions. *Sociology of Health & Illness, 35*(1), 147–161. https://doi.org/10.1111/j.1467-9566.2012.01488.x.

Macdonald, R., Shildrick, T., & Furlong, A. (2014). In search of "intergenerational cultures of worklessness": Hunting the Yeti and shooting zombies. *Critical Social Policy, 34*(2), 199–220. https://doi.org/10.1177/0261018313501825.

MacDonald, R., Shildrick, T., Webster, C., & Simpson, D. (2005). Growing up in poor neighbourhoods: The significance of class and place in the extended transitions of "socially excluded" young adults. *Sociology, 39*(5), 873–891. https://doi.org/10.1177/0038038505058370.

MacInnes, J. (1998). *The end of masculinity: The confusion of sexual genesis and sexual difference in modern society*. Buckingham: Open University Press.

Maguire, D. (2019). Vulnerable prisoner masculinities in an English prison. *Men and Masculinities*. https://doi.org/10.1177/1097184X19888966.

Majors, R., & Billson, J. M. (1993). *Cool pose: The dilemmas of black manhood in America* (Reprint ed.). New York: Touchstone.

Martin, P. Y. (1998). Why can't a man be more like a woman? Reflections on Connell's masculinities. *Gender and Society, 12*(4), 472–474. https://doi.org/10.1177/089124398012004008.

Martin, R., & Rowthorn, R. (Eds.). (1986). *The geography of de-industrialisation* (1st ed.). London: Macmillan.

Maruna, S. (2001). *Making good: How ex-convicts reform and rebuild their lives*. Washington, DC: American Psychological Association.

Maruna, S., & Roy, K. (2007). Amputation or reconstruction? Notes on the concept of "knifing off" and desistance from crime. *Journal of Contemporary Criminal Justice, 23*(1), 104–124. https://doi.org/10.1177/104398620629 8951.

Mason, J. (2002). *Qualitative researching*. London: Sage.

Mason, P. (Ed.). (2006). *Captured by the media: Prison discourse in popular culture*. Cullompton: Willan.

Massey, D. (1994). *Space, place and gender*. Cambridge: Polity.

May, T. (2001). *Social research: Issues, methods and process* (3rd ed.). Buckingham: Open University Press.

Maycock, M., & Hunt, K. (Eds.). (2018). *New perspectives on prison masculinities*. London: Palgrave Macmillan.

Mayock, P. (2005). "Scripting" risk: Young people and the construction of drug journeys. *Drugs: Education, Prevention and Policy, 12*(5), 349–368.

McAra, L., & McVie, S. (2013). Delivering justice for children and young people: Key messages from the Edinburgh Study of Youth Transitions and Crime. In A. Dockley (Ed.), *Justice for young people: Papers by Winners of the Research Medal 2013* (pp. 3–14). Howard League for Penal Reform. https://d19ylpo4aovc7m.cloudfront.net/fileadmin/howard_league/user/online_publications/Justice_for_young_people_web.pdf.

McConville, M., Sanders, A., & Leng, R. (1993). *Case for the prosecution: Police suspects and the construction of criminality*. London and New York: Routledge.

McCormack, M. (2012). *The declining significance of homophobia: How teenage boys are redefining masculinity and heterosexuality*. New York and Oxford: Oxford University Press.

McCrystal, P., Percy, A., & Higgins, K. (2007). Exclusion and marginalisation in adolescence: The experience of school exclusion on drug use and antisocial behaviour. *Journal of Youth Studies, 10*(1), 35–54. https://doi.org/10.1080/13676260701196103.

McDowell, L. (2003). *Redundant masculinities? Employment change and white working class youth*. Oxford: Blackwell.

McDowell, L. (2014). The sexual contract: Youth, masculinity and the uncertain promise of waged work in Austerity Britain. *Australian Feminist Studies, 29*(79), 31–49. https://doi.org/10.1080/08164649.2014.901281.

McDowell, L., & Bonner-Thompson, C. (2020). The other side of coastal towns: Young men's precarious lives on the margins of England. *Environment and Planning A: Economy and Space, 52*(5), 916–932. https://doi.org/10.1177/0308518X19887968.

McDowell, L., Rootham, E., & Hardgrove, A. (2014a). Politics, anti-politics, quiescence and radical unpolitics: Young men's political participation in an "ordinary" English town. *Journal of Youth Studies, 17*(1), 42–62. https://doi.org/10.1080/13676261.2013.825709.

McDowell, L., Rootham, E., & Hardgrove, A. (2014b). Precarious work, protest masculinity and communal regulation: South Asian young men in Luton, UK. *Work, Employment & Society, 28*(6), 847–864. https://doi.org/10.1177/095 0017013510757.

McNeill, F. (2006). A desistance paradigm for offender management. *Criminology and Criminal Justice, 6*(1), 39–62. https://doi.org/10.1177/174889 5806060666.

Merton, R. K. (1972). Insiders and outsiders: A chapter in the sociology of knowledge. *American Journal of Sociology, 78*(1), 9–47.

Messerschmidt, J. W. (1993). *Masculinities and crime: Critique and reconceptualization of theory.* Lanham, Md.: Rowman & Littlefield.

Messerschmidt, J. W. (1994). Schooling, masculinities and youth crime by white boys. In T. Newburn & E. A. Stanko (Eds.), *Just boys doing business? Men, masculinities and crime* (pp. 81–99). London: Routledge.

Messerschmidt, J. W. (1997). *Crime as structured action: Gender, race, class and crime in the making.* Thousand Oaks, CA and London: Sage.

Messerschmidt, J. W. (2000). Becoming "real men" adolescent masculinity challenges and sexual violence. *Men and Masculinities, 2*(3), 286–307. https://doi.org/10.1177/1097184X00002003003.

Messerschmidt, J. W. (2001). Masculinities, crime and prison. In D. Sabo, T. Kupers, & W. London (Eds.), *Prison masculinities.* Philadelphia, PA: Temple University Press.

Messerschmidt, J. W. (2004). *Flesh and blood: Adolescent gender diversity and violence.* Lanham, MD and Oxford: Rowman & Littlefield.

Messerschmidt, J. W. (2012). Engendering gendered knowledge: Assessing the academic appropriation of hegemonic masculinity. *Men and Masculinities, 15*(1), 56–76. https://doi.org/10.1177/1097184X11428384.

Messerschmidt, J. W., & Tomsen, S. (2018). Masculinities and crime. In W. S. DeKeseredy & M. Dragiewicz (Eds.), *Routledge handbook of critical criminology* (2nd ed., pp. 83–95). London, U.K.: Routledge.

Messner, M. A. (1990). When bodies are weapons: Masculinity and violence in sport. *International Review for the Sociology of Sport, 25*(3), 203–220. https://doi.org/10.1177/101269029002500303.

Messner, M. A. (1995). *Power at play: Sports and the problem of masculinity* (Reissue ed.). Boston: Beacon Press.

Messner, M. A., & Sabo, D. F. (1990). *Sport, men, and the gender order: Critical feminist perspectives.* Champaign, IL: Human Kinetics.

Miles, S. (2000). *Youth lifestyles in a changing world.* Buckingham: Open University Press.

Miller, J., & Glassner, B. (1997). The "inside" and the "outside": Finding realities in interviews. In D. Silverman (Ed.), *Qualitative research: Theory, method and practice* (pp. 98–111). London: Sage.

Mills, M., & Mills, K. (2001). *Challenging violence in schools: An issue of masculinities.* Buckingham: Open University Press.

Ministry of Housing, Communities and Local Government (MoHC&LG). (2019). *The English Indices of Deprivation 2019 (IoD 2019).* Statistical Release. London.

Ministry of Justice. (2012). *Prison population figures: 2011.* Available at https://www.gov.uk/government/statistics/prison-population-2011. Accessed 12 December 2014.

Ministry of Justice. (2013a). *Story of the prison population: 1993–2012 England and Wales.* London: Ministry of Justice.

Ministry of Justice. (2013b). *Criminal justice statistics quarterly: September 2012. Court Proceedings tables 2012.* Available at https://www.gov.uk/government/statistics/criminal-justice-statistics–2. Accessed 24 September 2015.

Ministry of Justice. (2018). *Education and employment strategy.* London: Ministry of Justice.

Moller, M. (2007). Exploiting patterns: A critique of hegemonic masculinity. *Journal of Gender Studies, 16*(3), 263–276. https://doi.org/10.1080/09589230701562970.

Monaghan, L. F. (2002). Hard men, shop boys and others: Embodying competence in a masculinist occupation. *The Sociological Review, 50*(3), 334–355. https://doi.org/10.1111/1467-954X.00386.

Moran, D., Pallot, J., & Piacentini, L. (2009). Lipstick, lace, and longing: Constructions of femininity inside a Russian prison. *Environment and Planning D: Society and Space, 27,* 700–720. https://doi.org/10.1068/d7808.

Morgan, R. (2002). Imprisonment: A brief history, the contemporary scene, and likely prospects. In M. Maguire, R. Morgan, & R. Reiner (Eds.), *The Oxford handbook of criminology* (3rd ed.). Oxford and New York: Oxford University Press.

Morris, T., & Morris, P. (1963). *Pentonville: A sociological study of an English prison.* London: Routledge.

Mosak, H., & Maniacci, M. (2013). *Primer of Adlerian psychology: The analytic—Behavioural—Cognitive psychology of Alfred Adler.* Philadelphia and London: Routledge.

Mosse, G. L. (1998). *The image of man: The creation of modern masculinity.* New York: Oxford University Press.

Mullen, K., Watson, J., Swift, J., & Black, D. (2007). Young men, masculinity and alcohol. *Drugs: Education, prevention and Policy, 14*(2), 151–165. https://doi.org/10.1080/09687630600997816.

Mullins, C. W. (2006). *Holding your square: Masculinities, streetlife, and violence.* Cullompton: Willan.

National Treatment Agency. (2009). *HMP Hull integrated drug treatment system: Treatment plan 2009/10.*

Nayak, A. (2003a). "Boyz to Men": Masculinities, schooling and labour transitions in de-industrial times. *Educational Review, 55*(2), 147–159. https://doi.org/10.1080/0013191032000072191.

Nayak, A. (2003b). Last of the 'Real Geordies'? White masculinities and the subcultural response to deindustrialisation. *Environment and Planning D:Society and Space, 21*(1), 7–26. https://doi.org/10.1068/d44j.

Nayak, A. (2006). Displaced masculinities: Chavs, youth and class in the post-industrial city. *Sociology, 40*(5), 813–831. https://doi.org/10.1177/0038038506067508.

Newburn, T. (2016). Social disadvantage, crime, and punishment. In H. Dean & L. Platt (Eds.), *Social advantage and disadvantage* (pp. 322–345). Oxford: Oxford University Press.

Newburn, T., & Stanko, E. A. (1994). *Just boys doing business? Men, masculinities and crime.* London: Routledge.

Noble, S., McLennan, D., Noble, M., Plunkett, E., Gutacker, N., Silk, M., & Wright, G. (2019). *The English Indices of Deprivation 2019* (Research Report). Ministry of Housing, Communities and Local Government.

Nuttall, A., & Doherty, J. (2014). Disaffected boys and the achievement gap: "the wallpaper effect" and what is hidden by a focus on school results. *Urban Review, 46*, 800–815. https://doi.org/10.1007/s11256-014-0303-8.

O'Brien, R., Hunt, K., & Hart, G. (2005). 'It's caveman stuff, but that is to a certain extent how guys still operate': Men's accounts of masculinity and help seeking. *Social Science & Medicine, 61*(3), 503–516.

O'Connor, C., & Kelly, K. (2006). Auto theft and youth culture: A nexus of masculinities, femininities and car culture. *Journal of Youth Studies, 9*(3), 247–267.

O'Donnell, M., & Sharpe, S. (2000). *Uncertain masculinities: Youth, ethnicity, and class in contemporary Britain.* London: Routledge.

Office for National Statistics. (2013a). *170 years of industrial change across England and Wales.*

Office for National Statistics. (2013b). *Focus on violent crime and sexual offences, 2011/12.*

Office for National Statistics. (2016). *Regional labour market statistics.* Available at http://www.ons.gov.uk/ons/rel/subnational-labour/regional-labour-market-statistics/index.html. Accessed 26 March 2016.

Office for National Statistics. (2018). A summary of violent crime from the year ending March 2017 Crime Survey for England and Wales and police recorded crime.

Office for National Statistics. (2019a). Health state life expectancies, UK: 2016 to 2018.

Office for National Statistics. (2019b). Suicides in the UK: 2018 registrations.

Office for National Statistics. (2019c). Deaths related to drug poisoning in England and Wales: 2018 registrations.

Office for Standards in Education. (1993). *Access and achievement in urban education*. London: Ofsted.

Office for Standards in Education. (2013a). *Unseen children: Access and achievement 20 years on*. London.

Office for Standards in Education. (2013b). *Her Majesty's chief inspector of education, children's services and skills annual report 2012/13*. Schools.

Office for Standards in Education. (2015). *The annual report of Her Majesty's Chief Inspector of Education, Children's Services and Skills 2014/15: Education and skills*. London: Ofsted.

Office for Standards in Education. (2020). *The annual report of Her Majesty's Chief Inspector of Education, Children's Services and Skills 2018/19*. London: Ofsted.

Office for Standards in Education in conjunction with the Audit Commission. (2003). *Inspection of Kingston upon Hull Local Education Authority*. London: Ofsted.

Pallot, J., & Piacentini, L. (2012). *Gender, geography, and punishment: The experience of women in carceral Russia*. Oxford: Oxford University Press.

Parker, H., & Egginton, R. (2002). Adolescent recreational alcohol and drugs careers gone wrong: Developing a strategy for reducing risks and harms. *International Journal of Drug Policy, 13*(5), 419–432. https://doi.org/10.1016/S0955-3959(02)00154-8.

Parsons, T. (1964). *Essays in sociological theory* (2nd ed.). London: Collier Macmillan.

Peacock, L .(2012). *Worst cities to find a job*. Available at http://www.telegraph.co.uk/finance/jobs/9094339/Worst-cities-to-find-a-job.html. Accessed 26 January 2016.

Pemberton, S. (2013). Enforcing gender: The constitution of sex and gender in prison regimes. *Signs, 39*(1), 151–175. https://doi.org/10.1086/670828.

Perrin, C., & Blagden, N. (2014). Accumulating meaning, purpose and opportunities to change "drip by drip": The impact of being a listener in prison. *Psychology, Crime & Law, 20*(9), 902–920. https://doi.org/10.1080/1068316X.2014.888429.

Phillips, C. (2010). Reading difference differently? Identity, epistemology and prison ethnography. *British Journal of Criminology, 50*, 360–378.

Phillips, C. (2012). *The multicultural prison: Ethnicity, masculinity, and social relations among prisoners*. Oxford: Oxford University Press.

Piacentini, L., Pallot, J., & Moran, D. (2009). Welcome to Malaya Rodina ("Little Homeland"): Gender and penal order in a Russian penal colony. *Social & Legal Studies, 18*, 523–542. https://doi.org/10.1177/0964663909345097.

Pleck, J. H. (1976). The male sex role: Definitions, problems, and sources of change. *Journal of Social Issues, 32*(3), 155–164. https://doi.org/10.1111/j.1540-4560.1976.tb02604.x.

Pleck, J. H. (1981). *The myth of masculinity.* Cambridge, MA: MIT Press.

Plummer, D. (1999). *One of the boys: Masculinity, homophobia, and modern manhood.* New York: Routledge.

Plummer, D. C. (2001). The quest for modern manhood: Masculine stereotypes, peer culture and the social significance of homophobia. *Journal of Adolescence, 24*(1), 15–23. https://doi.org/10.1006/jado.2000.0370.

Plummer, K. (2001). *Documents of life 2: An invitation to critical humanism.* London: Sage.

Polk, K. (1994). *When men kill: Scenarios of masculine violence.* Cambridge: Cambridge University Press.

Prior, D., Farrow, K., Hughes, N., Kelly, G., Manders, G., White, S., & Wilkinson, B. (2011). *Maturity, young adults and criminal justice: A literature review.* Birmingham: University of Birmingham.

Prison Reform Trust. (2012). *Old enough to know better?* London: Prison Reform Trust.

Prison Reform Trust. (2014). *Bromley briefings. Prison factfile.* London: Prison Reform Trust.

Prison Reform Trust. (2015). *Keeping children in care out of trouble.*

Reay, D. (2002). Shaun's story: Troubling discourses of white working-class masculinities. *Gender and Education, 14*(3), 221–234. https://doi.org/10.1080/0954025022000010695.

Reay, D. (2004). "Mostly roughs and toughs": Social class, race and representation in inner city schooling. *Sociology, 38*(5), 1005–1023. https://doi.org/10.1177/0038038504047183.

Reay, D. (2005). Beyond consciousness? The psychic landscape of social class. *Sociology, 39*(5), 911–928. https://doi.org/10.1177/0038038505058372.

Reay, D. (2007). "Unruly places": Inner-city comprehensives, middle-class imaginaries and working-class children. *Urban Studies, 44*(7), 1191–1201. https://doi.org/10.1080/00420980701302965.

Reay, D. (2018). *Miseducation: Inequality, education and the working classes.* Bristol University Press, Policy Press.

Reay, D., & Lucey, H. (2000). "I don't really like it here but I don't want to be anywhere else': Children and inner city council estates. *Antipode, 32*(4), 410–428. https://doi.org/10.1111/1467-8330.00144.

Reiner, R. (2010). *The politics of the police* (4th ed.). Oxford: Oxford University Press.

Renold, E. (2001). Learning the 'hard' way: Boys, hegemonic masculinity and the negotiation of learner identities in the primary school. *British Journal of Sociology of Education, 22*(3), 369–385. https://doi.org/10.1080/014256 90120067980.

Rhodes, C. (2020). *Manufacturing: Statistics and policy.* London: House of Commons.

Ricciardelli, R. (2015). Establishing and asserting masculinity in Canadian penitentiaries. *Journal of Gender Studies, 24*(2), 170–191. https://doi.org/10. 1080/09589236.2013.812513.

Ricciardelli, R., Maier, K., & Hannah-Moffat, K. (2015). Strategic masculinities: Vulnerabilities, risk and the production of prison masculinities. *Theoretical Criminology, 19*(4), 491–513. https://doi.org/10.1177/136248061456 5849.

Ricciardelli, R., & Moir, M. (2013). Stigmatized among the stigmatized: Sex offenders in Canadian penitentiaries. *Canadian Journal of Criminology and Criminal Justice, 55*(3), 353–386. https://doi.org/10.3138/cjccj.2012.E22.

Richards, M. (1992). The separation of children and parents: Some issues and problems. In R. Shaw (Ed.), *Prisoners' children: What are the issues?* (pp. 3–12). London: Routledge.

Riley, A. (2020, January 6). Every school in Hull and East Yorkshire ordered to improve by Ofsted. *Hull Daily Mail.*

Roberts, S. (2010). Misrepresenting "choice biographies"? A reply to Woodman. *Journal of Youth Studies, 13*(1), 137–149. https://doi.org/10.1080/136762 60903233720.

Roberts, S. (2011). Beyond "NEET" and "tidy" pathways: Considering the "missing middle" of youth transition studies. *Journal of Youth Studies, 14*(1), 21–39. https://doi.org/10.1080/13676261.2010.489604.

Roberts, R. (2012). "I just got on with it": The educational experiences of ordinary, yet overlooked, boys. *British Journal of Sociology of Education, 33*(2), 203–221. https://doi.org/10.1080/01425692.2011.649832.

Roberts, S. (2012). One step forward, one step Beck: A contribution to the ongoing conceptual debate in youth studies. *Journal of Youth Studies, 15*(3), 389–401. https://doi.org/10.1080/13676261.2012. 663896.

Roberts, S. (2013). Boys will be boys… won't they? Change and continuities in contemporary young working-class masculinities. *Sociology, 47*(4), 671–686. https://doi.org/10.1177/0038038512453791.

Roberts, S. (2014). Introduction: Masculinities in transition: Change, continuity, crisis? In S. Roberts (Ed.), *Debating modern masculinities: Change, continuity, crisis?* Basingstoke: Palgrave Macmillan.

Roberts, S. (2018). *Young working-class men in transition.* London: Routledge.

Roberts, S., & Evans, S. (2012). Aspirations' and imagined futures: Choices, aspirations and economic hardship in working class student experience. In

W. Atkinson, S. Roberts, & M. Savage (Eds.), *Class inequality in austerity Britain: Power, difference and suffering* (pp. 70–89). Palgrave.

Roberts, M., Stanley, C., & Cavadino, P. (2002). *Young adult offenders.* London: National Association for the Care & Resettlement of Offenders.

Rogers, L., Hurry, J., Simonot, M., & Willson, A. (2014). The aspirations and realities of prison education for under-25s in the London area. *London Review of Education, 12*(2), 184–196. https://doi.org/10.18546/LRE.12.2.04.

Ross, J., & Richards, S. (Eds.). (2003). *Convict criminology.* Belmont: Wadsworth Publishing.

Rowthorn, R., & Coutts, K. (2013). *De-industrialisation and the balance of payments in advanced economies* (Future of Manufacturing Project: Evidence Paper 31). London: Foresight, Government Office for Science.

Sabo, D., Kupers, T., & London, W. (Eds.). (2001). *Prison masculinities.* Philadelphia, PA: Temple University Press.

Sandberg, S. (2008). Black drug dealers in a white welfare state: Cannabis dealing and street capital in Norway. *British Journal of Criminology, 48*(5), 604–619. https://doi.org/10.1093/bjc/azn041.

Sandberg, S. (2009). *Street capital: Black cannabis dealers in a white welfare state.* Bristol: Policy Press.

Savage, M. (1988). The missing link? The relationship between spatial mobility and social mobility. *British Journal of Sociology, 39,* 554–577.

Sayer, R. (2005). *The moral significance of class.* Cambridge: Cambridge University Press.

Schofield, G., Ward, E., Biggart, L., Scaife, V., Dodworth, J., Haynes, A., et al. (2012). Looked after children and offending: Reducing risk and promoting resilience. *UEA and TACT.*http://tactcare.org.uk/data/files/resources/lac_and_offending_reducing_risk_promoting_resilience_fullreport_200212.pdf. Accessed 23 June 2014.

Schwartz, M. D., & DeKeseredy, W. S. (1997). *Sexual assault on the college campus: The role of male peer support.* Thousand Oaks, CA: London Sage.

Scraton, P., & McCulloch, J. (2008). *The violence of incarceration.* London: Routledge.

Seddon, T. (2006). Drugs, crime and social exclusion: Social context and social theory in British drugs—Crime research. *British Journal of Criminology, 46*(4), 680–703. https://doi.org/10.1093/bjc/azi079.

Segal, L. (1990). *Slow motion: Changing masculinities, changing men.* London: Virago.

Segal, L. (2007). *Slow motion: Changing masculinities, changing men* (3rd ed.). Basingstoke: Palgrave Macmillan.

Sewell, T. (1997). *Black masculinities and schooling: How black boys survive modern schooling.* Stoke-on-Trent: Trentham.

Shabazz, R. (2009). "So high you can't get over it, so low you can't get under it": Carceral spatiality and black masculinities in the United States and South Africa. *Souls, 11*(3), 276–294. https://doi.org/10.1080/109999409 03088309.

Shildrick, T., Blackman, S., & MacDonald, R. (2009). Young people, class and place. *Journal of Youth Studies, 12*(5), 457–465. https://doi.org/10.1080/13676260903114136.

Shildrick, T., & MacDonald, R. (2007). Biographies of exclusion: Poor work and poor transitions. *International Journal of Lifelong Education, 26*(5), 589–604. https://doi.org/10.1080/02601370701559672.

Shildrick, T., & MacDonald, R. (2008). Understanding youth exclusion: Critical moments, social networks and social capital. *Youth and policy, 99*, 46–64.

Shilling, C. (2003). *The body and social theory* (2nd ed.). Theory, Culture & Society. London: Sage.

Short, M. J. (2015). City rivalries: How Newcastle became a "poster child" for the new North. *The Guardian*. Available at http://www.theguardian.com/cit ies/2015/mar/20/newcastle-poster-child-north-sunderland-rivals. Accessed 11 June 2015.

Silverman, D. (2011). *Interpreting qualitative data: A guide to the principles of qualitative research* (4th ed.). London: Sage.

Sim, J. (1994). Tougher than the rest? Men in prison. In T. Newburn & E. A. Stanko (Eds.), *Just boys doing business? Men, masculinities and crime*. London: Routledge.

Skeggs, B. (2004). *Class, self, culture*. London: Routledge.

Skelton, C. (2001). *Schooling the boys: Masculinities and primary education*. Buckingham: Open University Press.

Smart, C. (1977). *Women, crime, and criminology: A feminist critique*. London: Routledge.

Smith, D. J., & Gray, J. (1985). *Police and people in London: The PSI report*. Aldershot: Gower.

Social Exclusion Unit. (2002). *Reducing reoffending by ex-prisoners*. London: Social Exclusion Unit.

Sparks, R., Bottoms, A. E., & Hay, W. (1996). *Prisons and the problem of order*. Oxford: Clarendon Press.

Stahl, G. (2013). Habitus disjunctures, reflexivity and white working-class boys' conceptions of status in learner and social identities. *Sociological Research Online, 18*(3), 2. https://doi.org/10.5153/sro.2999.

Stahl, G. (2014). White working-class male narratives of "loyalty to self" in discourses of aspiration. *British Journal of Sociology of Education, 37*, 1–21. https://doi.org/10.1080/01425692.2014.982859.

Stahl, G. (2015). *Identity, neoliberalism and aspiration: Educating white working-class boys*. London: Routledge.

Stahl, G., & Dale, P. (2013). Success on the decks: Working-class boys, education and turning the tables on perceptions of failure. *Gender and Education, 25*(3), 357–372. https://doi.org/10.1080/09540253.2012.756856.

Stamou, E., Edwards, A., Daniels, H., & Ferguson, L. (2014). *Young people at risk of drop-out from education: Recognising and responding to their needs.* Oxford: Oxford University.

Standing, G. (2011). *The precariat: The new dangerous class.* London: Bloomsbury Academic.

Stewart, D. (2008). *The problems and needs of newly sentenced prisoners: Results from a national survey.* London: Ministry of Justice.

Steel, N., Ford, J. A., Newton, J. N., Davis, A. C. J., Vos, T., Naghavi, M., et al. (2018). Health in the countries of the UK and 150 English local authority areas 1990–2016: A Systematic Analysis for the Global Burden of Disease Study 2016. *The Lancet, 392,* 1647–1661. https://doi.org/10.1016/S0140-6736(18)32207-4.

Strangleman, T., & Rhodes, J. (2014). The "new" sociology of deindustrialisation? Understanding industrial change. *Sociology Compass, 8*(4), 411–421.

Sturge, G. (2020). *Prison population statistics.* House of Commons Library. http://researchbriefings.files.parliament.uk/documents/SN04334/SN04334.pdf. Accessed 1 June 2017.

Suleiman, R. (2014). *Stepping stones: The role of the voluntary sector in future welfare to work schemes.* London: The National Council for Voluntary Organisations.

Sykes, G. (2007). *The society of captives: A study of a maximum security prison.* Princeton, NJ: Princeton University Press.

Tarrant, A., Terry, G., Ward, M. R., Ruxton, S., Martin, R., & Brigid, F. (2015). Are male role models really the solution? Interrogating the "war on boys" through the lens of the "male role model" discourse. *Boyhood Studies: An Interdisciplinary Journal, 8*(1). https://doi.org/10.3167/bhs.2015.080105.

Thomson, R., Bell, R., Holland, J., Henderson, S., McGrellis, S., & Sharp, S. (2002). Critical moments: Choice, chance and opportunity in young people's narratives of transition. *Sociology, 36*(2), 335–354. https://doi.org/10.1177/0038038502036002006.

Thurston, R. (1996). Are you sitting comfortably? Men's storytelling, masculinities, prison culture and violence. In M. Mac an Ghaill (Ed.), *Understanding masculinities: Social relations and cultural arenas* (pp. 139–152). Buckingham: Open University Press.

Toch, H. (1992). *Violent men: An inquiry into the psychology of violence.* Washington, DC: American Psychological Association.

Tomczak, P. (2018). *Prison suicide: What happens afterwards?* Bristol: Bristol University Press.

Tomlinson, J. (2020). De-industrialization: Strengths and weaknesses as a key concept for understanding post-war British history. *Urban History*, 1–21. https://doi.org/10.1017/S0963926819000221.

Tomsen, S. (2008). *Crime, criminal justice and masculinities*. Aldershot: Ashgate.

Tomsen, S., & Gadd, D. (2018). Beyond honour and achieved hegemony: Violence and the everyday masculinities of young men. *International Journal for Crime, Justice and Social Democracy*, 8(1), 17–30. https://doi.org/10. 5204/ijcjsd.v8i2.1117.

Tomsen, S., & Mason, G. (2001). Engendering homophobia: Violence, sexuality and gender conformity. *Journal of Sociology*, 37(3), 257–273. https://doi. org/10.1177/144078301128756337.

Tyler, I. (2015). Classificatory struggles: Class, culture and inequality in neoliberal times. *The Sociological Review*, 63(2), 493–511. https://doi.org/10. 1111/1467-954X.12296.

Tynan, R. R. (2019). *Young men's experiences of long term imprisonment: Living life*. London: Routledge.

Ugelvik, T. (2014). Paternal pains of imprisonment: Incarcerated fathers, ethnic minority masculinity and resistance narratives. *Punishment & Society*, 16(2), 152–168. https://doi.org/10.1177/1462474513517020.

Ulyatt, M. E. (1985). *Trawlermen of Hull: The rise and decline of the world's greatest fishing port*. Dalesman: Lancaster.

Van Hoven, B., & Hörschelmann, K. (2005). *Spaces of masculinities*. London: Routledge.

Walker, G. W. (2006). Disciplining protest masculinity. *Men and masculinities*, 9(1), 5–22. https://doi.org/10.1177/1097184X05284217.

Walker, L. (2010). "My son gave birth to me": Offending fathers—Generative, reflexive and risky? *British Journal of Social Work*, 40(5), 1402–1418. https:// doi.org/10.1093/bjsw/bcp063.

Wakeman, S. (2014). Fieldwork, biography and emotion doing criminological autoethnography. *The British Journal of Criminology*, 54(5), 705–721. https://doi.org/10.1093/bjc/azu039.

Ward, M. (2014). "I'm a geek I am": Academic achievement and the performance of a studious working-class masculinity. *Gender and Education*, 26(7), 709–725. https://doi.org/10.1080/09540253.2014.953918.

Watson, J. (2000). *Male bodies: Health, culture and identity*. Buckingham: Open University Press.

Weaver-Hightower, M. (2003). The "boy turn" in research on gender and education. *Review of Educational Research*, 73(4), 471–498. https://doi.org/10. 3102/00346543073004471.

Webster, C. (2008). Marginalized white ethnicity, race and crime. *Theoretical Criminology, 12*(3), 293–312. https://doi.org/10.1177/136248060809 3308.

Webster, C., Simpson, D., & MacDonald, R. (2004). *Poor transitions: Social exclusion and young adults*. Bristol: Policy Press.

Wellford, C. (1967). Factors associated with adoption of the inmate code: A study of normative socialization. *The Journal of Criminal Law, Criminology, and Police Science, 58,* 197–203. https://doi.org/10.2307/1140837.

West, C., & Zimmerman, D. H. (1987). Doing gender. *Gender & Society, 1*(2), 125–151. https://doi.org/10.1177/0891243287001002002.

Westmarland, L. (2001). *Gender and policing: Sex, power and police culture.* Cullompton: Willan.

Wheeler, S. (1961). Socialization in correctional communities. *American Sociological Review, 26,* 697–712. https://doi.org/10.2307/2090199.

Whitehead, S. (2002). *Men and masculinities: Key themes and new directions.* Cambridge: Polity.

Whitehead, S., & Barrett, F. J. (Eds.). (2001). *The masculinities reader.* Oxford: Polity.

Willis, P. (1977). *Learning to labor: How working class kids get working class jobs.* Farnborough, England: Saxon House.

Wilson, A. (2003). Nike trainers—My one true love, without you I am nothing. In J. Androutopolous & A. Georgakopoulo (Eds.), *Discourse constructions of youth identity.* Amsterdam: John Benjamins Publishing Company.

Winlow, S. (2001). *Badfellas: Crime, tradition and new masculinities.* Oxford: Berg.

Winlow, S. (2004). Masculinities and crime. *Criminal Justice Matters, 55*(1), 18–19. https://doi.org/10.1080/09627250408553590.

Woodman, D. (2009). The mysterious case of the pervasive choice biography: Ulrich Beck, structure/agency, and the middling state of theory in the sociology of youth. *Journal of Youth Studies, 12*(3), 243–256. https://doi.org/10.1080/13676260902807227.

Woodman, D. (2010). Class, individualisation and tracing processes of inequality in a changing world: A reply to Steven Roberts. *Journal of Youth Studies, 13*(6), 737–746. https://doi.org/10.1080/13676261.2010.506533.

Wright, S., Crewe, B., & Hulley, S. (2016). Suppression, denial, sublimation: Defending against the initial pains of very long life sentences. *Theoretical Criminology, 21*(2), 225–246. https://doi.org/10.1177/136248061664 3581.

Wright, C., Maylor, U., & Becker, S. (2016). Young black males: Resilience and the use of capital to transform school 'failure'. *Critical Studies in Education, 57*(1), 21–34. https://doi.org/10.1080/17508487.2016.1117005.

Wyn, J., Cuervo, H., Crofts, J., & Woodman, D. (2017). Gendered transitions from education to work: The mysterious relationship between the fields of education and work. *Journal of Sociology, 53*(2), 492–506. https://doi.org/10.1177/1440783317700736.

Young, M. D., & Willmott, P. (2007). *Family and kinship in East London.* London: Penguin.

INDEX

© The Editor(s) (if applicable) and The Author(s), under exclusive   237
license to Springer Nature Switzerland AG 2021
D. Maguire, *Male, Failed, Jailed*,
Palgrave Studies in Prisons and Penology,
https://doi.org/10.1007/978-3-030-61059-3

Printed by Printforce, United Kingdom